Personal Faith, Public Policy is a refreshing examination of a perpetually emerging political force. This book details what many have known but few want to acknowledge—the power of unity among conservative Christian entities in the political arena. Jackson and Perkins have opened the door of understanding regarding the genesis of moral change in America.

—LYLE DUKES
Senior Pastor, Harvest Life Changers Church, International

Are you ever frustrated with the way our nation is headed? Do you feel powerless to do anything about it? And even if you had the power, would you know where to begin? Harry Jackson and Tony Perkins have brought a wealth of experience to answer these questions from a Christian perspective in *Personal Faith, Public Policy*. They have crossed racial, cultural, and party barriers to look at America from a joint perspective based on God's Word. These men are not armchair quarterbacks who point their fingers at a mismatched group of legislators. They have rolled up their sleeves with others and have been instrumental in changing laws that affect each one of us. And we can do it too! This book will enable anyone reading it to understand complex issues and know how to vote in the upcoming elections based on a biblical worldview. Read this book and make a difference.

—DR. WALT KALLESTAD
Senior Pastor, Community Church of Joy
President, ReignDown USA

Tony Perkins and Bishop Henry Jackson have written a thoughtful book on how Christians, black and white, can work together for the greater good to help solve many of the pressing issues of our times, especially the battle to preserve our first freedom—religious liberty.

—ALAN E. SEARS
President, CEO, and General Counsel, Alliance Defense Fund

Tony Perkins and Harry Jackson chart a course for evangelical cultural engagement that is equal parts courage, wisdom, and heart. Their broad and bold vision will challenge, inspire, and may at times even offend. May it ignite a fresh passion to apply our faith in the public square for the good of humanity and the glory of God.

—JIM DALY
President, Focus on the Family

Few evangelical leaders have their finger on the pulse of both Congress and the evangelical community like Tony Perkins. As he teams up with Bishop Harry Jackson, an emerging leader in the African American community, they present an insightful and challenging prescription to both the white and black evangelical community for shaping the nation's future.

—CONGRESSMAN MIKE PENCE
Former Chairman of the House Republican Study Committee

Bishop Harry Jackson and Tony Perkins have been—and are—two of the most courageous watchmen on the wall in the struggle to help people of faith be the salt and the light that they have been commanded to be in our society and in our government. These two men from very different backgrounds have been united by their common faith concern for the troubling moral trajectory of our society. Every person of faith should read this book. It will challenge them concerning their responsibilities as people of faith and citizens of this blessed country.

—DR. RICHARD LAND
President, The Ethics & Religious Liberty Commission

These two authors are on the front lines of the policy and faith battle-fields of our culture. They know the issues and they are solidly grounded in the faith. Christians can learn much for their perspective on the challenges facing us as concerned and involved citizens.

—JANICE SHAW CROUSE, PhD
Director and Senior Fellow
The Beverly LaHaye Institute and Concerned Women for America

In *Personal Faith, Public Policy*, Bishop Harry Jackson and Tony Perkins powerfully contextualize the nexus of a personal faith narrative with viable solutions to major public policy issues. This book will revolutionize how mainstream America defines evangelicalism and will provoke Christians to look beyond just a few issues and embrace the collective ethos of a transformational faith. This book engages problem solvers with a biblical worldview.

—REV. SAMUEL RODRIGUEZ JR.
President, National Hispanic Christian Leadership Conference

PERSONAL
FAITH
PUBLIC
POLICY

HARRY R. JACKSON JR.
& TONY PERKINS

FRONTLINE

A STRANG COMPANY

Most STRANG COMMUNICATIONS/CHARISMA HOUSE/SILOAM/FRONTLINE/EXCEL BOOKS/
REALMS products are available at special quantity discounts for bulk purchase for sales
promotions, premiums, fund-raising, and educational needs. For details, write Strang
Communications/Charisma House/Siloam/FrontLine/Excel Books/Realms, 600 Rinehart
Road, Lake Mary, Florida 32746, or telephone (407) 333-0600.

PERSONAL FAITH, PUBLIC POLICY by Harry R. Jackson Jr. and Tony Perkins
Published by FrontLine
A Strang Company
600 Rinehart Road
Lake Mary, Florida 32746
www.frontlineissues.com

Unless otherwise noted, all Scripture quotations are from the King James Version of the
Bible.

Scripture quotations marked NAS are from the New American Standard Bible. Copyright ©
1960, 1962, 1963, 1968, 1971, 1972, 1973, 1975, 1977 by the Lockman Foundation. Used
by permission. (www.Lockman.org)

Scripture quotations marked NIV are from the Holy Bible, New International Version.
Copyright © 1973, 1978, 1984, International Bible Society. Used by permission.

Scripture quotations marked NKJV are from the New King James Version of the Bible.
Copyright © 1979, 1980, 1982 by Thomas Nelson, Inc., publishers. Used by permission.

Scripture quotations marked NLT are from the Holy Bible, New Living Translation, copyright © 1996, 2004. Used by permission of Tyndale House Publishers, Inc., Wheaton, IL
60189. All rights reserved.

Cover Designer: Karen Grindley
Design Director: Bill Johnson

Library of Congress Cataloging-in-Publication Data

Jackson, Harry R.
  Personal faith, public policy / Harry R. Jackson and Tony Perkins.
    p. cm.
  ISBN 978-1-59979-261-3
  1. Christian conservatism--United States. 2. United States--Politics
and government--2001- I. Perkins, Tony. II. Title.
  BR526.J33 2008
  261.0973--dc22

                                                      2007049789

First Edition

08 09 10 11 12 — 9 8 7 6 5 4 3 2 1
Printed in the United States of America

Contents

Preface

We have written this book together because we share two deeply held beliefs—one is the absolute truth of God's Word, and the other is that we are at a point when, perhaps more than any other time in recent history, our nation's public policy is in need of moral clarity.

Growing up with different backgrounds has given us different experiences and perspectives. Harry, an African American, is a registered Democrat, while Tony is a white Republican. But by working together, we have found that because of our relationship with God we have far more in common than we had been led to believe.

We first came together when organizing a project called Justice Sunday in 2005. As we joined our organizations for this common cause, we had the opportunity to share with each other our passion for affecting public policy decisions with values based on God's Word.

This book grows directly out of that shared passion and the many conversations we've had since. In writing this book, we have gone through the process of hammering out policy positions that have required give-and-take from both of us. We have wrestled through seven key issues facing our nation and have attempted to establish a point where all evangelicals—white, black, and brown; Republican and Democrat; young and old—can stand together. Will it be to everyone's liking? Perhaps not. But like iron sharpening iron, we've worked through the issues in this book yielding to the ultimate truth test—not what do Republicans or conservatives say or Democrats or liberals think, but rather what does God's Word say. We have done our best to step out of our cultural conditioning and our typecasting and reason together. We wish to be clear that the ideas and policy suggestions in this book are our personal views and do not represent the views of the Family Research Council, Hope Christian Church, or the High Impact Leadership Coalition. Rather, they are the fruit of an exchange between two evangelical Christians about issues facing our nation.

We have done this not because we believe we have all the answers, but because we see not only an opportunity but also an absolute need to bring evangelicals and conservative Christians, regardless of color, into unity on key public policy matters that will shape our nation's future.

We pray that this book will serve as a call to action in your life. Pray with us that God will guide our nation's policy makers and that conservative Christians from all walks of life will come together and lead the way with the biblically based solutions our country—and indeed the world—has been waiting for.

—HARRY R. JACKSON JR.
—TONY PERKINS

Introduction

IS THE RELIGIOUS RIGHT REALLY DEAD?

The reports of my demise were greatly exaggerated.

—MARK TWAIN

Everywhere you turn, pundits and politicos are writing the obituary of the religious Right. We are told in ponderous articles that the movement is fracturing, splintering, losing momentum, losing heart, stumbling, fighting among themselves, and on the verge of falling into irrelevance. Is it true? Or is this wishful thinking on behalf of those who have always despised what the religious Right stands for? We're not betting men, but we are pretty sure it's the latter.

Today, the religious Right continues to mature as a movement and grow in its influence in American politics. Few other constituencies can match it for size and, more importantly, unity. But the missing story that perhaps only people like us can see, because we are in the trenches and on the front lines every day leading church services and meeting with the movement's leaders, is that the religious Right is not falling apart. Rather, it is growing, expanding, and being rejuvenated. The range of issues on which its leaders are willing to take a stand is expanding, and the movement is finding surprising partners and creating new coalitions. What our critics see as "splintering" is actually the growing pains that precede a healthy expansion. To their frustration, critics of the religious Right will soon realize that the movement is neither losing steam nor walking dejectedly away from the public policy arena. Rather, it is adapting to the changing political environment and broadening its ranks while holding firmly to the principles that have united us thus far.

But let's rewind the tape to nearly thirty years ago and set the stage for what we intend to argue in this book: the religious Right is poised for greater influence in the decades to come than it has ever experienced as it pursues a unified agenda on seven key issues. But first, just how did this cultural and political movement that we know as the religious Right come to be?

The Moral Majority Is Born

The course of modern American politics was forever changed in a small meeting in Lynchburg, Virginia, in 1979. The meeting, a follow-up to an earlier meeting between Dr. Jerry Falwell, Howard Phillips, and the late Ed McAteer, was held in a local hotel. Paul Weyrich, Alan Dye, and the late Bob Billings joined the original trio for what would become a historic meeting. While the participants were few in number, their efforts would launch a movement that would bring Christians back to a place in American public life they had retreated from decades earlier.

In those preceding decades, America had undergone an ugly and extreme transformation at the hands of radical secularists. All that had once defined America was being blurred or erased, one principle at a time. Bible reading and prayer were banned from public schools by the courts. And with a single ruling, America was changed overnight from a pro-life nation to a country that condoned the killing of innocent, unborn children.

In this atmosphere of accelerating moral decay, the groundwork for the meeting in Lynchburg had been laid by McAteer, a retired salesman from Colgate Palmolive, and Phillips, a former member of the Nixon administration. Both were convinced of the need for an organized response to the Left, which had been operating unchallenged in attempting to dismantle and rebuild America in its own godless image. McAteer's main task was to persuade Falwell to step into the public square and be the voice of the movement.

Weyrich, one of the key architects of the modern conservative political movement, came armed with a strategy. He had studied the successes of the Left in the 1960s and early 1970s and identified what the Right lacked. The missing component, which the Left had successfully employed to oppose the Vietnam War and advance President Lyndon B. Johnson's Great Society, was religion. They used religion in the pursuit of their goals.

In Weyrich's opinion, the Right had to get its own religion, in a political sense, if they were to be a lasting force in American politics.

At one point during the wide-ranging discussion, Weyrich is reported to have said that there was a moral majority who wanted to maintain the traditional Christian values that were under assault in America. Falwell asked Weyrich to repeat the statement and then spun around and declared to one of his assistants, "That's the name for this organization— the *Moral Majority*."

That day marked the beginning of a new force in the American political landscape, as people of conservative Christian faith began returning en masse to the realm of politics and public policy. More than fifty years earlier, Bible-believing Christians had trekked into the political wilderness following the infamous Scopes Monkey Trial held in Dayton, Tennessee, over the summer of 1925. Although Christian statesman William Jennings Bryan had successfully argued the case in court, biblical fundamentalists, who opposed the teaching of evolution, lost the bigger battle in the court of public opinion. They were not prepared to stand in the face of the relentless assaults by the media and academic elites who attacked their values as outdated and portrayed them as "uneducated, unthinking and reactionary."[1]

At the rebirth of conservative Christian civic involvement in 1979, the new leaders were determined not to repeat the "sins" of the fathers. They would not shy away from controversy, nor would they yield to criticism; they would work with others to restore the moral foundations of the nation. In a short time the new movement would become highly influential in American politics. Its commitment to nonnegotiable, explicitly moral and biblical values caused it to be revered and ridiculed, embraced and eschewed, loved and loathed. But there was one thing few politicians could afford to do: ignore it.

Premature Death Notices

The reawakened movement was most unwelcome by the Left, and from the start the media and liberal Christians busied themselves writing the religious Right's obituary. With almost predictable regularity, like the paper they were written on, headlines were recycled, heralding the so-called waning influence of evangelicals and their splintering unity. With each election cycle, hope sprung anew in editorial rooms and political back offices that this would be the year the religious Right's strength would begin to fade. Some observers even had the audacity to actively explore what American politics would look like once the religious Right was gone.

Consider the *New York Times* article of Monday, June 1, 1981, which read, "Views of Religious Right Are Assailed by Carter."[2] President Carter was an active evangelical and Southern Baptist lay minister. But he believed, then and now, that separation of church and state meant that the pulpit must be silent and that the voice of the church in public policy must be muted. The body of the *Times* article said, "Former President Jimmy Carter has told a group of Baptist writers and editors that the measuring rod for Christianity of the so-called 'religious right' is a 'distortion' and will not long prevail."

This was just three years after the launch of the Moral Majority! Already, liberal media and politicians were trying to strangle the movement in the cradle. Carter has been sparring with the religious Right ever since. His 2006 book, *Our Endangered Values: America's Moral Crisis*, repeated his long-standing argument in favor of his conception of "separation of church and state" in a manner that was perhaps more strident than any of his previous statements throughout the years.[3] Perhaps he remains frustrated that the religious Right has not faded into the woodwork as he hoped and predicted it would.

The obituaries continued throughout the movement's first decade, even as Ronald Reagan, the Moral Majority's preferred candidate, won a second term by a landslide. Then, almost a decade after the *New York Times* first played grave digger, the *Washington Post* decided it was ready to notify the next of kin that the conservative Christian movement was now truly on its deathbed. Just after Thanksgiving in 1990, the paper ran this headline: "Bloom Is Off Religious Right, Scholars at Conference Agree; Movement Criticized for Lacking Political Finesse." It read, in part: "The religious right has fallen on hard times, torn by sectarian division, hindered by the uneasiness of some in its ranks with coalition building, dispirited by scandals involving television preachers and hurt even by some of its successes, according to scholars and movement partisans."[4]

Three years later, when the movement failed to expire as predicted, the *Washington Post* in a now infamous article, published on February 1, 1993, attributed the movement's success to the members of the religious Right who were "largely poor, uneducated and easy to command."[5] Whether this was bitterness at their failed forecast or the reporter's (and editor's) simple ignorance, we still do not know, but it's possible that these are the most discriminatory words to be written about any single group in a major U.S. paper in the past thirty years.

Then on January 19, 1996, the headline in the *New York Times* read, "G.O.P. Candidates Divide Religious Right." The story was once again of an ailing and splintered movement: "Religious conservatives are a political force fractured, their allegiances divided among several Republican candidates."[6] To put this article into context, it was written just a little over one year after Newt Gingrich was elected Speaker of the U.S. House of Representatives after the Republicans won control of the House—the first time in nearly half a century that a Republican had held this position. Just months before, former executive director of the Christian Coalition Ralph Reed was on the cover of *TIME* magazine as they called him "the right hand of God."

Fast-forward to the *Miami Herald* on May 8, 2007, and an article whose tone was eerily similar to that of the early 1990s, with its gleeful expectation that the religious Right was finally about to collapse under its own weight or perhaps tear itself apart with internecine squabbles. Alexandra Alter wrote an article headlined, "Religious Right at Political Crossroads." She intoned convincingly that, "[They] see a crumbling conservative Christian base deflated by ethical scandals in the Republican Party, the Democratic victory in the 2006 congressional elections and...new leaders...."[7] In the article, Clyde Wilcox, a professor of government at Georgetown University, said, "Some evangelicals are tiring of electoral politics in the wake of ethical scandals involving lobbyist Jack Abramoff and Christian conservative poster boy Ralph Reed. Some of them are beginning to say, 'Maybe we've been had in the electoral arena.'"

Then the *New York Times Magazine* weighed in with an article titled "The Evangelical Crackup" in October 2007. It said:

> Just three years ago, the leaders of the conservative Christian political movement could almost see the Promised Land. White evangelical Protestants looked like perhaps the most potent voting bloc in America. They turned out for President George W. Bush in record numbers, supporting him for re-election by a ratio of four to one. Republican strategists predicted that religious traditionalists would help bring about an era of dominance for their party. Spokesmen for the Christian conservative movement warned of the wrath of 'values voters.' James C. Dobson, the founder of Focus on the Family, was poised to play kingmaker in 2008, at least in the Republican primary.

And thanks to President Bush, the Supreme Court appeared just one vote away from answering the prayers of evangelical activists by over-turning *Roe v. Wade*.

Today the movement shows signs of coming apart beneath its leaders.... The 2008 election is just the latest stress on a system of fault lines that go much deeper.[8]

These represent only the high points—or rather, low points—of journalistic attempts to bury a movement many wish had never been born. We could cite dozens more examples of deliberate efforts by some in the media to deflate conservative evangelicals, hoping they might become discouraged by the negative press reports and retreat into the political wilderness as their fundamentalist forefathers did eighty years ago. To evangelicals and other religious groups, it naturally seemed that the liberal media had joined hands with the liberal political community to marginalize people of faith. Ann Coulter's book *Godless* makes the case that liberals adhere to a set of "religious" principles that are as unbendable as the basic doctrines of any religious faith. She argues that liberals have been evangelistic in their attempts to convert the world to their secular point of view.[9] Our experience certainly has shown us that liberals often act, vote, and participate with greater "religious" zeal than many Christians do.

New Alliances Against the Religious Right

Now there is a new twist to this old trend of prematurely burying the enemy. Lately, we see a new level of cooperation between various members of the press and liberal Christians, who are allies of convenience against the religious Right. Liberal Christians are stepping up efforts to crack the unity of evangelicals by sponsoring antiwar rallies, fomenting debate about the environment, and becoming increasingly harsh and public in their criticism of the various views and tactics of the religious Right. Liberal Christians are perfectly welcome to express their views as loudly as they wish and to frame their arguments from a biblical point of view. This kind of debate can be healthy. But the press, seeing an opportunity to chip away at the unified foundation of the religious Right, is clearly slanting their coverage to use the efforts of liberal Christians like a battering ram.

For example, the national media virtually ignored the May Day for Marriage rally in October of 2004 in Washington DC. The event brought tens of thousands of participants and many social conservative leaders, including Dr. James Dobson, Chuck Colson, Gary Bauer, and Dr. Richard Land, to the National Mall to give a last-minute push to state marriage amendments that were on the ballot in eleven states. They wanted to keep the issue of marriage at the forefront of the debate heading into the national elections. Yet there were few print stories on the event.

Compare that to the media's response to an antiwar protest held in March 2007 that attracted about three thousand people. The event was sponsored in part by Jim Wallis, founder of the magazine *Sojourners* and spokesman for the new Christian Left. Wallis urged political action at the rally, while at the same time calling upon the nation to "repent of this war!" The coverage was fawning and outsized with many stories about the antiwar march.

Liberal newspapers and periodicals have also gone out of their way recently to play up an internal debate about environmental stewardship that is occurring behind the closed doors of the evangelical movement. Reporters have happily reported on letters leaked to the press that expose so-called deep fissures within the ranks of this movement. Never mind that every movement has internal debates and genuine, even intense dialogue about issues. Never mind too that this movement had demonstrated astonishing unity, delivering 60 million voters to the polls in past elections. The only angle these reporters could see was the one that fit their overall agenda: that the movement was somehow falling apart over issues like the war and the environment.

Why is the Christian Left so quick to attack the religious Right? Probably because as a movement, the Christian Left has yet to build any lasting political or policy influence. The only power they have at the moment is in their shared goal with liberal non-Christians of reducing the influence of Bible-believing, conservative Christians in American politics and policy. They have tried to gain traction by playing to the media on the one or two issues on which they can muster some temporary consensus, like the war in Iraq or the overly broad topic of poverty, which we will address in detail in this book.

The media readily allow the Christian Left to claim scriptural authority based upon selective reading of the Bible. But the failure of the Christian Left to gather any noticeable momentum, other than with East Coast media outlets, points to a fundamental difference it has with the Christian : many constituents of the Christian Left reject the Bible as authoritative, meaning every opinion and idea is just as valid as the next. Try building a coalition on that framework! By contrast, the mortar that has kept the religious Right together and strong is the agreement that, come what may, the Word of God is infallible and inerrant, making it the final word on all matters of life and policy.

Let us be clear again that we believe those on the Left have every right to speak out, and we welcome the public discourse over the important issues of our day. We have no doubt that during the next election some valid positions will be put forth by the Christian Left. But it's also true that their goal, at least in part, is to raise doubts and questions about specific social debates, such as global warming and the war, in an effort to weaken the heart and fracture the unity of the religious Right on core moral issues. And we have little doubt that some in the media will continue to be complicit in this goal.

Thankfully, there are clear biblical answers to each cultural concern and policy, and we will address the seven most important policy and cultural issues facing America in this book.

Rising Influence

Those who argue the religious Right is losing influence need only look over their shoulder to the election results of 2004, which we will discuss in greater detail in the next chapter. That election thrust evangelicals back into the center of the political stage as they helped defy modern political precedent by expanding the president's party's control of Congress in a midterm election. Not only did the party identified with the "values voters" gain more seats, but also every state that put a marriage amendment on the state ballot passed it overwhelmingly.

This election seems to have served as a wake-up call to some media outlets that conservative Christians weren't going anywhere, and that if you can't beat 'em, you might as well join 'em. Take CNN as just one example. This network had not historically had a pro-evangelical editorial bent. Members of the faith community quickly fled to FOX News or other cable networks when those options became available because they perceived them to be more supportive of their values. Yet in 2007, CNN took a radical plunge into serving Christian viewers. Just before Easter, CNN devoted nearly five days of prime-time broadcasts to discuss religion in the United States. Catholics, Protestants, evangelicals, and Jews were each represented. By our count there were at least five different specials repeated strategically during the holiday weekend.

CNN's programs were evenhanded and objective. At times they even seemed faith affirming and inspirational. The most comprehensive of these presentations was a two-part series hosted by the network's current news luminary, Anderson Cooper. His special, called *What Is a Christian?* explored the tension between science and faith. The segments were diverse, fast paced, and informative. The tone of each vignette was, for the most part, objective and civil. Cooper himself displayed intellectual curiosity and openness to each presenter as they sought answers to the central question of the program: "How is the faith community in the U.S. changing in both force and focus?"

A second, equally engaging program titled *What Would Jesus Really Do?* was also aired during that Easter season. Although this program was more overtly critical of the evangelical Christian movement, the host, Roland Martin, asked important questions about evangelical views on global warming, the Iraq war, and the divide between the rich and poor. Martin featured Bishop T. D. Jakes, Rick Warren, Jerry Falwell, and other evangelical ministers. He also made space for black evangelical clergy to present their positions, which sometimes diverge from those of their white counterparts. Martin is to be commended for not simply trotting out Rev. Jesse Jackson and Rev. Al Sharpton as "black experts." The overall presentation was, dare we say, fair and balanced.

We could add that after pastors contacted Lou Dobbs expressing concern over an unbalanced treatment of religion, he has added a frequent segment on his show titled "God and Politics," to which Tony is a regular contributor.

Excelling in the Time of Transformation

While some in the liberal press continue to pen eulogies for our movement, and while others commendably present more evenhanded coverage, the major story still is being missed: the religious Right is not fading away; it is transforming, broadening its base and its focus, sharpening its arguments, and honing its tactics for a new generation of cultural engagement. Our personal observations and connections with pastors and churches across the country tell us with certainty that Bible-believing Christians are not shying away from the pubic debate. They are as engaged as ever.

But they are also looking for leadership, guidance, and unity on the major issues of the day. We hope to provide a portion of what is needed in this book to help them succeed.

To successfully navigate this transformation of the religious Right and the challenges that will accompany its ascendance to a new level of influence, we must accomplish two very important tasks. First, we must keep the core values that have defined the movement—the sanctity of human life, the preservation of marriage, and the defense of our Christian faith—as our top priorities. Secondly, without neglecting these core issues, we must also reshape our message and agenda to include other important issues that face our generation—issues like immigration, poverty, the environment, and racial reconciliation. The purpose of this book is to examine these issues in greater detail and lay out a strong moral platform and a strategy that will enable Bible-believing Christians of every color to stand together at this defining moment in the history of our nation.

The Old Testament gives us a biblical precedent for talking about a moral platform for America. The prophet Jeremiah spoke to his nation in a time of moral decline. His words expressed the displeasure of God with Israel as a nation. They had lost their moral orientation and had begun to stagger like drunken men after a night of carousing. Jeremiah told them that they would be punished but that God had a plan for the nation. Specifically the prophet says the following:

> For thus says the Lord of hosts, the God of Israel: Do not let your prophets and your diviners who are in your midst deceive you, *nor listen to your dreams which you cause to be dreamed*. For they prophesy falsely to you in My name; I have not sent them, says the Lord.
> —Jeremiah 29:8–9, nkjv, emphasis added

Preachers, prophets, and "political pundits" of Jeremiah's day were developing dreams for the nation, but these dreams were of human origin and lacked the perspective and favor of the Lord. Jeremiah boldly spoke for God and said in the first person in Jeremiah:

> "For I know the plans I have for you," declares the Lord, "plans to prosper you and not to harm you, plans to give you hope and a future. Then you will call upon me and come and pray to me, and I will listen to you."
> —Jeremiah 29:11–12, niv

Thousands of years later, and halfway around the world, Chaplain Robert Hunt planted a cross on a Virginia beach in April of 1607, days before the founding of the settlement at Jamestown. With this act he dedicated himself to God's purposes and the land to be used as an instrument in the hand of the Lord. America has been uniquely blessed from that time forward, despite the nation's flaws, faults, and failures. Is there a set of public policies and personal choices Americans can make that will ensure another four hundred years of God's blessing upon this nation? We do not presume to speak for God as the Old Testament prophets would have. We do, however, believe that God has a plan for our nation that begins with the principles of Scripture, requires the involvement of the church, and will be empowered by His Holy Spirit. This prescription, we believe, will not *just* be embraced by people of faith, but also many in the secular community will embrace this approach for America because of its fairness, simplicity, and clarity. In the pages of this book we will lay out the policies and the underlying beliefs that provide such a framework.

These seven key issues are:

1. Value human life, both abroad in our war against terrorism and at home.
2. Reform immigration policy.
3. Reduce poverty and ensure justice, including health care.
4. Cultivate racial harmony and diversity.
5. Protect religious freedom.
6. Restore marriage and family.
7. Care for creation.

We are convinced that the church must take bold action on each of these issues to reverse America's present moral and cultural decay. The statement that America has lost its moral compass has become a cliché today. But the average American Christian, with the exception of major elections, appears to be in denial of the true depths of moral depravity that has gripped the nation in hopes that it will go away. Therefore, there is only a muted sense of outrage and urgency attached to the church's assignment to be the moral and cultural conscience of the nation. But through careful discussion, detailed presentation, and prayerful consideration of the issues we now face, we believe that the church can enter this battle well armed and able to stand uncompromisingly for the truth that can turn America around.

America's future can be as bright as the promises of God. To realize the dream, we must take action on these seven critical steps in our private lives, as churches, and in our public policy. The question is, do you want a revolution?

Chapter 1

WHO IS THE RELIGIOUS RIGHT ANYWAY?

The evangelical movement, or more specifically the religious Right, has long been caricatured as a group of prudish old men who are on some kind of strange, moralistic power trip. The movement has been painted as antiblack, antiwoman, antipoor, antigay—antieverything but lower taxes and war. The press and Hollywood are almost addicted to portraying the religious Right with stereotypes that make it seem downright un-American and anti-Christian.

But the average reporter or screenwriter has apparently never been in an evangelical church and is certainly not in touch with the dramatic transition that the religious Right is going through. The movement is literally changing before our very eyes, becoming more diverse in a number of important ways, from race to age to political affiliation. Although the numbers are difficult to quantify, and no formal study has been done, to our knowledge, we can point to significant signs of a groundswell of support coming from unexpected quarters. People of all different races, cultures, ages, and religious backgrounds now find a home on the religious Right. The movement is building bridges and alliances with people and organizations some might find surprising. But this isn't a story you're likely to hear about on the cable channels or the evening news. Many of our opponents hope to confine us to a narrow margin on the sidelines of policy. But because of the expansion and growth of the movement beyond its traditional constituencies, we are destined to remain in the center of any policy debate in America, perhaps more so than at any time before.

Broad-based Support

The reason the religious Right is in much better shape than many believe is because the values so often talked about by the movement are shared by many more Americans than the media would like to acknowledge. While people may not identify themselves as belonging to the religious Right, they hold the same values that the movement promotes and defends. Consider the elections of 2004. As we all watched the results come in, tracking the states that had marriage amendments on the ballot that day, the early reports based on exit polling showed President Bush going down in defeat. Early in the evening Tony began to receive calls from media outlets seeking comments on these ominous numbers. His cell phone began to ring as some within the Bush administration called with messages of panic. The network anchors seemed almost gleeful at the speculated outcome.

Then the actual returns from across the nation started coming in, and President Bush won. The conservative majority was expanded in the Senate by five seats. Frowns and grimaces replaced the earlier smiling faces of some talking heads as real results replaced the exit polls. The term coined that night was "values voter"—that mysterious person who played a decidedly influential role in the election results.

Who were these "values voters"? Some said they were evangelicals who turned out in historic numbers. Many would like to say that was the entire picture, but it wasn't. Evangelicals did vote in large numbers, representing about half of the votes cast,[1] and 78 percent of them voted for George Bush.[2] But they did not sway the election alone. They had help. The term "values voter" came from a category of questions asked of voters as they exited their voting locations on election day. There were also follow-up polls conducted, one by the Pew Research Foundation, which verified the results. Here are the issues that voters identified as being the deciding factor(s) in how they cast their votes, according to Pew Research:[3]

Moral values	27%
Iraq	22%
Economy/jobs	21%
Terrorism	14%
Health care	4%
Education	4%

Taxes	3%
Other	4%
Don't know	1%

The poll asked even more specific questions and discovered that, among people who said moral values was a deciding factor in how they voted, the largest segment, 44 percent, identified policy issues like same-sex marriage, abortion, and embryonic stem cell research. Other respondents who did not specify policy issues "pointed to factors like the candidates' personal qualities or made general allusions to religion and values."[4]

While some commentators talk about the impressive ability of religious Right organizations to mobilize voters on election day, that is not the whole truth. Rather, what is at work is the power of those moral values across a broad spectrum of voters. While Bible-believing Christians are pointedly identified with these values, and often are painted as self-acclaimed public guardians of America's morality, far more Americans share a common or similar set of values than just those dismissively labeled "the religious Right." Why is this important? Because it shows that the moral fiber that has been a key element of America's unity and success as a nation still abides, despite decades of assault by the secularists. Americans want moral values in their public policy. No amount of contrary court decisions or left-wing propaganda over the past sixty years has changed that.

We would never claim that America was ever a country made up 100 percent of heaven-bound Christians. In fact, we are unable to identify a point in the history of America where we can say that America was a Christian nation from a strictly spiritual perspective. Certainly no one would say that there was a time in the history of the nation when everyone living in this country was a true believer in Jesus Christ. Billy Graham has pointed out that we can't even say that about our churches.

What we have said, and what others have said based upon an abundance of evidence, is that America was shaped by, and for most of its history has been guided by, values that come from biblical Christianity. In fact, in *Divided by God*, Jewish author and law professor Noah Feldman points to "nonsectarianism" as America's effort to embrace a common morality that was founded upon the Christian faith without the particular theological beliefs of the various Christian sects.[5] This idea of common values has been the glue that has held this diverse republic together.

Harvard professor Samuel P. Huntington elaborates upon this point even further in his book *Who Are We?* when he identifies religion, and primarily the Christian religion, as a central element of the American identity.[6] This American identity is greatly influenced by the "Protestant emphasis on the individual conscience and the responsibility of individuals to learn God's truths directly from the Bible." In fact, according to a Gallup poll released in the spring of 2007, about one-third of adults in America believe the Bible is in fact the Word of God.[7]

It is these values, Huntington states, that "promoted American commitment to individualism, equality and the rights to freedom of religion and opinion. This American creed that supports the American identity, that has been fundamental to our success as a nation, is," according to Huntington, "the unique creation of a dissenting Protestant culture."[8]

The work of Feldman and Huntington supports our strong belief that today's Bible-believing Christians who are actively engaged in influencing the world around them through social and political engagement are not a part of some "vast, right-wing conspiracy" to impose their values on everyone. Rather, they are defending the common values, rooted in biblical Christianity, which have unified Americans for generations and helped make America uniquely successful as a country.

Reacting to Unrighteousness

Yet many opponents of the religious Right still paint the movement as an aggressor, assaulting the freedoms of a secular culture. We suggest they brush up on their history. What prompted Jerry Falwell and others to challenge the public policies of our government and the direction of the broader culture in the early 1980s after years of isolationist neglect by Christians was the aggression of the Left against America's long-held common values. The denizens of the religious Right, then and now, didn't have a driving desire for power, nor did they want to establish a theocracy. They did not see themselves as savvy politicians or radical religious terrorists bent on taking over the country by any means necessary. Rather, they saw themselves as people of conscience who over the last half a century have awakened to a terrible reality similar to what King David saw in his day.

> When the foundations are being destroyed,
>   what can the righteous do?" . . .
> For the LORD is righteous,

> he loves justice;
> upright men will see his face.
>
> —PSALM 11:3, 7, NIV

The religious Right is made up of people who have been awakened by real concern over government policy and cultural initiatives that were being influenced and shaped by a postmodern worldview that was radically secular and hostile toward the Christian faith. The specific galvanizing issue that launched and rapidly advanced the cause of the Moral Majority was school prayer, which had been banned by the federal courts. These courts had become a virtual candy store for people promoting the radical secular agenda. Stripping public schools of prayer was merely one in a string of legal victories that went against the popular will, but it was also the issue that finally caused millions of Christian voters to march back into the public policy arena. In spite of broad support from the American people, running as high as 80 percent, a constitutional amendment allowing voluntary school prayer failed to get the two-thirds support it needed in the Senate on March 21, 1984, by a vote of 56 to 44.[9] It remains to this day an issue that a vast majority of Americans support in one form or another. A 2005 Gallup poll of teens revealed that 84 percent were in favor of some kind of prayer within public schools.[10]

So while the rise of the religious Right is often portrayed as some type of conspiracy to impose Old Testament law or a biblical moral code upon the nation, the truth is that the movement was a reaction to a series of court decisions beginning in the late 1940s with organizations intent on carrying out a secular agenda through the judicial system. In fact, many of the groups that today claim they are defending America from the religious Right predate all of the public policy organizations associated with the religious Right. In other words, they picked the fight. We're just trying to end it.

Take the American Civil Liberties Union (ACLU), founded in 1920 by Roger Baldwin and Crystal Eastman, who had strong socialist and communist ties.[11] Or look at the antireligion organization presently headed by Barry Lynn, Americans United for the Separation of Church and State, founded in 1947. The timing of the founding of that particular organization is interesting as it coincides with a seminal decision by the United States Supreme Court in *Everson v. Board of Education* that resurrected a previously little-known metaphor, the "wall of separation between church and state" from Thomas Jefferson's correspondence. This decision has shaped all of the subsequent decisions by the courts on issues pertaining to religion in the public square.

Organizations like the Moral Majority, founded in 1979, and the one Tony now heads, the Family Research Council, which was founded in 1983, or the Christian Coalition, founded in 1989, were all a response to the radical secularist agenda of organizations like the ACLU and Americans United for the Separation of Church and State who found the only fertile ground for their anti-Christian agenda in the courts. Consider just a few of the major assaults that have been successfully launched against the Christian faith in the last forty to fifty years through these and other organizations:

▸ *Torcaso v. Watkins*, 367 U.S. 488 (1961): Court holds that the state of Maryland cannot require applicants for public office to swear that they believe in the existence of God. The court unanimously rules that a religious test violates the establishment clause.

▸ *Engel v. Vitale*, 370 U.S. 421 (1962): Any kind of prayer composed by public school districts, even nondenominational prayer, is unconstitutional government sponsorship of religion.

▸ *Abington School District v. Schempp*, 374 U.S. 203 (1963): Court finds Bible reading over school intercom unconstitutional, and in *Murray v. Curlett*, 374 U.S. 203 (1963), the court finds obliging a child to participate in Bible reading and prayer unconstitutional.

▸ *Epperson v. Arkansas*, 393 U.S. 97 (1968): State statute banning teaching of evolution is deemed unconstitutional. A state cannot alter any element in a course of study in order to promote a religious point of view. A state's attempt to cite a nonreligious motivation will not be given credence unless that state can show a secular reason as the foundation for its actions.

▸ *Lemon v. Kurtzman*, 403 U.S. 602 (1971): Creates a three-part test for determining if an action of government violates the First Amendment's separation of church and state: (1) the government action must have a secular purpose; (2) its primary purpose must not be to inhibit or to advance religion; (3) there must be no excessive entanglement between government and religion.

▸ *Stone v. Graham*, 449 U.S. 39 (1980): Court finds posting of the Ten Commandments in schools unconstitutional.

▸ *Wallace v. Jaffree*, 472 U.S. 38 (1985): State's moment of silence at public school statute is unconstitutional where legislative record reveals that motivation for statute was the encouragement of prayer. Court majority silent on whether "pure" moment of silence scheme, with no bias in favor of prayer or any other mental process, would be constitutional.

▸ *Edwards v. Aguillard*, 482 U.S. 578 (1987): Unconstitutional for state to require teaching of "creation science" in all instances in which evolution is taught. Statute had a clear religious motivation.

▸ *County of Allegheny v. American Civil Liberties Union*, 492 U.S. 573 (1989): Court finds that a nativity scene displayed inside a government building violates the establishment clause.

▸ *Lee v. Weisman*, 505 U.S. 577 (1992): Unconstitutional for a school district to provide any clergy to perform nondenominational prayer at elementary or secondary school graduation because it involves government sponsorship of worship. Court majority was particularly concerned about psychological coercion to which children, as opposed to adults, would be subjected by having prayers that may violate their beliefs recited at their graduation ceremonies.

▸ *Santa Fe Independent School District v. Doe*, 530 U.S. 290 (2000): By a 6-3 decision the court ruled that the district's policy allowing students to pray at graduation ceremonies and over the public address system at home football games was unconstitutional.

▸ *Lawrence v. Texas*, 539 U.S. 558 (2003): The court ruled that homosexuals have a constitutional right to engage in sodomy. The decision paved the way for a direct assault on traditional marriage.

Despite how liberal organizations try to portray Bible-believing Christians as being on a crusade to impose their values on people, the truth is we are simply responding to the attacks that have been waged by a small but significant minority aided by the courts.

The New Religious Right

Today, the religious Right is not shrinking and becoming outdated and irrelevant to mainstream voters, as those on the Left hope. Rather, it is undergoing a renewal. As we have already said, the day when the words *religious Right* brought to mind a stern-looking, gray-haired white man raised on prune juice are over—or should be. The new religious Right has expanded to include not just Protestants from every denomination but also millions of Roman Catholics, conservative Jews, and secular people of moral conscience. The religious Right is racially diverse, as we'll explore here and in a later chapter. The fact that this book is being authored by two men of different races and very different backgrounds is emblematic of the Right's present demographic.

This growth goes beyond the addition of African American evangelicals to include Asian and Hispanic evangelicals. In April of 2004 Tony met with a small group of Chinese pastors in San Francisco over an authentic Chinese lunch. Tony was encouraged to find a vibrant and growing network of Asian churches that were committed to defending biblical truth in the very challenging environment of San Francisco. Two weeks later the network of conservative Asian churches turned out over seven thousand people for a rally in support of traditional marriage held at the foot of the Golden Gate Bridge.

While that is evidence of culture diversification among the religious Right, the movement is also becoming younger. To illustrate this point, we'd like to introduce you to Rachel, Laura, Jesse, and Deron. Rachel Alade is eighteen years old—bright, energetic, and motivated. Her dad, Moses, is a previous vice president of taxation of the Discovery Channel. Her mom is a pharmacist who has nurtured Rachel in faith and practical wisdom. The Alades' original dream was for Rachel to attend a prestigious university like Harvard and then medical school. But those possibilities were put on hold because, though Rachel had the intellect and talent to make it at any Ivy League school, she first decided to pursue a year-long internship with Teen Mania, a youth ministry organization whose purpose is to "provoke a young generation to passionately pursue Jesus Christ, and to take His life-giving message to the ends of the earth."

One other thing makes Rachel different from the evangelical stereotype. Her mom and dad are Nigerian immigrants. Now instead of sending her to a fancy finishing school, which the family could readily afford, they have chosen to give their eldest child a spiritual boot camp experience.

Teen Mania itself is an example of the new wave of youth support within the religious Right, and there are many stories like Rachel's. Teen Mania founder Ron Luce ran away from home at the age of fifteen and became involved in drug and alcohol abuse before finding Jesus Christ. Today, Luce holds bachelor's and master's degrees in counseling and psychology, respectively. He is also a graduate of the Harvard Business School's Owner/President Management Program. Luce has created a robust organization that is committed to reach and disciple the next generation of conservative Christians. Teen Mania hosts Acquire the Fire and Battle Cry events that bring teens together during weekends to praise, pray, and be challenged to live out their faith. They enjoy live music by popular Christian recording artists and bands. In 2005, there were more than thirty Acquire the Fire/Battle Cry weekends, with an estimated 250,000 youth attending. That's no small constituency. We received the following e-mail report from Ron in November 2007:

> God has greatly blessed Teen Mania Ministries in continuing to bestow on it growth in the areas of effectiveness and support. Over 2.5 million teenagers have been affected by one or more aspects of the ministry. In touring over 30 cities each year doing youth events, Acquire the Fire has had over 205,000 choose to follow Christ at live events. There have been over 57,104 missionaries to over 65 countries through Teen Mania's Global Expeditions branch. As a result of their ministry, over 1,266,772 people have committed to following Christ all across the Globe! In addition to these, various aspects of Teen Mania Ministries have been televised. We also have many individuals getting equipped to go and reach teenagers today on www .battlecry.com.
>
> With this growing amount of effectiveness, God has blessed us in support as well. Teen Mania has about 30 million dollars of annual

income. These funds have been used to make all of these things a possibility.

Teen Mania's theme for the 2007–2008 season is, "Let Your Voice Be Heard." We know what we believe, yet all too often we sit back while the world is crumbling around us. It's time to make a stand and speak up for what we know is right. Our biblical views go outside the church walls; they should apply to every area of our life. As a follower of Christ, we must get involved with politics. Do you know who your congressmen are? Are you trying to serve them in any way? Do you know who the candidates for the upcoming presidential election are? Are you planning on voting? These are things that will allow us to get our voice out there.

It is said that 98 percent of people follow the 2 percent of people that shape culture. If we are not of that 2 percent that is involved in the leadership of this nation, then whose ideas are we following? We need to dig deep into our beings and pull out our values and line them up with the candidates. We need to make a decision based on our values and know that the person we choose is someone who will make policies based on their convictions. We need to move from being the influenced to be the influencers of this society.

Here is another story of a young person who is changing the face of the religious Right, illustrating the way many young evangelicals are pushing back against secularism that has been steering the courts in running over the rights of students to pray and recognize God in our schools. On September 15, 1999, Laura Watson attended a See You at the Pole post-rally in Fort Worth, Texas. That night, a forty-seven-year-old man fired his gun at the adults and youth who were attending the evening rally at a local church. He wounded seven people and killed seven others before he killed himself. Laura says of her experience, "It was eight minutes of tragedy, but God is still using it for triumph."[12]

Today, Laura is a teacher at a Chinese senior middle school in Changzhi, China. She sees herself as a lifestyle evangelist. In 2007, she promoted a See You at the Pole (SYATP) rally at her school in China. Laura is one of the millions of young people who have been impacted by SYATP since it was founded in 1990. The movement began when a few teens gathered for a discipleship weekend in Burleson, Texas. As they met together, God moved on them powerfully. They became burdened for their friends at school. As they began to pray, they decided to drive to three schools that night. When they arrived, they went to the flagpoles at each school and prayed for their friends, their schools, and their youth leaders.[13]

This group of teens joined with others who were having similar meetings at their schools. Together, they birthed a vision that students all over Texas would meet at their school flagpoles simultaneously to pray. This vision was shared with 20,000 students in Dallas that June. A challenge was put forth to gather as many as possible to "See You at the Pole" on September 12, 1990. At 7:00 a.m. on that date, more than 45,000 students met at their school flagpoles in four different states to pray.[14]

The news about this prayer movement spread to youth ministers at a national conference in Colorado. Even though there were no plans for a second SYATP event, it was clear that students wanted one. One million students gathered on September 11, 1991, at flagpoles from Massachusetts to California. Again they prayed for their friends, schools, leaders, and their country.

See You at the Pole has continued to grow. More than two million students from every state participate, joining with students in twenty countries, including Japan, Turkey, Australia, and the Ivory Coast. Testimonies flood the SYATP office as students share stories of how their friends have found Christ while watching the other students pray at the flagpoles. Some share how their schools have changed. Paul Fleischmann, president of the National Network of Youth Ministries, says, "Every year we have seen this day serve as a springboard for unity among teenagers on their campuses. See You at the Pole unites students in prayer at the beginning of the semester. Young people have taken unprecedented leadership through this to have a positive impact at their schools."[15]

The other two young people we'll briefly introduce you to who represent the new religious Right are Jesse Engle (then eighteen) and Thomas Hall (then nineteen). Three years ago they and five of their friends felt directed by the Lord to move to the Castro District of San Francisco. Their new home was fifteen blocks from a place called "Boys Town." On any given Sunday afternoon, hundreds of men flocked the streets of this area, walking hand in hand, kissing openly, and even performing sex acts upon each other right on the streets. It was like a modern-day Sodom, but these young men did not write off the people there. Instead, they established a nightly prayer watch from 10:00 p.m. to 6:00 a.m. They faithfully asked God for three things:

1. To burden them to cry for mercy over San Francisco and the homosexual community

2. Mass deliverance from sexual addiction and personal bondage for the people of San Francisco

3. To give them divine love for the people of that region

These prayer meetings gave birth to what is now known as the Justice House of Prayer, which currently operates from a headquarters on the infamous Haight Street, birthplace of the free love movement of the 1960s. Jesse is the eldest son of Lou Engle, the founder of a movement titled TheCall. Thomas's mother, Sherry Hall, leads a dynamic outreach ministry in Nashville, Tennessee, that ministers to homeless people and drug addicts. These young men are continuing the work of their parents in the next generation.

Both Jesse and Thomas are currently working as part of TheCall that began on Labor Day weekend in 2000, when four hundred thousand people (mostly under the age of thirty) gathered on the National Mall in Washington DC to fast and pray for a spiritual revival in America. During the eight years following the initial event, Lou Engle and his team have hosted numerous regional events, including rallies in:

▸ New York City, with over eighty-five thousand people
▸ San Francisco, with over one hundred thousand attendees
▸ Nashville, attended by over seventy thousand people
▸ And others, including Boston, London, and the Philippines

Harry serves on the board of this prayer and revival movement, which has been growing in racial diversity over the years.

White and Black Partnerships

Not only is the religious Right getting younger, but it's also changing color. There are encouraging signs of a broadening ethnic base within the movement, including a burgeoning coalition of black and white values voters. Consider what happened in Ohio in 2004, when the Buckeye State stepped into the pivotal, election-deciding role that Florida had been placed in four years prior. Ohio's political apparatus, controlled by

Republicans, refused to legislatively place the marriage amendment on the November ballot. But a massive grassroots effort was launched in the churches throughout Ohio. The effort, spearheaded by Phil Burress, president of Citizens for Community Values, collected 557,085 signatures in sixteen weeks.[16] The effort had to overcome not only political opposition but also forty-two court challenges that attempted to keep it off the ballot.

The only statewide elected official who openly supported the marriage amendment was Secretary of State Ken Blackwell, the first statewide elected African American in Ohio. Blackwell was not the only African American who supported marriage. Based upon exit polling, six in ten African Americans voted in support of the marriage amendment. Not coincidentally, in Ohio, President Bush almost doubled the percentage of votes he received from African Americans over the 2000 election, receiving 16 percent of their vote.[17] According to Edison Media Research, a similar outcome was seen among black voters in the other critical battleground state of Florida. In northern Florida, a Bible Belt region stretching from Jacksonville on the Atlantic side westward across the panhandle, 27 percent of black voters supported President Bush in 2004.[18] Clearly, marriage was a major issue from the top to bottom of the 2004 ballot.

Behind these numbers is something of great significance. The imminent threat to marriage and the broader assault on Judeo-Christian values have prompted a powerful new conversation between white and black evangelicals, which led to the successful passage of the marriage amendment in Ohio and nearly two dozen other states. Relationships were fostered through these conversations, like the one between Tony and me, and these relationships are in part fueling the transformation of the conservative evangelical movement.

Deron Cloud is a good example. He is a 6 foot 3 inch black man in his early forties who has a no-nonsense attitude and is reaching the hip-hop generation with a powerful message of grace and peace.[19] During standing-room-only plays or "dramanars," Cloud gives biblically based answers to the most pressing problems of the twenty-something crowd. Many of the young black adults whom Cloud is reaching have been ignored by the rest of the world.

His approach is similar to that of playwright Tyler Perry, whose movie *Diary of a Mad Black Woman* put him on the map. Cloud has worked at his craft of acting and playwriting for over fifteen years. He preaches a message

of personal responsibility and tough love. Central to his church's evangelistic outreach is preaching against teen sexuality, abortion, drug use, gang
involvement, and absentee parenting. As one listens to Cloud's preaching,
one hears the heart of a revolutionary. He would not identify himself as a
Republican, nor would he sign up as a loyal Democrat. He does, however,
believe that an unseen kingdom influences the world in which we live. The
King of that kingdom, Jesus Christ, has not made blacks inferior or created
them to be victims. In fact, they can become victorious soldiers if they
wholeheartedly choose the kingdom of God.

CNN recently featured Cloud and his church, The Soul Factory, in a
segment that discussed the church's unique worship style and its use of
dramatic arts.[20] They referred to it as the "un-church" because of its down-
to-earth, come-as-you-are appeal. The Soul Factory has five thousand
attendees in the DC area and recently opened a branch in Atlanta. Their
first evangelistic event in Atlanta drew over eleven thousand mostly
unchurched people.

So what makes Cloud and other young leaders like him different from
old-school black pastors? They are both biblical and social conservatives.
Their focus on public policy has shifted to put a priority on protecting the
unborn, as the African American community has been disproportionately
affected by abortion. They are placing a priority on traditional marriage as
they see the results of public policy that has deemphasized the importance
of marriage in their communities. In addition, leaders like Cloud do not
believe that government programs alone can stop crime, cure poverty, or
improve poor schools. Cloud's cultural understanding coincides with that
of many new-guard national thinkers.

Commentator Juan Williams, for example, gives some excellent prescriptions for turning around the black community's doldrums. In his
book *Enough*, Williams writes:

> Black Americans, including the poor, spend a lot of time talking
> about the same self-defeating behaviors that are holding back too
> many black people. This is no secret. It's practically a joke. And black
> people are the first to shake their heads at the scandals and antics of
> the current crop of civil rights leaders who are busy with old-school
> appeals for handouts instead of making maximum use of the power
> black people have...[21]

It seems there is a changing of the guard within the black community to leaders who are willing to partner and stand with the religious Right. This has been evident in Harry's ministry as well.

On May 19, 2005, Harry called a press conference at which he hoped to present Justice Janice Rogers Brown's record to the nation and break the tyranny of left-leaning African American leaders as it related to blacks who were nominated for high posts. A year before Harry's press conference, pastors of the largest black churches in America were unable to get the media to attend any press conference convened for the purpose of the protection of marriage, so the task was daunting. Churches of fifteen thousand and twenty-five thousand members had found themselves ignored by the media because the Reverend Al Sharpton or Reverend Jesse Jackson were not involved. But Harry, Tony, and the team worked with Senator Frist, Senator Brownback, and other white, conservative political leaders to draw a large group from the press to attend this black-tie event. They drew over a hundred pastors from around the country to the press conference and lobbying event for a values-oriented judicial appointment, marking a new day in American politics. It also showed that blacks and whites were finally coming together—not just in national rallies about faith but also on judicial policy. They were ready to roll up their sleeves and go to work.

Our first big project together, an event called Justice Sunday, was organized by the Family Research Council in April 2005. Justice Sunday was intended to rally values voters and put pressure on the United States Senate to confirm the judges who were being blocked by a filibuster. This event turned out to be a spiritual family reunion that showed the diversity of the new religious Right. Yet it completely puzzled the three hundred media reporters and even more political activists who attended. The event, held in Louisville, Kentucky, was simulcast to a thousand churches. It is probably best remembered because the appearance of Senate Majority Leader Bill Frist by video created a stir that was covered by all the major news outlets.

But on that day the media missed the underlying story that, with the exception of some rabid bloggers, almost went unnoticed. Justice Sunday was a major step toward the forging of a broad, new coalition of values voters. Christians of many different backgrounds—both Republicans and Democrats, Protestants and Catholics—participated with great enthusiasm.

Harry was one of the speakers, but he and others were dismissed by the skeptics as tokens. Max Blumenthal wrote in *The Nation*:

> Justice Sunday also featured a token Catholic, William Donohue, who heads the nation's largest "Catholic civil rights organization," the Catholic League. In the battle to confirm far-right judicial nominees like William Pryor, who happens to be Catholic, Donohue has become a key asset for the Christian right's evangelical faction. He has argued that Democratic senators opposing Pryor and others are motivated by anti-Catholicism.[22]

Just in case his readers did not get his implications of tokenism, Blumenthal went on to write:

> As the emcee of Justice Sunday, Tony Perkins positioned himself beside a black preacher and a Catholic "civil rights" activist as he rattled off the phone numbers of senators wavering on President Bush's judicial nominees. The evening's speakers studiously couched their appeals on behalf of Bush's stalled judges in the vocabulary of victim-hood, accusing Democratic senators of "filibustering" people of faith.

We can forgive this fear response more readily by keeping in mind that this rally was the first major political event held after the 2004 election. Opponents of the religious Right were still reeling from the loss of the presidency due to an unexpectedly strong response to moral issues that the Left did not detect before election night. But instead of seeing the ascendant religious Right as a positive force in America—an advocate for the poor and the alien, for the right to life, and for religious liberties— they instead perceived the religious community as a major threat to the very foundation of the nation.

Several books published in the interim sought to present the religious Right as a dangerous, un-American, divisive force bent on seizing power and imposing antiquated morals on all people. One of the harshest critiques was Kevin Phillips's *American Theocracy*.[23] The *New York Times* book review all too predictably lauded the book on March 19, 2006, stating:

> *American Theocracy* may be the most alarming analysis of where we are and where we may be going to have appeared in many years. It is not without polemic, but unlike many of the more glib and strident

> political commentaries of recent years, it is extensively researched and frighteningly persuasive.... By describing a series of major transformations, by demonstrating the relationships among them, and by discussing them with passionate restraint, Phillips has created a harrowing picture of danger that no American reader will welcome, but that none should ignore.[24]

Notice the language: "alarming," "frighteningly," "harrowing," and "danger." This reviewer saw bogeymen everywhere he looked. He wasn't alone. On September 5, 2006, Rosie O'Donnell, then a cohost of ABC's *The View*, compared the terrorists of 9/11 to Bible-believing Christians. During a diatribe against the United States' involvement in the war in Iraq, O'Donnell was challenged by cohost Joy Behar, who made reference to the threat of radical Islam. O'Donnell responded with these now infamous words:

> One second. Radical Christianity is just as threatening as radical Islam in a country like America where we have a separation of church and state. We're a democracy.[25]

Aside from embarrassing herself, O'Donnell demonstrated a general ignorance that many people in the secular culture share about who conservative Christians really are. Some people think we are professional politicians who work cynically under the guise of religiosity. Others believe we are theologians who have taken too much interest in public policy and should go back to our seminaries and churches. Others, particularly members of the secular Left, think we are scary old-time fundamentalists, ready to whack someone with a Bible or bring out the snakes. To these poor souls, we really are viewed as being on the same level as the Taliban in our religious toxicity and danger.

Political Diversity

The religious Right is also becoming more diverse in its political affiliations. While the religious Right began as a movement with deep roots within the Republican Party, it is now maturing into an ideologically anchored movement that is becoming independent of a political party. Early evangelical leaders had hoped that they could influence the Republican Party's platform and then direct the party to arrest the moral and social decline of the nation. They were partially successful; they significantly influenced the party's platform. However, generally speaking, they were never able to advance beyond the ranks of the party's foot soldiers, and moderates were repeatedly supported over social conservatives for key leadership posts and as candidates for high office.

Supporters of the religious Right acknowledge more and more that the movement has been too wedded to the Republican Party. (A similar complaint has been lodged against the black Christian community for being linked too closely with the Democratic Party.) This close association has not necessarily given the movement greater clout. One need only read excerpts of the book by former White House employee David Kuo, *Tempting Faith*, to conclude that the faith community has often been tolerated as a needed constituency instead of celebrated as a strategic ally.[26] Although Kuo's observations were extreme and perhaps imbalanced, they offered one insider's opinion that even in a "Christian" administration there can be the tyranny of the secular strategists.

This growing revelation, combined with the fact that younger evangelicals are much less partisan, is signaling that unconditional allegiance to the Republican Party, or to any major political party, may soon come to an end. Evidence is already at hand in the last two elections where black evangelicals voted for Republican candidates based upon their support of marriage in 2004, and white evangelicals voted for Democratic Congressional candidates who were pro-life and pro-family in 2006. Because of this untethering of white and black evangelicals from the major political parties, evangelicals are poised to become more powerful across party lines than ever before. While some argue that evangelicals lose influence when they fail to vote as a bloc for a particular political party, the ability to seed both parties and to operate as a political "free agent" could prove to have a much greater impact on actual public policy. As a result of the broadening of the evangelical movement, both political parties will increasingly have to compete for the support of evangelicals to succeed. This, we believe, will ultimately result in policies that are more faith friendly.

In 2008 and beyond, conservative evangelicals will advocate policy initiatives within both parties. Additionally, it will be more difficult to marginalize social conservatives by characterizing them as mean-spirited spoilers because their ranks will have become more diverse, their message increasingly redemptive, and their words more clearly associated with acts of personal ministry.

Sound far-fetched? It's already happening. Consider the presidential candidate forum called "Faith, Values, and Politics," hosted and broadcast on CNN in June 2007. The program, featuring the three leading Democratic Party presidential contenders, was revolutionary not for its questions, speeches, or choice of clergy but because it was being held at all. It was nothing short of amazing to see candidates who typically say they want to keep faith out of politics openly discussing aspects of their faith.

Yes, this may have been a clever gambit by liberals to make a new statement: "We have faith too!" (Some shrewd element of the liberal community must have finally realized that the 60 million evangelical voters represent a political force that can no longer be ignored.) Yes, the questions asked by the host and guest panel were softballs. Yes, the candidates were insulated from the tough policy and moral questions of our day. Yes, each candidate's answer was winsome, clear, and well rehearsed, amounting mostly to a glorified photo op. But putting this all aside, the program was still a major demonstration of the breadth of influence of the religious Right on the American dialogue. The leading Democratic candidates are responding to the American people. A Pew poll on religion and politics, conducted in September 2007, revealed that 72 percent of Americans want a president with "strong religious beliefs." Regardless of political party, a candidate for president of the United States cannot win without passing a minimal hurdle of declaring faith in God.[27]

The new openness won't be seamless. The week after the CNN Presidential Values Forum, Howard Dean, chairman of the Democratic National Committee, put both feet in his mouth again by making the following statements about faith in the keynote address at the Washoe County Democratic Party's annual Jefferson-Jackson dinner in Reno, Nevada:

> I haven't seen gay marriage in the Bible once. . . . But I've seen a lot about helping people who are poor and including people and not leaving anybody behind. Those are core values of the Democratic Party, and they also are core values of an awful lot of evangelicals.[28]

Many evangelicals use this as a biblically illiterate observation aimed at accusing conservative Christians of hypocrisy. Dean and others like him have not learned how to lift up biblical values without inadvertently slamming people of faith. Their lack of reverence for the Scriptures exposes their confusion. We can't help but recall that when Dean was asked about his favorite book of the New Testament during his campaign for president, he responded, "Job."

Fortunately, while some Democrats may be confused about the Bible, others are beginning to understand that they must moderate their tone toward issues of faith, if not the substance of many of their policies. Indeed, the presence of the religious Right in the realm of public policy has perhaps toned down the antireligious rhetoric Democrats have often used to drum up votes. Liberals and secular politicians are finding it increasingly difficult to use religious folks as whipping boys, while seeking to attract our votes at the same time. Perhaps that's why both Hillary Clinton and Barack Obama hired strategists to focus on reaching religious voters. John Edwards made this revealing statement: "I think the majority of Americans, the people who largely decide elections, what they are looking for—particularly in these times—is a really good and decent human being to be president. If you are a person, a man or woman, of faith, that has an impact on how they view you as a human being, whatever your faith is."[29]

Isn't that what the religious Right has been saying for over three decades? It seems that Edwards and the other candidates learned something from John Kerry's defeat in 2004: it was in part due to his lack of respect for his personal faith community (the Catholic church) and his disregard for the fears of the values voters about same-sex marriage. Insiders report that President Clinton privately encouraged Kerry to come out with a moral-sounding response to gay marriage just before the election, thus cooling off the millions who were going to the polls to support a marriage amendment and a pro-marriage candidate. But Kerry ignored the issue, and he ignored the nationwide rallies conducted by Focus on the Family Action and FRC Action and dozens of other pro-family organizations. He instead chose an immoral hill to die on.

Democrats are tentatively embracing people of faith this time around because, if for no other reason, they do not want a repeat of Election Day 2004. For the religious Right, this means new influence in public policy, new partnerships, and less dependence on one party to advance our ideas. The 2006 backlash against the Republican Party shows that values voters can both reward and punish those in office. They are a powerful voting bloc that must be sought out and convinced during each election cycle.

In 2008 and beyond, Democrats and Republicans will no longer be able to take their traditional bases for granted. This ultimately will give both parties a new respect for the voting power of people of faith. As Democrats vie for the Christian vote, they will be affected by our message.

Jesus said this concerning the transforming effect of the kingdom of God: "The kingdom of heaven is like unto leaven, which a woman took, and hid in three measures of meal, till the whole was leavened" (Matt. 13:33). As both parties tune in to faith, they will be impacted by the powerful truths of the Christian faith and the conviction of the Christian community in the United States. If the parties fail to respond, it may fuel further discussions about the creation of a third party that would more clearly represent the interests of evangelicals from both political parties. Considering that evangelicals roughly represent half of Republican voters and two-fifths of Democratic voters,[30] a third party is a potentially powerful possibility.

Young Evangelicals More Independent

A 2007 study by Pew Research confirms a trend toward nonpartisanship among young evangelicals, meaning that it's unlikely that the Republican Party will ever have the kind of unanimous support from evangelicals that it once enjoyed.[31] The study found that from 2001 to 2007, the percentage of younger white evangelicals who identify themselves as Republicans dropped from 55 percent to 40 percent. "However," says the study, "the shift away from the GOP has not resulted in substantial Democratic gains; instead it has produced a small increase in the number of Democrats (five-point increase) and a ten-point increase in the number of independents and politically unaffiliated Americans."

This means the votes of these young, white evangelicals will be up for grabs. But to appeal to them, candidates will have to be conservative on key issues. As the study notes:

> The trends toward dissatisfaction with Bush and away from the Republican Party by younger white evangelicals suggest that the Democratic Party may have a new opportunity to appeal to this group. Yet, while this group seems to be less loyal to the Republican Party than older white evangelicals, they remain much more conservative than the overall population in the same age group. Young white evangelicals remain largely committed to politically conservative values and to conservative positions on a variety of issues, including the war in Iraq, capital punishment and abortion. Indeed, in 2007, more white evangelicals ages 18–29 describe their political views as conservative (44%) than moderate (34%) or liberal (15%), almost identical to their ideological leanings in 2001. So although younger white evangelicals

are 14 percentage points less conservative on this measure than white evangelicals ages 30 and older, they are 17 points more conservative than young people as a whole.[32]

According to the Pew Research Center, the vast majority (72 percent) of younger white evangelicals favor the death penalty for convicted murderers, compared to only 56 percent of all Americans ages eighteen to twenty-nine. "And when it comes to abortion, younger white evangelicals are even more conservative" than older white evangelicals.

> For example, 70% of younger white evangelicals favor "making it more difficult for a woman to get an abortion," compared with 55% of older white evangelicals and 39% of young Americans overall who share this view.[33]

In addition to producing a greater sense of social and political responsibility among Christians, the work of the religious Right over the past three decades has spawned a new generation of Christian young people, studying at schools as diverse as Liberty University and Harvard, who are equipped with a sense of spiritual purpose and are quietly preparing to enter the public square through politics and law.

The religious Right is in a time of healthy transformation. It is finding an expanded message, vitality, and an emerging generation of leaders. After being demoralized, vilified, and declared dead by its enemies, the religious Right is poised to build upon the foundation laid by its pioneers. As America heads for what we pray and believe will be a new great awakening—that is, a historic realignment of America's ideals and practice—the religious Right is in a much better position to lead American public policy and private piety than any other constituency. The movement is embracing new constituencies and new arguments that resound with the American people while staying true to the movement's core principles.

Prayer Points

▸ Thank God that, as Christians, we are still able to make our values known without risking our lives in this country.

▸ Repent for where you have not actively pursued righteousness on behalf of this country (Prov. 14:34). Ask the Lord's

forgiveness for any lethargy or slothfulness in researching
candidates and their platforms before election day.

▸ Ask the Lord to strengthen those who are fighting for a
moral agenda within the government (Job 8:6)—from
governors to congressmen and the Cabinet of the president
to the Supreme Court justices.

Chapter 2

CONSCIENCE TO THE NATION

In May 2006, we met with national leaders and members of the Bush administration for a summit that, whatever its intent, signaled a turning point in the relationship of evangelicals to the Republican Party. By that time the religious Right was restless. The president and Congress had failed to follow through on the values voters' agenda except to veto stem cell research. The administration seemed to be backing away from its original commitment to pass a constitutional amendment that defined marriage as a union between only a man and a woman. The president's priorities over the previous eighteen months had not included any of the evangelical community's major concerns. In fact, we had been told repeatedly that the president would get around to addressing the issue of marriage as soon as he won the battle for Social Security reform. That victory never came. President Bush ended up losing a great deal of credibility in that fight. Then his response to Hurricane Katrina and the devastation of New Orleans and the Mississippi Gulf Coast radically shifted the nation's view of the administration's competence and character. In addition, the Iraq war was by this time a constant source of emotional turmoil for many Americans.

As the president's credibility slipped, in many ways so did his commitment to the moral agenda of the evangelical Christian community. Many evangelicals felt as though they had been faithful foot soldiers for the Republicans in an expensive war for political turf but now had little to show for it. While what was accomplished was not insignificant with two solid Supreme Court justices in place, President Bush also held the line against congressional efforts to expend taxpayer-funded research on human embryos. Congress did pass and the president did sign into law the Unborn Victims of Violence Act, partial-birth abortion ban, and the Born-

Alive Infant Protection Act, but there was so much more promised and so much more needed. For us, the confirmation that there was little to show for all we had done came in the disheartening discussion with various members of the administration, the Republican National Committee, senators, and congressmen at this summit. Karl Rove, the president's chief political strategist, addressed the group via phone and described the dynamics of the 2004 presidential victory. He communicated a view that left many of us shaking our heads in disbelief. According to Rove, the grassroots evangelical activism in Ohio generated by the state marriage amendment had not been a decisive factor in the outcome of the presidential election in the state and therefore the nation.

As we mentioned in chapter 1, the effort to pass the marriage amendment in Ohio was opposed by every statewide elected Republican except Ohio Secretary of State Ken Blackwell, who would later become the Republican gubernatorial candidate for the Buckeye State. The amendment only got on to the ballot and passed because of the initiative and work of Phil Burress, the president of Citizens for Community Values, who was aided by almost $2 million from FRC Action. Rove's statement was either convenient amnesia or an attempt to rewrite history. Rove's cavalier manner served to convince us that the Christian moral values agenda would no longer be a priority of the administration.

After Karl Rove had finished speaking, leaving some in the room in shock and others visibly angry, Harry spoke up. He explained that he was a registered Democrat but had felt compelled to work with the Republicans because of the moral agenda that many Republicans supported, primarily the defense of marriage. Harry went on to say that it was beginning to appear that the Republican Party was taking Christians for granted just as the Democrats had taken blacks for granted. Harry's statement angered Rove, who then tried to dismiss our concerns as trivial and naïve. Several major national leaders spoke up and voiced their displeasure with both Rove's attitude and the administration's lack of follow-through on the issues like marriage that were featured prominently in the 2004 campaign, only to disappear after the election.

A few days later Harry and thirteen others were in the West Wing of the White House for a meeting in which the president opined that he had done everything he could to protect marriage. He implied that the Senate was not doing its share. He ended the forty-five-minute discussion by asking the group to educate their constituencies and told them that he needed their help to change the nation. In our opinion, the administration was effectively "passing" on the debate. They had written it out of their agenda. Our movement had failed to push the president and his party to action. Instead, we lost a strategic battle because we had not leveraged our influence for fear of losing what stature we had in the party.

For many evangelical leaders, this led to a painful self-examination about the fruit of this close alliance between the Right and the Republican Party. What had been accomplished in this thirty-year courtship? The three most visible goals of this alliance over the last three decades were to pass the Human Life Amendment, a school prayer amendment in the early 1980s, and most recently to pass the Federal Marriage Amendment in 2006. Unfortunately, none of these amendments succeeded. The Human Life Amendment failed by a vote of 50 to 49 in 1983. The school prayer amendment failed by a vote of 56 to 44 in the U.S. Senate in 1984, and the marriage amendment met a similar fate, when a cloture motion failed 49 to 48 on June 28, 2006. One might argue that our Republican-only alliance has not successfully advanced our agenda. In hindsight, we can easily acknowledge our need to impact both political parties.

Regaining Our Voice to the Nation

The church is not called to be a mouthpiece for a political party; rather it is to be a moral voice to the nation, and the public role of Christians is to be a sort of moral conscience to society. To operate in that role, we must remain faithful to the principles of the Scriptures and the character of Jesus Christ. As much good as we see in the track record of the religious Right, we do believe that many in the faith community have either been apathetic in their silence concerning the moral issues of our day or have transgressed by functioning as just another special interest group. It is especially unfortunate that in the eyes of many, the religious Right has been seen as an appendage of the Republican Party as opposed to being seen as guardians of truth and ambassadors of Christ.

Some would argue that to be ambassadors for Christ we must withdraw from the political process. However, if we are to be truly obedient, withdrawal is not an option. Instead, we must rise above the seductive draw of power and partisan myopia and be consistent voices, speaking the truth in love.

Let us warn you, this is not the path of least resistance. Some within our movement frown on party disloyalty. During the page scandal in the fall of 2006, Tony was interviewed by every major news network about Representative Mark Foley and the fact that congressional leadership had taken no action to address his overtures to underage male pages even though it had been brought to their attention on several occasions. Tony said that the revelation was the final straw for many conservatives and that the incident would impact turnout and enthusiasm of social conservative voters in the election that was only weeks away. The prediction was accurate. But in the process he was assailed by a prominent Christian talk show host and other party loyalists for honestly assessing the situation because they saw it as harmful to the party's prospects at the polls.

As long as we as Christians are willing to tolerate or overlook duplicity in our self-identified party, it will be clear to the world that our allegiance is to a party and not the truth, regardless of what we claim. Unfortunately, the Christian community is not now seen as an objective voice—received and respected by all. To become that objective and prophetic voice to the culture and government, we must change the way we relate to power. The civil rights leaders of the 1950s and 1960s often used the phrase "speaking truth to power." They were more committed to truth than to power. They were aware that if they remained true to their calling they might lose their access to powerful politicians and businessmen, hence the statement coined by civil rights leaders that "we have no permanent friends, only permanent interests." The permanent interests of civil rights leaders were the welfare and equal rights of African Americans. But as black religious leaders strayed from their objective cultural advocacy in subsequent decades, they stopped "speaking truth to power." Leading black ministers and civic leaders became nothing more than an extension of the Democratic Party, which threw them a bone every now and again.

In the same way, the evangelical movement has been guilty of preferring access over accountability. All too often evangelicals have tolerated major breaches of character or competence within the Republican Party or certain "pet" conservative groups. But if we are ever to speak as the moral conscience of the nation, we must consistently stand for a clear set of values and principles, no matter if that leads to a temporary loss of political power.

At the risk of being overly simplistic, it is important to remember that we must earn the right to be heard. We cannot assume that because the Bible is the basis for our social involvement we will be received by all Americans. Daniel (Dan. 9:1–21) and Nehemiah (Neh. 1:4–11) are excellent biblical examples of godly men who participated in something theologians call "identificational repentance." They repented before God for the shortcomings of their people and became responsible for leading massive national reform. In a unique way, their humility qualified them for leadership and the right to be heard.

We believe that these biblical examples of political leaders who came before us did their best to honor both God and His Word. They attempted to reflect the character of God in dealing with the secular world. Most importantly, they realized the need to be a true witness for the Lord in all they said and did. We yield to these same tenets and know that while many of the movement's intentions were good, there are some areas in which we missed the mark.

The apostle Peter's teachings explain the spiritual dynamic behind this phenomenon of "identificational repentance." Peter said, "Be clothed with humility: for God resisteth the proud and giveth grace to the humble. Humble yourselves therefore under the mighty hand of God, that he may exalt you in due time" (1 Pet. 5:5–6).

As Daniel and Nehemiah took personal responsibility for the sins of their nation, grace to lead their people and make changes was imparted to their lives. In a similar way, we as a movement need to ask the Lord to forgive us for our faults whether they are past or present. In years past, there have been several examples of churches and governmental bodies formally repenting for past actions. In 2005, the U.S. Senate, under the leadership of Senator Frist, apologized to the nation for not having intervened to prevent the lynching of 4,700 African Americans from the Reconstruction Era to the present. Similarly, in 2007, the Commonwealth of Virginia apologized for the damage done through slavery that they had allowed to flourish within their state borders. This was especially significant because Jamestown, Virginia, was the first place African slaves touched American soil in 1619. It was the "Plymouth Rock of Slavery" in what is now the United States. In 1995, the Southern Baptist denomination repented for racism and drafted a document that expressed their regrets, which was signed by the leadership of their movement. As a result, Dr. Richard Land has stated that their denomination has grown in black membership by more than 750,000 people since the resolution. The Southern Baptist repentance demonstrates that there is more than a natural or political phenomenon occurring here.

As an expression of our repentance, we believe leaders in our movement, including us, need to apologize to the nation for not being the godly example we should have been for them. Here are the main points of the apology we wish to offer:

First of all, we must ask forgiveness for falling into the trap of aligning with one party too closely. While impacting the Republican Party was a necessary first step for our movement, our message and influence must extend to both parties. Secondly, we must apologize for failing to show the world a unified church. They have seen us as being separate and disconnected—a black church, a white church, and a Hispanic church. Therefore we must ask the Lord to give us wisdom concerning increasing the momentum of racial reconciliation within the entire body of Christ. In fact, later in the book we will address our need to heal the racial divide in much more depth.

Finally, we acknowledge that our movement has unintentionally allowed itself to be characterized as insensitive and uncaring concerning the poor and needy. Nothing could be further from the truth. Unwisely, we have just shrugged off the numerous declarations that we lack Christlike compassion. Our chapter on poverty will address that criticism, but we must take responsibility for having been silent in many public policy matters concerning the poor who need our advocacy. Our national voice must rise to the same level as our local works in this arena.

For both of us, writing the things in this book has become a way of following in the footsteps of Nehemiah and Daniel. We recognize the country's need for the power of God's grace that comes only through this kind of humility and repentance, and we long for the massive transformation that can follow.

Dealing With Failed Leadership

Whether conservative Christians like it or not, we are held to higher standards than liberals. Conservatives, and Bible-believing Christians especially, must remember that we have chosen these high standards for ourselves. The culture did not ask for the standards we espouse; in fact, most people reject them. We are attempting to rescue a resistant society that essentially thinks it does not need help, and we must remember this.

In the face of skepticism from many of our fellow Americans, some of whom paint us as passé moralists who are out of touch with the modern world, we must strengthen our right to be heard by the culture. Our nonreligious neighbors must sense that our desire to serve the nation and keep it from self-destruction is genuine. For this message to be received there has to be integrity of lifestyle, clarity of thought, and a sense of mission among our leaders that restore conservative credibility. Anytime someone is so bold as to try to be the conscience of a nation, their motives and integrity will be closely examined by skeptics. This is especially true of the leaders we choose for ourselves.

The same standard should apply to leadership within the church. Previous scandals that have rocked the church show that there is structural accountability that will expeditiously resolve these moral failures in a biblical manner. However, no amount of structural accountability can replace personal holiness and personal accountability. Like it or not, evangelical leaders are held to a higher standard because we represent a higher standard. Perfection is not possible, nor is it demanded, But we *are* demanding personal integrity and accountability. The nation has a right to expect our civil and religious leaders to walk the walk, not just talk the talk. The personal failure of conservative leaders has tarnished the credibility of our movement and may lead many Americans to reject our moral positions on the grounds of personal hypocrisy. We must demand greater personal accountability among our leaders in the pulpits and in politics.

2006

If our nation's political leaders from both parties don't clean up their act, they may soon experience both providential and political repercussions. Each election is like a report card issued by voters, grading our elected officials on how they have done. Voters reacted very harshly to the Republican scandals in the fall of 2006 and removed them from the majority on Capitol Hill. Contrary to what some self-satisfied liberal commentators and reporters wish us to believe, Christian ideology was not defeated in those elections, despite the fact that the party with the greater religious rhetoric was ousted. Rather, the election was a multifaceted referendum on the Republican Party because of scandal, corruption, out-of-control spending, and its clumsy handling of the Iraq war effort. It was a failing grade on competency and character. The message was: "If you ever want to have governing power again, you'd better straighten up and fly right."

Anyone who has been involved in family counseling recognizes that reestablishing trust is a difficult task. It is vastly more difficult to restore a broken relationship than it is to begin a new one. In our nation, the restoration of trust will occur just as it does in a family. Healing always starts with someone recognizing their own shortcomings instead of pointing the finger at someone else.

This is not a time for Christian conservatives to hang their heads or to run for cover. This is a time for a moral, political, and spiritual renewal to grip the heart of the nation. Our prayer is that this revolution will begin with us personally. We want to be model Christians. We want to see America populated by Christians who live so loudly that their actions are heard around the world. St. Francis of Assisi expressed what we are feeling in this way: "Preach the gospel at all times, and, when necessary, use words."

It's also time for Bible-believing Christians to influence both major parties to pull up their grades on both character and competency. This first means that social conservatives have to bump up their game by walking the walk themselves and putting the issues before both parties by hosting additional town hall forums, writing more books, and being more public about our failures as well as about the tenets of our faith and how they should intersect with the culture and public policy.

A Biblical Model

Christians are called to perform a "prophetic" role in modern-day culture. What does that mean? In both the Old and New Testaments, prophets were charged by God to deliver important messages to their contemporaries. They served as God's conscience to their people. In addition to speaking, they often demonstrated their messages to the culture in which they lived. They were like walking, talking billboards placed at key intersections in their nation to relay God's messages.

It isn't always a comfortable lifestyle. Isaiah went around naked, Ezekiel was not allowed to mourn the death of his wife, and John the Baptist wore the most unusual clothes. We're not calling for bizarre or spooky behavior, but we are calling for Christians to act and believe as though each one of us has a prophetic assignment to the nation that begins right where we live and work. We have been assigned to speak and live out the truths of God. The majority of the prophets of Ezekiel's day were corrected by the Lord because they did not get involved in the major social problems of the nation. The Lord figuratively referred to the cultural problems of Ezekiel's day as "breaches in the wall." Ezekiel 13:4–5 reveals the problem:

> O Israel, thy prophets are like the foxes in the deserts. Ye have not gone up into the gaps, neither made up the hedge for the house of Israel to stand in the battle in the day of the LORD.

According to this scripture, the spiritual protection of Jerusalem was not up to armies, presidents, or governments alone. The Lord made it clear that prophetic voices must "stand in the gap" before Him in order to protect their land. This concept of a social "gap" is repeated in Ezekiel 22:30 and is consistent with the major themes of this and other books. Drawing from the Scriptures as a whole, we believe that the church must do five things correctly in order to fulfill its prophetic role in our day:

1. Live right

This simply refers to the church's need to meet the standard of Scripture before it attempts to talk to the culture. We must have strong, individual, personal testimonies of victory in the areas in which we want to offer help to others. It is not just enough to speak the way; we must lead the way. This means that in an area like marriage it is not enough to tell everyone else that marriage is important. Rather, Christians should work to make their marriages models of success so that we as a community will have greater authority to speak to the nation about marriage.

The church's ability to defend God's institution of marriage has been greatly hindered by our lack of reverence for marriage. With divorce rates in the church that rival the nonchurch community, we are failing to honor and uphold marriage as God designed it to be. We know that this is a sensitive subject for many Christian leaders who have congregations made up of families that have been broken by divorce, but our silence on the matter does not help. Our message on marriage and divorce should be very clear, because God is very clear. God says He hates divorce. Why? For one, we believe He hates it because of what it does to men, women, and children. But God does not say He hates people who are divorced. He cares very deeply about them and for them. We must minister to those who are hurting because of divorce, but at the same time warn others and prepare them to succeed in marriage.

2. Do right

We need to minister within our local communities. The Christian community has a responsibility to serve the nation before it can credibly confront the nation. Crisis pregnancy centers are an excellent example of a way in which churches and outreach ministries have addressed the problem of abortion. There are approximately twenty-eight hundred crisis pregnancy centers in the United States that help pregnant girls and women find alternatives to abortion. These ministries show that our opposition to abortion is not just a matter of meddling. We are willing to help people. Unless we are willing to give people godly options, helping them to do the right thing, we become judges instead of servants.

The Christian community as a whole must be much more involved personally in the public life of the nation. We must become not just advocates for the poor, the homeless, the widows, and for those who are being treated unjustly, but we must personally and corporately serve their needs. By the same token we are also called to function corporately in a manner similar to the prophets of the Bible proclaiming God's truth to the culture and to the government.

3. Move right

We live in a media-savvy world in which public opinion is a part of the culture. Our community must make sure that we consider the way the nation views what we do. Romans 14:16 makes an amazing declaration as we consider our service to the community. It says, "Do not allow what you consider good to be spoken of as evil" (NIV).

One of the most problematic aspects of Christian activism in our day is the fact that we are often labeled and typecast. Our good is "spoken of as evil." We need to reconsider our practices and methods to insure we are not fueling those stereotypes. For example, the Moral Majority was unable to shake its image within the black community of being racially prejudiced. There were lingering jokes in the black community that the city of Lynchburg—the headquarters of Jerry Falwell's Liberty University, Thomas Road Baptist Church, and the Moral Majority movement—was given its name because of the huge number of blacks who had been "lynched" in that town. Many blacks would snicker as they spoke about Dr. Falwell's political efforts, as if to imply that they knew what he was really doing. Some folks went so far as to state that the Moral Majority was an extension of previous political or social movements such as the Dixiecrats and the KKK, which had opposed equal rights for blacks. While the claims have no merit, the movement has not yet shaken this image of racial bigotry. This racial divide has hurt both blacks and whites. There is much we can do together in the future. Moving right means developing campaigns to overcome the stereotypes that our opposition uses to divide us.

4. Pray right

All the prophets of the Bible were prayer warriors who sought God regularly, worshiped Him intimately, and obeyed Him faithfully. The story of Jonah is an excellent account of the way the Lord used prayer to change the heart of His servant and bring him to maturity. Every Sunday school child can speak about the prophet who was swallowed by a whale, but very few of them understand the length of the personal growth journey this man embarked upon. Initially, he ran the opposite direction of God's call because he didn't want to speak the Lord's message to a great heathen city. He was arrested by a storm and then thrown into the ocean at his own request. In the end, Jonah obeyed, and the Lord showed mercy to the people of the great city after they repented.

We believe that the story of Jonah is literally true, yet we see an amazing allegorical quality to it as well. It is interesting to note that Jonah's father's name was Amittai, which means "truth." This means Jonah was "son of truth." God had to deal with Jonah's heart to make him courageous enough to carry the message, compassionate enough to love sinners who violate the Word of God, and composed enough to respond to the sovereign dealings of God in his life. As with Jonah, the greatest victory for us would be for the people who seem to be our greatest enemies to repent of their sins, enter into a personal relationship with God, and see their lives and lifestyles changed. To reach that end, we must be courageous, compassionate, and composed. The quickest way to take on those attributes is to spend time with God in prayer.

James 1:20 summarizes the spiritual lesson from the life of Jonah. "For the wrath of man worketh not the righteousness of God." No servant of God can become self-righteous, assuming that the Lord feels the same way toward the people as the prophet feels about them. The old phrase "love the sinner and hate the sin" has a great deal of truth. It is helpful if we constantly remind ourselves that "we do not wrestle against flesh and blood, but against principalities, against powers, against the rulers of the darkness of this age, against spiritual hosts of wickedness in the heavenly places" (Eph. 6:12, NKJV). In other words, prayer is often the real battlefield on which we fight.

5. Speak right

We must succeed in speaking the truth in love. Our words to the culture must not be judgmental. They must be helpful and redemptive. This means our hearts must be filled with the desire to reach the lost and heal the sick. If our hearts are not right, our words will not be right—"for out of the abundance of the heart the mouth speaks" (Matt 12:34, NKJV).

We are not saying that a Christian should never offend. Any Christian engaged in the reformation of our culture is bound to offend, perhaps more often than not. But the defining question is, is it the truth we speak that offends, or it is the attitude with which we speak it? Do we love people? Are we motivated to speak out of both temporal and eternal concern for those we confront?

Tony likes to refer to many of the cable talk shows as "gladiator TV" because of the verbal assaults that are intended to draw blood from the opponent. The more controversy and the shriller the voice, the higher the ratings. Tony, while appearing on television almost more than any other Christian leader in the policy arena, refuses to attack his television opponents. He discusses the issue at hand, points to the inconsistencies or flaws in his opponent's position, but never attacks. In fact, he often uses the time in the "green room" and the time between segments to find out more about them.

The bottom line is, we as Christians must love people, and our words must reflect that love, even when we speak the truth.

These are a few of the steps we believe the religious Right, and the church at large, must take to restore its prophetic, credible, objective, and powerful voice in America's culture and policy.

From Revival to Reformation

One of the reasons we have written this book is to give Christians a positive, biblically based blueprint for activism. But our country's greatest need is for spiritual revival in American churches. We see the fire of revival in our churches; we must fan those flames with our prayers so that from a spiritual revival we can see an awakening in America that will lead to cultural reform.

Evangelicals are poised to lead such a spiritual awakening. But in addition to seeing souls saved, Christians must aim to reform the culture. This implies new laws, new public policies, and a new focus upon biblical justice. (We use the words *biblical justice* because the term *social justice* has been become overly identified with the Left and with socialism, heavy government spending, and antifamily policies and approaches.)

True societal reformation will go beyond rhetoric or feelings and create new realities for everyday people. The First Great Awakening in America created a desire for the abolition of slavery. The Second Great Awakening reinforced the first and created a broader spiritual base for the inevitable abolition of slavery and recognition of human rights. The civil rights movement of the 1950s and 1960s under Dr. King's leadership was a "mini-awakening" that opened doors for all Americans. King's message was so persuasive that many other groups were given freedom in its wake. Revival is a kind of spiritual shock wave that reverberates throughout society and government.

But when revival becomes reformation, the personal becomes public. Inner faith becomes outward policy. Righteousness is incorporated into the entire culture. In an awakened America, people would walk in love toward their fellow man. Racism, sexism, and classism would be washed away. The privileged would serve the poor. Blacks, whites, and Hispanics would live in harmony and create a color-blind nation that loves God and strives to do His will. In an awakened America, child abuse would be banished from our shores, and pornography would not destroy the intimacy of marriage. In an awakened America, the dream of personal achievement and Dr. King's dream of social harmony would both be realized.

In an awakened America, more families would stay together. Babies would not be aborted. Rather, unwanted babies would be adopted and discipled instead of aborted or discarded. In an awakened America, opportunity will replace oppression and racism will give way to relationship.

Every great awakening in America has brought us back to the powerful foundations of our faith and erased social barriers that would destroy us. In these times of awakening and intense spiritual vibrancy, we believe the church should seek to reform the structure of society.

Both revival and reformation are needed in our land. Think of them as two wings of a bird. Without strength in both wings, a nation cannot soar into God's purposes. These two wings do not compete with each other; they complete each other. For Christians, political involvement must be an expression of a vital personal faith. In days of revival, God renews our hearts, creates fresh spiritual brokenness, and releases new compassion. And when that revival becomes reformation, biblical justice for others becomes the cry of the revived. Momentary spiritual renewal is coupled with thoughtful, strategic action, which makes permanent gains in society and government. Bible readers are aware that when Jesus was resurrected, other people were also raised from the dead (Matt. 27:52–53). Revivals work like Jesus's resurrection; they can awaken many moral aspects of a culture or society.

Reformation of an entire nation will take the entire Christian community working in unity and with a prophetic voice. Now let's move into the seven core values of personal faith and public policy that we believe will set the agenda for our movement in the years to come.

Prayer Points

▸ Thank the Lord for His mercy upon the nation, despite the sin that has mounted in every generation since the founding of the nation (Ps. 79:8).

▸ Repent on behalf of the American church, that we have not been a consistently true voice that represents God's kingdom agenda in the way we should. Ask Him to forgive every Christian leader.

▸ Ask the Lord to lead you into His righteousness as a light to those around you. Ask Him to bring you to a place of practical justice by actively engaging in the political process. Ask His Spirit to show you specifically what you should do (Matt. 5:16).

Chapter 3

CORE VALUE #1: THE VALUE OF LIFE (PART 1)

TERRORISM, WAR, AND THE SWORD

A s an eighteen-year-old, not yet a month out of high school, Tony was forced to ask himself if he could kill another human being. The thought had never crossed his mind during the visit with the Marine Corps recruiter or during the initial screening process or testing that preceded his arrival at Marine Corps Recruit Depot San Diego in the summer of 1981. Unlike today, America was not at war, but the threat of war loomed heavy over the nation as the cold war continued.

Tony was in basic training at the time. Basic training is designed to transform boys and girls who won't follow the simplest instructions from their parents to clean up their rooms into young men and women who will follow orders even in the face of death. They are shaped into some of the most skilled and courageous warriors in the world. Part of this process is not only training them in the mechanics of how to fight, but also spurring the psychological changes needed to prepare someone to take the life of another human being.

For Tony, this became a key moment not only in his training but also in his life. It required much prayer and deep soul-searching. Could he take the life of another human being? At that time the most likely enemy would have been the communists. Was he prepared to send someone from an atheistic country, who almost certainly did not know God, into a godless eternity? Tony was apparently not able to hide his dilemma. His drill instructor saw it all over his face and gave him a tongue-lashing laced with expletives. So Tony retreated to a closet to secretly pray through an issue that most Christians never have to confront in reality.

The religious Right is often described by its opponents as being hawkish, promilitary, and even warmongering. On our home soil, we support law-and-order policies, causing some to see us as mean-spirited, judgmental, and violent. But our stance on war, terrorism, and the use of military force is part of a seamless and consistent philosophy toward life. Above nearly all other values, conservative evangelical Christians stand for protecting life, whether it's the life of the unborn, the life of the aged, the life of people like Terri Schiavo who are severely handicapped, or the lives of innocent citizens throughout our country. Our defense of life springs from the Bible's repeated commands to defend the weak and defenseless.

While most people don't see an immediate connection between issues like abortion and terrorism, to members of the religious Right, the connection is clear. In this chapter we will tackle the thorny question of how to wage war and combat terrorism in a way that upholds our fundamental goal of supporting and defending innocent human life.

What the Bible Says About the Use of Deadly Force

Terrorism used to be a minor matter of foreign policy. Prior to leaving the Marine Corps in 1987, Tony was assigned as his unit's antiterrorist noncommissioned officer. Little training accompanied the additional responsibility because the idea of a terrorist strike occurring at a facility in the United States was not even entertained. Today, that same facility is ringed with concrete barriers, and a sentry stands guard to screen all persons who enter.

Upon leaving the Marine Corps, Tony joined a private consulting firm in Washington DC that trained foreign police officers to combat terrorist threats overseas. Again, there was no thought that such specialized training, such as what was needed to fight the Shining Path in Peru or November 17 in Greece, would one day become regular training for law enforcement in this country as it is today.

The present war against Islamic terrorism now brings to the fore an age-old argument: can a Christian be in favor of war, and in what circumstance? We are often asked, "How can a man of the cloth be pro-war?" or "How can a peace-loving Christian deal so harshly with terrorists?" We respond by saying that we are not pro-war. War, at its root, is based in the sin nature of man and should be strenuously avoided. Unfortunately, there are times when war cannot be avoided. In a fallen world, war is sometimes the only option we have to defend innocent life.

There are issues where the Bible is very explicit, such as the Ten Commandments or Jesus's summation of the commandments (Matt. 22:37–40). One does not have to consider whether or not an adulterous relationship or stealing is right or wrong. Scripture is clear. In other cases we rely upon the principles found in the biblical accounts of how God instructed His people to live. Engaging in war is one of those areas. We know that God does not prohibit a nation from engaging in war (Deut. 20), but there are clear guidelines.

When and how to make war centers around the question that defines the whole value of life debate: who has the right to engage in armed combat that will terminate human life? The primary verse that will guide our discussion of the Bible's approach to life is part of the Ten Commandments. The sixth commandment reads: "Thou shalt not kill" (Exod. 20:13). Most Bible scholars say that this commandment forbids the intentional taking of human life by an individual, unless it is in self-defense. In today's vernacular the scripture could be more accurately translated as a commandment against murder. In fact, the New American Standard version of the Bible says exactly that: "You shall not murder" (Exod. 20:13, NAS).

This commandment is only repeated directly three additional times in the Bible—Deuteronomy 5:17, Matthew 5:21, and Romans 13:9. Despite the limited number of references, these passages make it clear that taking a human life is in the domain of God, not man. There were procedures for dealing with accidental death, but the intentional taking of human life has always been seen as a heinous crime punishable by death. Killing another human being for personal reasons, whether out of passion or premeditation, is an act of rebellion against God, for He has said, "Vengeance is Mine, I will repay" (Rom. 12:19, NKJV; see also Deut. 32:35). Life is His responsibility. It's His domain. We must treat it with utmost respect in every form in which we find it.

However, since the time of Noah, governments have had biblical authority to execute people who commit capital crimes or violate national law. Further, governments—not individuals—are charged by God to wage war. Wars often result in large numbers of human casualties. The apostle Paul confirms the government's authority to use lethal force in the Book of Romans:

> Let every soul be subject unto the higher powers. For there is no power but of God: the powers that be are ordained of God. Whosoever

therefore resisteth the power, resisteth the ordinance of God: and they that resist shall receive to themselves damnation. For rulers are not a terror to good works, but to the evil. Wilt thou then not be afraid of the power? do that which is good, and thou shalt have praise of the same: For he is the minister of God to thee for good. But if thou do that which is evil, be afraid; for he beareth not the sword in vain: for he is the minister of God, a revenger to execute wrath upon him that doeth evil. Wherefore ye must needs be subject, not only for wrath, but also for conscience sake.

—ROMANS 13:1–5

The "sword" Paul talks about is symbolic of the civil government's authority. It is used to defend, punish, or execute, and the threat of punishment helps to keep people within the law. For many years, most denominations have therefore endorsed an understanding of the Scriptures called the Just War Theory. We will explain this theory in greater detail later, but essentially, this approach to the Word of God maintains that although God is not the author of mortal conflict on the earth, there are moments in which governments must take up arms and engage in just wars. Most people would agree that the war against Hitler's Germany was an important war for world freedom—a just war. Unfortunately, in today's postmodern world the conflicts are seen as less sharply defined, and more people insist that there are reasonable sides to every conflict.

In the Scriptures most wars that Israel entered into were seen as just and holy. On the other hand, the military aggressions by Babylonian and Assyrian armies that led to the captivities of the Israelites were manifestations of God's discipline and judgment upon Israel. But when they cried out to God in humility, the Lord delivered them from the hands of their enemies. The often-quoted 2 Chronicles 7:14 says, "If my people, who are called by my name, will humble themselves and pray and seek my face and turn from their wicked ways, then will I hear from heaven and will forgive their sin and will heal their land" (NIV). This essentially guaranteed divine intervention in Israel's international conflicts, nationwide epidemics, or famine. When they were walking with God as a nation, the Israelites consulted God before each battle. There was a sense that success in combat was tied to the divine blessing and provision of God. In fact, the Lord was seen as the captain or supreme commander of the nation. Jehovah was Israel's ultimate war hero. (See Psalm 24:8.) When Israel was delivered from Egyptian captivity, they called God a man of war (Exod. 15:3). This concept differs from the Islamic concept of jihad in that these just wars are under the authority of the civil government, not the church or the individual, which has clearly been given distinct areas of responsibility. The Bible is clear on the separate but complementary areas of responsibility of the individual, the family, the church, and the state. In Christian nations, governments, not individuals, wage wars. While the practice of suicide bombing is condoned by some Islamic states and encouraged by some Islamic leaders, it is in many cases personally initiated and carried out. This stands in stark contrast to the biblical principles that Christian nations follow in entering into armed conflict.

The highest priority when considering war should be peace (Deut. 20:10). Every effort should be made to resolve matters without the use of deadly force. The use of military force is seen in Scripture as justifiable when it is in defense of the nation from external or internal attack and to assist other nations who share the same moral value system (1 Kings 22:3–4). We will readily admit that these are not firm and fixed "thus says the Lord" principles. Rather, they are open to interpretation, which is why Christians must think them through carefully and prayerfully and come to conclusions in each particular situation.

We do not believe that pacifism is in keeping with Christian teachings. Consider this passage from the Book of Ecclesiastes:

> There is a time for everything,
>> and a season for every activity under heaven:
>> a time to be born and a time to die,
>> a time to plant and a time to uproot,
>> a time to kill and a time to heal,
>> a time to tear down and a time to build,
>> a time to weep and a time to laugh,
>> a time to mourn and a time to dance,
>> a time to scatter stones and a time to gather them,
>> a time to embrace and a time to refrain,
>> a time to search and a time to give up,
>> a time to keep and a time to throw away,
>> a time to tear and a time to mend,
>> a time to be silent and a time to speak,
>> a time to love and a time to hate,
>> a time for war and a time for peace.
> —Ecclesiastes 3:1–8, niv

The Evolution of Modern War Theory

St. Augustine, known as a father of modern Christianity, is often credited with developing foundational, biblical premises of how national armed conflict should be viewed. He did not promote war because of self-defense. Augustine believed that it was never permissible to kill someone in order to defend our personal lives or property. Rather, based on Jesus's teaching of turning the other cheek (Matt. 5:39; Luke 6:29), he felt that Christian love required a nonviolent response to imminent personal danger. But this rule of "turning the other cheek" did not apply to the Christian obligation to care for the defenseless and weak. Therefore, according to Augustine, Christian rulers were obligated to make war in order to protect subjects—even if force of arms was the only way to stop an attack upon the defenseless.

Augustine's biblical views became the basis of the medieval Christian doctrine called the Just War Theory. St. Thomas Aquinas built on the writings of Augustine as he crystallized this doctrine. He taught that there were three conditions necessary for a morally legitimate war:

1. Legitimate authority
2. Just cause
3. Right intention

In the interest of time we will not attempt to trace the concept of just wars from Aquinas's day to the present. We will simply look at Just War principles, the modern principles derived from Augustine's and St. Thomas Aquinas's doctrines and that are accepted by most nations. They are divided into two categories:

1. *Jus ad bellum* (justice in resort to war) principles, which apply to political leaders. These include:

    ‣ Just cause
    ‣ Legitimate authority
    ‣ Comparative justice
    ‣ Right intention
    ‣ Last resort
    ‣ Reasonable chance of success

2. *Jus in bello* (justice in the conduct of war) principles, which
    apply to military commanders and soldiers. These include:

    ‣ Proportionality
    ‣ Discrimination

Most of the points are self-explanatory. But we want to zero in on three of them—right intention, proportionality, and discrimination. As we think about the concept of right intention, we must keep in mind that war is most moral when its primary objective is to stop genocide or accomplish some other noble aim. Unfortunately, many nations wage war based on less honorable purposes. Wars to gain access to natural resources such as oil, minerals, or even water rights violate the primary concept of right intention. A few examples of immoral reasons for war are ethnic cleansing, economic gain, expansion of territory, and increased international influence.

The second point that needs to be explained is proportionality, also sometimes referred to as the "principle of macro-proportionality." This is in keeping with the words of Jesus in Luke 14:31–32:

> Or what king, going to make war against another king, sitteth not down first, and consulteth whether he be able with ten thousand to meet him that cometh against him with twenty thousand? Or else, while the other is yet a great way off, he sendeth an ambassage, and desireth conditions of peace.

This principle suggests that the amount of force used should be in proportion to the military objective pursued. In other words, moral warriors would not kill soldiers simply to kill them. Further, they would certainly not kill or maim innocent civilians. This leads us to the third point that we want to highlight—discrimination. This concept says essentially that soldiers should fight soldiers. It is sometimes called "the principle of noncombatant immunity." The unfortunate reality of war is that there will always be some "collateral damage" or loss of life of innocent civilians. But the principle still holds: we should seek to minimize the number of noncombatants that are hurt. "Weapons" such as land mines are especially reprehensible because they kill noncombatants for years after the conflict.

What about preemptive strategies for preventing war? It is easy to decide to wage war against someone who has attacked your nation. It is more difficult to gauge whether a preemptive strike should be made against a potential attacker. The most obvious example of this in the last decade has been the question of whether or not we should have invaded Iraq. The morality of this invasion has been questioned by many. While we don't seek to reargue that here, we do believe the preemptive strikes are sometimes justified. Similar to a man standing in the entrance way of his house seeing an armed robber who may harm innocent family members, a quick preemptive strike may be the wisest course of action.

Is Terrorism a "Just War"?

What about terrorism? Is it a moral option for people who view themselves as oppressed? We do not think so. It violates both the principles of discrimination and proportionality. It is especially immoral in the way that it is carried out in the world today, with brutal acts such as beheadings, torture, and marketplace bombings. These are not confined to the Middle East; the IRA in Ireland and other resistance movements have violated these principles as well. The objective of terror tactics is always the same: to generate fear so as to force a superior or occupying military force to give in to the terrorists' objectives.

In the summer of 2007, terrorism was on the mind of Harry and his wife, Michele, who were in Greece when a botched terrorist attack in Glasgow, Scotland, made international news. The Greeks they spoke with were painfully aware of the nearly four hundred years of domination and suffering their ancestors had experienced under Turkish Muslims. Churches and historic buildings were desecrated during the Muslim occupation of the land. The Greek light of democracy and freedom was nearly snuffed out during a long night of national fear. One of the greatest civilizations in human history lay ravaged and imprisoned by a backward, brutish occupation force that only understood the politics of the sword. Further, religious intolerance was practiced in Greece just as it is in every nation in which Islam has the upper hand. For example, "nonbelievers" paid higher taxes, had no say in the government, and were not free to evangelize others.

Greece was set free because of a religious revival along with military and political action in 1822. God's grace helped them overcome terrible odds. Many people died during Greece's four hundred years of occupation, but when Greek apathy died, they were able to break the bonds of this oppression.

Only the naïve believe that the flare-up of radical Islam today is a temporary response to the wars in Iraq and Afghanistan. So why is Islam again
trying to dominate the world through violence? And how is it that tolerant,
politically correct societies like Britain and the United States, which are
more than accommodating to Islam, provoke Muslims to attack in such a
manner? We are observing an age-old pattern of Islamic imperialism. This
is not the result of U.S. and British foreign policy errors. Rather, these are
the pervasive and dangerous manifestations of an ancient ideological war.
Fundamentally minded Islamic families and mosques are raising a new
generation of terrorists to be intolerant advocates of their idea of jihad.
While we would be the first to say not all Muslims are evil or terrorists, we
would be very quick to add that we find it hard to see a line of distinction
that separates Islam's spiritual goals of world domination from its political
goals. Also, the Islamic terrorists who oppose us do not think about their
actions from a Western worldview that has been shaped by Christianity
and that gives great value to the individual. Terrorists have a very different
set of moral parameters. The common American sentiment that terrorists
are human too and only want what we want is a gross misunderstanding
of the culture and philosophical foundations of terrorist actions. This puts
us in the difficult situation of deciding how to respond to enemies who act
without a similar moral compass.

Unfortunately, in the name of religious tolerance, Western cultures
may actually be emboldening terrorists in their society. One example is
the Church of England and others discussing the dropping of the Cross of
St. George, the patron saint of England, from the flag because it reminds
Muslims of the crusades. Western governments are starting to look the
other way as Islamic groups incite terrorism and attempt to set up Sharia
law—which violates their nation's internal laws—on Western soil. Islamic
radicals do not feel that these concessions are olive branches of peace; they
see them as weakness that is inherent in depraved Western culture. They
also believe it will logically result in the infidels eventually recognizing
and honoring the "superiority" of Islam. The perception of weakness is
not without merit. Consider how many leaders in the West are afraid of
making Muslims angry or appearing racist, so they often violate basic
principles of domestic justice.

We believe that no amount of diplomacy will permanently reverse the
efforts of Islamic imperialists and terrorists today. Our hope for peace lies
in educating the next generation while justly and swiftly defending against

those who do not value human life. Unfortunately, that means we will live more or less at war for a long time to come. And in that ongoing conflict there will be many moral questions to face. One of them is torture.

Torture

The unusual dynamics of the war in Iraq, and the problems of interrogating combatants in the Middle East, have led many people to conclude that torture is acceptable. We believe, however, that America should hold itself to a higher standard that distinguishes the Christian West from the rest of the world. At a minimum, we should adhere to the international standards of warfare established by the Geneva Convention. Granted we understand that the Geneva Convention is not clear on illegal combatants, leaving their treatment open to debate. Despite the lack of international clarity, America must maintain a sense of dignity and justice in all that we do, even in war. The debate about torture defines who we are. If we cross a certain line we become sadistic, barbaric, and part of the problem rather than the solution. It's instructive to note that over the last century of warfare, the countries that have engaged in torture of prisoners of war have been non-Christian nations. (We include Hitler's Germany in this list because it manifestly was not a Christian nation by the time of World War II. Hitler had led it astray.) We cannot allow the end (peace) to justify the means (torture).

The reason America is having a debate about torture at all is because we are losing our grip on what defines us as a people and nation. The fact that we would even consider torturing our enemies tells us we have lost something foundational in our character. It's this erosion of values that led to things like the Abu Ghraib scandal. When torture becomes more acceptable to our leaders, it will be practiced by people down the chain of command. It becomes almost impossible to draw the line on where it should stop. Tony's first assignment in law enforcement was the parish (county) prison where he quickly learned that if you are not tethered to the truth that there is right and wrong and everyone is accountable for their actions, you can get sucked into a moral black hole where anything is allowed and standards are no longer fixed. This leads to loss of morale, loss of conscience, and a state of hateful lawlessness even among "the good guys." As angry as we may be at our enemies, we shouldn't put Jack Bauer in charge of interrogation.

Torturing another human being is damaging to both parties. The way we treat foreign nationals on the field has a psychological impact on our soldiers, our citizens, and our culture. It also sends the message to our allies and enemies that we no longer respect the dignity of human life. It signals that despite our rhetoric, we are no different than our enemies.

What constitutes torture? At the very least, our definition of torture would include any infliction of intense suffering that causes long-term, irreparable physical damage. We are hesitant to define torture in psychological terms because it's much harder to measure and because war itself has a negative psychological impact.

How the Church Can Fight Terrorism

We recently attended a meeting in New York City with fifty or so bishops and church leaders from Europe and Africa. Their core message to us was this: radical Islam is on the march around the world, and the church in America is a key player in meeting this challenge. They asked us to redouble our efforts at personal evangelism around the world. This is a great example of what everyday believers can do to truly fight terrorism over the long term. We should support ministries that go into the Middle East and present the gospel and missionaries who evangelize Muslims in this country.

There is a strong public policy element to this as well. Many countries, including allies of the United States, do not allow Christians to live and move freely. An example is Saudi Arabia, which is a close ally but which will not even allow a church to be built within its borders. Some have outlawed conversion to Christianity, with the punishment for such crimes being death. In February of 2006, Abdul Rahman, an Afghan citizen, was arrested and was facing the death penalty for his earlier conversion to Christianity. The Family Research Council was made aware of Abdul's situation and immediately sought the intervention of the U.S. State Department. When the State Department was reluctant to act, FRC helped make Abdul's plight a national story as Tony appeared on every major network calling for the U.S. government to act. The rationale for the United States to intervene was simple. The Afghan government that was prosecuting Abdul was in place because of the U.S. intervention in Afghanistan that toppled the Taliban regime in 2001. The construction of the constitution that Afghanistan was operating under was supervised by the United States and was supposed to guarantee religious freedom. International pressure began to build as Australia, Germany, the United Kingdom, and even the European Union spoke out in opposition to the actions of the Afghan government.

President George W. Bush released a strong statement saying, "It is deeply troubling that a country we helped liberate would hold a person to account because they chose a particular religion over another."

On the morning of March 27, Tony was called to the White House for a briefing on Abdul by a senior member of the National Security Council. At that meeting Tony was informed that Abdul had been released and was being taken by UN transport to Italy.

This is a good example of the United States pressuring an ally to tolerate Christian activity. Countries like Afghanistan, Iraq, and many others receive aid from the United States. Our nation's policy should be that they must maintain the free passage and free exercise of religion of Americans who come to help rebuild and ideally for their own citizens. We have to flex our muscle, because if Christian witness is excluded from these countries, then radical Islam will grow and terrorism will flourish. We must demand that our government open doors for evangelism in places where Muslim rulers have slammed that door shut. Before countries like Turkey become full members of the European Union (EU), the United States should encourage our allies, who are members of the EU, to insist that Turkey and others who join the union are tolerant of all faiths. The United States can promote this policy in many ways, including trade agreements, subsidies to other nations, and diplomatic pressure.

After World War II, General MacArthur was overseeing reconstruction in Japan. He called for missionaries to come to prepare the soil for the seeds of democracy in Japan. While sending missionaries is the work of the church, providing for their safety is the work of the government. The U.S. Department of State should ensure at the negotiating table that these missionaries will be protected and given free passage to move around the country and share the gospel.

We need to raise awareness about the challenge of radical Islam in many different ways. Christians should build relationships with politicians who are open to this issue. We can also influence opinion making through public forums (especially the media), resourcing, and building relationships with journalists. It is also important to teach students in Bible colleges and seminaries about the challenge of radical Islam and the best means of response.

A nation's strength ultimately is found in God. We cannot rely solely upon our military to fight radical Islam. The strongest military on earth, absent a declared trust in God, is of little use and should be of little comfort to its people. As the English Bible commentator Matthew Henry wrote, "Weapons of war stand men in little stead without a martial spirit, and that is gone if God is gone." In keeping with our value of life, we should be antiwar unless circumstances make it necessary to defend innocent life. And in everything we do in war and peace, America should strive to maintain the moral high ground so that friends and foes alike will see the justice of our cause.

Prayer Points

▸ Thank God for His faithfulness to America that we have seen little in terms of terror or war on our soil. Praise Him for the protection He gives to us as a nation against many forms of evil (Ps. 5:11).

▸ Pray for wisdom for our leaders who must make tough decisions concerning the complex international relationships of our country on a daily basis (Ps. 105:22).

Chapter 4

CORE VALUE #1:
THE VALUE OF LIFE (PART 2)

FROM CONCEPTION TO RESURRECTION

n 1992, Tony realized that "pro-life" was more than a slogan when he came face-to-face with his own conscience. Since the age of five his family had attended church; he had accepted Jesus Christ as his Savior at age nine. Though he doesn't recall ever hearing a sermon about abortion, he always thought of himself as pro-life because Christians, after all, are pro-life.

In July 1992, the controversial organization Operation Rescue arrived in Baton Rouge for a demonstration in front of what used to be known as Delta Women's Clinic (it has since closed). At the time, Tony was a reserve police officer with the Baton Rouge police department. For the previous five years he had worked as a contractor with the U.S. State Department in antiterrorism training. When the police department received notice that Operation Rescue was coming to Baton Rouge, Tony heard talk of how some planned to "teach" these people a lesson. He too thought the protestors were a little over the top. It was his opinion that you could be pro-life without creating a scene. Still, he chose not to work during the weeklong protest.

Throughout the week, the protestors assembled at the clinic during the day and packed out a local church at night. Tony went to the clinic each morning equipped with his personal video camera, not to join the protestors or to film them, but simply to observe the actions of a few police officers. Most of the officers apparently thought he was working intel for the department and paid no attention to him. But the use of excessive force that was caught on tape was shocking and explosive. The video was given to a local independent television station, which aired the footage each night, feeding the flames of the controversy.

At night Tony and his wife attended the church services, where the roles were reversed. Abortion supporters did the picketing, trying to block cars from entering the church. It was at one of these evening services that he was confronted with the idea that being pro-life was more than a bumper sticker on your car or even a guide to voting—it was the heart of God.

At that point no one knew the source of the video that was creating the stir. But then Tony decided to go public and write an article for a local Christian newspaper, detailing what had been taking place. The article linked him to the video, and he was summoned to the chief of police's office and ordered to hand over his badge and commission. He received a six-month suspension for violating department policy by speaking against department actions. At the end of the suspension his badge was offered back to him by the chief on the condition that he agree to never speak out against department actions again. He could not agree to the terms and left the department.

In the meantime, Tony was offered a position as a reporter for the television station to which he had provided the video. His assignments as a reporter, and later as the news director, were primarily to the Louisiana legislature, which eventually led to the next stage of his career. But through it all, Tony had come to terms with what God said regarding innocent human life. He could not stand passively by and let his silence contribute to the continuation of a practice that would ultimately bring God's judgment upon our nation. He had to come out strongly on the side of the unborn. There was no longer any middle ground for him.

Support of unborn children has long been the cornerstone issue of the religious Right. But with the advance of technology and medicine, there are a host of new and novel life issues confronting our movement. Technology is presenting moral and ethical questions that were not even contemplated when the pro-life movement began in the 1970s. But the heart of the matter remains unchanged: How do we as Bible-believing Christians uphold the sanctity of human life? What should be our policy objectives in 2008 and beyond? What are the personal steps we must take to truly build a life-honoring culture?

The challenge and mandate for us are to establish a consistent, principled pro-life position that we can apply across the board to all issues. This will not only help us evaluate candidates for the nation's highest offices and to give them guidelines for future policies, but it will also equip each of us with a practical guide in our quest to advance a culture of life. If we don't define where we stand, we will find ourselves caught flat-footed by new technologies that affect how life is created, altered, and destroyed.

Let's see what the Bible says to us today about the sanctity of life and how this biblical approach affects the following policy issues that are especially impacted by our understanding of the value of life:

1. Abortion
2. Cloning
3. Stem cell research
4. Child abuse and neglect
5. Elder care
6. Euthanasia
7. Slavery and sex trafficking
8. Capital punishment

Abortion

Abortion is wrong based upon God's injunction not to murder human beings. An unborn child is a person with a calling and destiny ordained by God. In the eyes of God, killing an unborn child is just like killing an adult, because life begins at conception—a fact that even science confirms. Scripture makes clear that God acknowledges and has His hand upon the unborn (Job 31:15; Ps. 139:13–14; Isa. 44:2; Jer. 1:5). The sacrificial killing of children is also forbidden in the Scriptures. Molech, the national god of the Ammonites, was worshiped by people who presented their own children to him in ritualized murder. The nation of Israel was exhorted not to follow in the ways of the Ammonites and kill their children. The scripture below makes a specific reference to this practice.

> And thou shalt not let any of thy seed pass through the fire to Molech, neither shalt thou profane the name of thy God: I am the LORD.
> —LEVITICUS 18:21

While the church was slow to respond thirty-five years ago when the Supreme Court opened the door to legalized abortion in the infamous *Roe v. Wade* decision, Christians have since responded in remarkable ways.

The nationwide network of crisis pregnancy clinics and homes for unwed mothers operate on the time of dedicated volunteers and the donations of engaged Christians reaching out to women in need. In 2004, Focus on the Family launched the Option Ultrasound Program (OUP), a project that provides ultrasound machines for these centers. As of November 2006 over 270 machines have been put in place, resulting in literally thousands of babies being saved as their mothers saw the remarkable images on the screen.[1]

What if the church had initiated just a portion of these outreaches prior to the court's decision in 1973? Could the decision have been prevented? We would like to think so. There also is no doubt in our minds that because of the church's successful reaction to the legalization of abortion on demand, slowly but undeniably a culture of life is being reconstructed.

As Christians, we must continue to actively, boldly, and compassionately work to reduce abortions. We believe it's possible to decrease the number of abortions by 50 percent over the next ten years. We should encourage more crisis pregnancy centers to open, especially in black and Hispanic neighborhoods. These centers are even more effective when they have sonogram equipment and more medical staff—a great opportunity for donations or funding by churches or individuals. Churches can also educate women about the risks associated with abortions, including the potentially heightened risk of breast cancer.[2]

Harry feels strongly that the high number of black children aborted every day in our nation is a form of black genocide. He is especially grieved that he was not more vocal about abortion in the black community prior to the 1980s when some black clergy doubted white evangelical sincerity about abortion. The net result of this deception is that both black and white political leaders tolerated this crime against God and man for far too long. To help bring solutions to this problem, he, along with the High Impact Leadership Coalition, has begun encouraging black churches to prioritize this kind of outreach.

As Christians, we should also advance a cultural public relations campaign that shows that not only does the faith community care about unborn children, but we also care for mothers and their children once they enter the world.

In the policy arena, we should continue to promote abstinence until marriage as the standard. We should support the funding of abstinence programs available under Temporary Assistance to Needy Families, the federal program that funds welfare. The movement also needs champions of abstinence in every racial category. We should continue to lobby for the elimination of state subsidies for abortion and to protect and enhance parents' rights in the pregnancy-related decisions of their children.

Cloning

Cloning is a new frontier in the pro-life battle. It burst into the news when Dolly the sheep was cloned in 1996. DNA was taken from an oocyte (an unfertilized egg) of a Scottish Blackface ewe, and through somatic cell nuclear transfer, or SCNT, Dolly was created.[3] Theoretically, human clones can be created using the same technology. If this thought repulses and horrifies you, you're not alone. The United Nations has gone on record against human cloning, but strangely the United States has yet to pass a prohibition on the practice of human cloning. Our Congress has not even been able to agree to a ban on the Frankenstein science of human/animal hybrids made through cloning.

Here is why Congress has refused to prohibit human cloning. To ban human cloning would also ban what opponents of these ethical restrictions call "therapeutic cloning." What's the difference? Only that in therapeutic cloning, the embryo is made and then destroyed before it reaches a certain age, normally fourteen days—hence the name "clone and kill" that has been attached to this procedure. Keep in mind we are still talking about a human embryo that if given time and the right environment would become a full-grown human.

The compromises that have been offered are to set timelines by which the embryos have to be destroyed so that they cannot become a full-grown clone. That's not much of a compromise. In fact, it is a slippery slope. If we as a society agree that it is OK to conduct research on human embryos up until they are fourteen days old because it may improve the quality of life for others, what is to stop us from redrawing that line to four weeks or four months? There are actually some who advocate allowing the embryos to fully develop and then harvesting the parts before birth.

As Christians we should support scientific advancements and celebrate the benefits they bring to the human race, but we must take the lead in insisting that science should not violate the principle of valuing life. Rather, we must control scientific advancements within a life-honoring ethical framework. Science unbridled from morality will take us places we don't want to go, and we will only realize it too late. The fact that something *can* be done does not mean it *should* be done. We need to continue to push for a total ban against the cloning of human beings and the creation of human/animal hybrids through use of cloning or any other means.

Embryonic Stem Cell Research

On January 18, 2007, Noah Markham was born in Covington, just outside of New Orleans, Louisiana. Noah's birth would not normally have made national news, but he was the youngest survivor of the devastating hurricanes that hit Tony's home state in September 2005. On September 11, 2005, two weeks after Katrina hit New Orleans and left the city under water, seven Illinois conservation police officers and three Louisiana state troopers rescued Noah and fourteen hundred other embryos that had been frozen at Lakeland Hospital.[4]

It is frozen embryos like Noah that are at the heart of the debate over stem cell research. In 2003, there were an estimated four hundred thousand frozen embryos in the United States.[5] Most are the result of in vitro fertilization where multiple embryos are produced by parents to be used for fertility treatments; the "extras" are frozen for possible future use. Some of these frozen embryos have actually been adopted by infertile couples, giving birth to the name "snowflake babies." The question lies with what to do with the four hundred thousand "excess" embryos that lie in wait within laboratories across the country. The Left wants to use these embryos for research purposes. We strongly disagree. These are living beings who have identities in God's kingdom. Tony shows pictures of over one hundred adopted "snowflake babies" at crisis pregnancy centers to help potential mothers understand the human face behind the embryo. Tony stood side by side with young children who began as snowflake babies at the White House. They watched as President Bush announced the first veto of his administration, his veto of a bill that expanded taxpayer funding of research on these frozen embryos. We applaud that President Bush has stood resolute on his commitment that taxpayer money should not be spent to conduct research on human embryos.

There's another good reason to not go down the path of stem cell research. It's ineffective! In the ten years that human embryonic stem cell research (ESCR) has been done, there have yet to be any successful treatments of any medical condition.[6] In fact, ESCR is problematic in that the cells divide and multiply so rapidly that they create tumors. There are also problems of host rejection. There is, however, a successful and ethical alternative: adult stem cell research.[7]

Adult stem cells are derived from umbilical cord blood as well as a variety of other sources. In many cases, adult stem cells are extracted from the body of the person being treated, which eliminates the issue of rejection that is so problematic in embryonic stem cells. Adult stem cells have been successfully taken from various areas of the body, bone marrow being one of the most common. Adult cells have also been successfully used from the blood, kidneys, eyes, nasal tissue, and fat cells (no shortage there!). Blood and tissue from the umbilical cord are also sources of adult stem cells. At present, over seventy different types of medical conditions have been treated with adult stem cells, yielding remarkable success in many cases.[8]

Presidential candidate Senator Fred Thompson summed up our views against embryonic stem cell research with a convincing argument that silenced even the liberals. The senator notes that seventy-three breakthroughs have been made in adult and cord blood research, while to date, there are "still no embryonic stem cell breakthroughs." These breakthroughs are addressing major health concerns, such as ovarian and breast cancer, diabetes, and heart disease among others. With the success of adult stem cell research, Thompson believes it is only logical to "put out money where the breakthroughs are happening" and cease cloning embryonic cells.[9]

We should be investing our resources in this kind of medical and scientific research that is not only effective but is also ethical in that it does not require the destruction of a human embryo. In this debate over human life, regardless of whether it's abortion, embryonic stem cell research, or end-of-life issues, we must have a fixed reference point from which we do not deviate. That point is simply this: *all innocent human life is deserving of our collective protection.*

Research that involves the destruction or manipulation of embryonic human beings should be eliminated from universities. And higher institutions affiliated with religious institutions must understand the indictment they bring on our beliefs if they participate in research involving human embryonic cells. College alumni must take the time to find out if their alma maters are participating in morally suspect research. If an institution is using human embryos, its alumni should petition to halt such research.

The academic community should set standards that define the precious and unique nature of each human life.

Congress should ban federal involvement in human embryonic stem cell research based on the fact that it destroys a human being. We can never approve the destruction of living human beings to preserve or promote the health of other living human beings in the name of science. We should also encourage the use of alternative sources of stem cells, such as adult stem cells, those from umbilical cords or placentas, or other new sources of reprogrammed skin cells by increasing federal funding for this type of research.

In a legal brief filed by Mother Teresa in a court case in New Jersey a number of years ago she wrote:

> I have no new teaching for America. I seek only to recall you to faithfulness to what you once taught the world. Your nation was founded on the proposition—very old as a moral precept, but startling and innovative as a political insight—that human life is a gift of immeasurable worth, and that it deserves, always and everywhere, to be treated with the utmost dignity and respect.[10]

The goal of life should not be to enrich and prolong our own lives at all costs, especially when that cost is the next generation. If we follow this path of cloning and embryonic stem cell research, not only will we become the first generation of Americans to fail to make sacrifices so that our posterity might prosper, but also we will commit to sacrificing our posterity in the pursuit of that elusive fountain of youth.

Child Abuse and Neglect

In a major meeting on Capitol Hill attended by a high-profile group of black and white urban clergymen, the head of one of the nation's largest black denominations stood up and made a surprisingly transparent comment. He said that many black Americans feel as though white Christians have great compassion for the unborn but forget about children after they are born. His message was clear: many people of color feel that the religious Right fails to emphasize the "right to life" of young adults, prisoners, and the elderly. The leader's statement was not an accusation against his white brothers but was meant to explain one of the many reasons unified action across racial lines is sometimes difficult. He was essentially saying, "Let's broaden our battle to protect life at all stages so that our 'good will not be evil spoken of.'"

To survive and thrive as a movement in the coming years, Bible-believing Christians must expand the discussion about the value of life. This "expansion" is not a euphemistic way to describe a new compromise. Rather, the expansion we're calling for reflects the ever-changing moral challenges facing our nation.

One often-overlooked aspect of the life issue is child abuse and neglect. There were 2.6 million reports of child abuse filed in 2002 in the United States. Through the investigations that followed, about 896,000 children were identified as positively being victims of either abuse or neglect. This stunning figure amounts to more than 2,450 children who are abused each day. Of these cases, 60 percent of these children were neglected—the caretaker had not provided for their basic needs. Physical abuse victims amounted to 20 percent, sexual abuse victims were 10 percent of the total cases filed, and 7 percent were victims of emotional abuse.[11]

Based on these statistics from 2002, an average of four children die every day as a result of child abuse or neglect in the United States. This amounts to nearly 1,400 kids per year.[12] Compared to the 1.2 million children killed by abortion every year, this number may seem small, but even one child's death because of abuse is too many.[13]

Yet the immediate death statistics are not the whole picture of abuse. An abused young person suffers ongoing misery. Survivors of abuse may become depressed, withdrawn, violent, or even suicidal, and they may become abusers themselves. Abused children may also grow up to refuse discipline, use drugs, or run away from home. Child abuse inflicts long-term damage to the survivors and significantly impacts their quality of life.

God gives children to parents, and along with this gift comes the responsibility for shaping their children's lives. Child abuse and physical neglect are crimes and should be treated as such. When a parent seriously harms a child through physical abuse or neglect, he or she should not be dealt with by social service agencies but by the criminal justice system. Treating child abuse as a crime not only restores justice but also provides the parent with due process, which is often lost in the administrative hearings of social service agencies.

There is another form of neglect we'll point out, and we go again to the scripture from the Old Testament that we referenced earlier.

> And thou shalt not let any of thy seed pass through the fire to Molech, neither shalt thou profane the name of thy God: I am the LORD.
>   —LEVITICUS 18:21

Does this scripture even remotely relate to modern life? Yes, in our view it does. God's injunction against sacrificing children speaks to the experience of contemporary America. Every day, unborn children are sacrificed for the elusive promise of an education, economic security, or maintaining a reputation. But in less obvious ways even Christians are often tempted to "sacrifice" and neglect their children on the altar of personal convenience by not investing the time to properly raise them to know and follow the Lord. They either overschedule themselves or their children, or they work long hours out of concern for the economic future. They sacrifice time with and training of their children and so harm their souls and minds. This is a far cry from actually sacrificing children in the flames or criminally neglecting them, but the principle is the same. With the increase of two-income families, children are educated and socialized primarily by day-care facilities and school systems. Parents draw back and do not have as strong a bond with their children as in past generations.[14]

The answer is to recognize this error and restructure our lives so that raising our children becomes a top priority. Our public policy should encourage this focus on our families through tax policies that make it easier for parents to leave the workforce and raise and educate their children. Both state and federal governments can encourage employers to adopt flexible work schedules where possible through business tax incentives and credits. The bottom line is that we must make our children a priority. As parents this may mean making financial sacrifices for a season with one parent leaving the workforce. It may mean no outside hobbies or activities beyond church, work, and family. Because every person and every family situation is unique, only you know what steps you need to take to give your family the attention God would have you give them. Whatever those steps are, we encourage you to take them, not just for the well-being of your family and your children, but also for the well-being of our country.

The church has a clear-cut opportunity to show our love and compassion to the nation. Will we discard these lives or disciple an overlooked generation?

Caring for the Elderly

The sanctity of human life includes preserving the quality of life of the weakest and most vulnerable among us. The fastest-growing population segment within the United States is people aged sixty and older. The

United Nations Department of Economic and Social Affairs has calculated that one out of every ten people in the world is sixty years of age or older. At the current rate, by 2050 this will grow to one out of five.[15]

As the numbers increase, so does the abuse of the elderly. In Ohio, for example, there are more than forty reports of elder abuse each day.[16] Who would abuse an elderly person? Surprisingly, it is not typically a worker in an institution but a family member. Elder abuse crosses all cultural and economic barriers. Most of the victims are females, seventy-five years or older, who live with family members and experience poor mental or physical health.

Stress has been determined to be a strong contributing factor to this kind of abuse. Many family members are under pressure financially due to the senior living with them. The demands of physical care combined with the continuation of career and family pursuits bring anxiety and overwork. This type of abuse includes giving improper or very little care to the person, keeping him or her in isolation, denying food or medication, verbal abuse, physical restraint or hitting, and misusing the person's money or property.[17]

The challenge to protect the unborn and to protect the elderly may seem to have only a casual connection, but a deeper look suggests they are more closely related than one might think. In 1916 Planned Parenthood was launched by Margaret Sanger with the aid of wealthy industrialists.[18] The genocidal motivation behind Planned Parenthood was to prevent the unwanted and the unproductive from entering the population. Today, Planned Parenthood is the largest abortion provider in the world, having performed 264,943 abortions during its 2005–2006 fiscal year.[19] The organization that had a 2005–2006 budget of $847 million also receives millions in federal tax dollars every year to help them in their task.[20]

The idea of eliminating the potentially unproductive and unwanted is utilitarian. It does not consider what the person has to offer but only what they have to take of our allegedly finite resources.

It only stands to reason that the same utilitarian standard would be applied to the elderly. The aging baby boomers, who ushered in abortion on demand to accommodate their sexual liberation, will soon be entering their golden years only to come face-to-face with a generation who has grown up under this utilitarian view of life. How tragic that the policy of abortion on demand that many supported could soon be turned on them.

How do we care for our elderly and ill? Christians should offer to help those providing home-based health care and volunteer at nursing homes, assisted-living facilities, and hospices. The church should model how the elderly are to be treated. We should promote laws that insure that ill and elderly people are given appropriate medical care and pass tax relief measures for families who must care for elderly loved ones and/or ailing family members.

The value of life continues to be the bedrock of the religious Right, and our principled voices must be heard on every issue that touches life. With a consistent voice, we can turn the tide of the culture of death in America so that life is again celebrated, nurtured, and affirmed in our private lives and our public policies at every stage.

Euthanasia

In 2005 the right-to-life issue was thrust before the American people, this time not over the unborn but over the disabled. America watched as food and water were withheld from Terri Schiavo, a woman who had suffered from severe brain damage, until she died. The nation was gripped by the real-life drama as an estranged and divided family, the courts, and Congress wrestled over Terri's right to live. Liberals immediately began to twist and distort the facts, paving the way for politicians and others to attempt to capitalize on the distortions of the truth. Tony was very involved in this issue. He worked closely with the congressional leadership at the time to seek a resolution that was within the limits of the law and provided due process for Terri Schiavo.

Here are the facts in Terri's case. She was injured under suspicious conditions in February of 1990. Almost thirteen years later, in 2003, a Florida judge, George Greer, ruled that if Terri Schiavo were competent to make the decision, she would choose to end life-sustaining measures such as receiving food and water. Terri was not on mechanical life support, but she had to be given food and water. Under state law the decision that she would want food and water to be withheld from her had to be reached by the presence of "clear and convincing" evidence. Amazingly, this standard is less than is required in criminal cases, which calls for evidence "beyond a reasonable doubt." The evidence presented in Judge Greer's court was little more than hearsay both in support of and in opposition to ending her life. Legal experts in support of saving her life argued that the Florida court had abandoned their "clear and convincing" standard and therefore failed to insure Terri Schiavo the due process she was guaranteed under the constitutions of both Florida and the United States. But Judge Greer issued a court order that no food or water be given to Terri Schiavo, which would thereby cause her death.

At this point Congress became involved, but its role was greatly misunderstood. Congress did not create a special law to save Terri Schiavo or interject itself into a family dispute between Terri's husband and her parents and siblings. Congress, by a bipartisan majority, simply asked the federal court to review the evidence in the case to insure due process. However, the federal court rejected the request of Congress and did not issue a temporary injunction stopping the removal of life-sustaining food and water in order to review the evidence.

The case revealed something deeply wrong with our justice system: criminals are afforded more legal protections than the disabled. It also revealed something wrong with our culture: euthanasia is becoming more acceptable and even has the support of some states.

According to the *American Heritage Dictionary*, the word *euthanasia* means, "the act or practice of ending the life of an individual suffering from a terminal illness or an incurable condition, as by lethal injection or the suspension of extraordinary medical treatment." Dr. Jack Kevorkian of Michigan popularized the practice of assisted suicide in the previous decade. More and more people in secular society seem to believe that it is appropriate for people with terminal illnesses to commit suicide or to be assisted to commit suicide. This is a logical outcome of the illogical idea that life is a choice made by man. If a mother, in consultation with her doctor, can choose to end the life of her unborn child, why can't someone else in consultation with a doctor such as Mr. Kevorkian make the same choice for themselves or a disabled family member? With each concession we make in the value of innocent human life, we erode the foundation upon which all life stands.

Currently, there are no federal laws that specifically address the issue of euthanasia or assisted suicide. Proposals for these measures are determined at the state level. The District of Columbia and all fifty states include the prohibition of euthanasia under the homicide laws. Thirty-eight states prohibit assisted suicide through specific laws. Seven other states have banned assisted suicide under common law. The District of Columbia and four states do not have any specific laws banning assisted suicide, nor do they recognize the common law in terms of this issue. Oregon is the only state with laws that legalize assisted suicide.[21]

In fact, Oregon voters approved the "death-with-dignity" referendum twice in four years. Many doctors have criticized this law because it puts physicians in direct conflict with their Hippocratic oath. In 2001, former Attorney General John Ashcroft attempted to stop the measure by saying the Oregon law violated the federal Controlled Substances Act (CSA) by allowing a physician to prescribe a lethal dose of medicine to end the life of a terminally ill person, which was not a legitimate use of the federally controlled substance. The State of Oregon challenged the attorney general in federal court. The case eventually went to the U.S. Supreme Court as *Gonzales v. Oregon*. The Family Research Council filed an amicus brief in the case supporting the attorney general's position. Unfortunately, the Court decided in 2006 against the attorney general's use of CSA.

The main arguments made by the proponents of euthanasia are that people do not want to endure unbearable pain, that they should have the legal right to commit suicide if they so desire, and that people should not be forced to remain alive against their will. Those against euthanasia argue that passing euthanasia laws would open the door for performing life-ending treatments on those who are not terminally ill. They also see euthanasia as being used as a means to contain health-care costs for the elderly. Additionally, there is concern that euthanasia may increasingly become used involuntarily for the elderly and disabled.

But at its base, euthanasia is a total rejection of the value and importance assigned by God to all human life. We only need to look to history to learn the danger of those who have utilized euthanasia. Only two countries currently have legalized euthanasia. Almost every society, whether religious or not, has made euthanasia a crime for thousands of years. Corrupt leaders and deceived authorities have blemished the human race through their indiscriminate killing of millions of "undesirables." Nazi Germany and present-day Darfur alone have proven this to be true. We continue to bear the scar of these horrendous incidents on the human race.[22]

Slavery and Sex Trafficking

The FBI estimates that well over 100,000 children and young women are trafficked in America today. This is an especially shocking statistic for most

Americans because most of us don't see it happening or understand how it's possible in a free country. We tend to believe that this is only an international problem. There was a time when many of the victims were runaways and kids who had been abandoned. But many of today's sex slaves come from intact families.[23]

Research from the University of Pennsylvania reveals that each year between 244,000 and 325,000 American children are at risk of becoming victims of commercial sex exploitation.[24] Dr. Melissa Farley of Prostitution Research interviewed 130 working prostitutes in the San Francisco Bay area. Fifty-seven percent of these women were sexually abused as children, and most were exploited by pimps and brothel owners because of their vulnerability due to former abuse, homelessness, and other needs.[25] World Vision gave a report to Congress on the trafficking of children and women inside the United States. The State Department estimates anywhere from 14,500 to 17,500 women and children are brought into the country annually for the purpose of commercial sex.[26]

We cannot help but surmise that the rise of child pornography and lax enforcement of obscenity laws have fed this problem. One study in the Federal Prison System focused on 155 male inmates who volunteered to take part. Each of the inmates was serving a sentence for the possession or distribution of child pornography. The eighteen-month treatment program included three six-month anonymous questionnaires that asked the inmates about their sexual history and asked them to create a "victims list" from previous abuse. These questionnaires were compared to the inmates' original sentencing confessions. During sentencing, only 26 percent were known to have committed any "hands-on" sexual offenses. Yet, during the treatment, more than 85 percent admitted to participating in other acts of sexual abuse. Also striking was the fact that at sentencing, 75 victims had been identified as compared to 1,777 victims named during treatment. This twentyfold increase seems to indicate that the link between child pornography and sexual abuse may be much higher than we realize.[27]

We also know that the number of sexual predators is growing nationally. Our lawmakers need to prioritize prevention of these kinds of crimes. Sadly, many good pieces of legislation have been struck down by the courts, including the virtual child porn law that the U.S. Supreme Court struck down in 2002 (*Ashcroft v. The Free Speech Coalition*), saying that it violated the First Amendment guarantee of the freedom of speech.[28]

Tony knows from experience that passing a law is just half the battle. Many good pieces of legislation are passed into law, only to be left unenforced. During the last seven years, pro-family groups have held multiple meetings with officials in the Bush administration, including two U.S. attorney generals, seeking a commitment to enforce present obscenity laws, yet the Bush administration has only prosecuted a percentage of the most egregious cases of obscenity. Protecting children and women from abuse that arises from illegal pornography and obscenity should be a priority.

Capital Punishment

In January 2000, former Republican governor of Illinois George Ryan imposed a moratorium on the state's death penalty after the courts had overturned thirteen of twenty-five death penalty sentences. One of the cases that prompted his action involved Anthony Porter, who spent fifteen years on death row for a double homicide. Porter was within two days of execution when he won a reprieve from the Illinois Supreme Court in late 1998. His conviction was eventually overturned as a result of evidence uncovered by Northwestern University Professor David Protess, private investigator Paul Ciolino, and a team of journalism students.

Porter's case, along with dozens of other death sentences that were overturned as a result of DNA evidence, has given rise again to calls to ban capital punishment. We would agree that everything possible should be done to insure that innocent individuals are not executed, nor should they be incarcerated and deprived of their liberty. But are these concerns reason enough to do away with capital punishment entirely?

Executions for crimes in the United States date back to the first settlement of Jamestown when Captain George Kendall was shot by a firing squad in December of 1607 for sowing discord and mutiny. (Some sources say he was also accused of spying against the British for Spain.)[29]

The debate over capital punishment is not just about innocent individuals being executed. Rather, some people believe that all life is sacred and should not be taken by anyone, including the government and even as the result of a heinous crime. Others argue from a utilitarian viewpoint that executions have been proved to not be the best deterrent to crime.

As with the other topics in this book, we turn to the Bible for direction on the issue. There are references in both the Old and New Testaments to capital punishment for various crimes, but primarily for the taking of another life. Following the Flood, God told Noah, "Whoever sheds man's blood, by man his blood shall be shed…" Just in case Noah wished to ask why, God told him, "For in the image of God He made man" (Gen. 9:6, NKJV). That gives us an important basis for supporting capital punishment. It was not designed to be a deterrent; it was designed to be a punishment for a crime committed not only against another human being but also against God. As we have already mentioned, in the New Testament there is clear delegation of this authority to take a life. (See Romans 13:1–5.)

The Old Testament gives specific guidelines for the use of capital punishment. The execution of an individual for a capital offense required the testimony of two witnesses. Punishments were also instated for perjury to prevent false witnesses. And cities of refuge were established so that those accused of murder could seek protection while establishing the facts of their case. These allowances show God's great concern for justice. This biblical principle of requiring two witnesses before a sentence of death is found in our U.S. Constitution. These days, because of advancements in technology, the "witnesses" don't need to be two persons who physically saw the crime committed. DNA, satellite imagery, and photo surveillance in many big cities mean that the two witnesses may be electronic. But the principle is clear—if government is to take the life of a human being for a capital offense, there must be at least two corroborating sources upon which the individual's guilt is established. The cornerstone of our justice system should in fact be justice, and as Bible-believing Christians we should be as concerned about the life of a possibly innocent death row inmate as we are about the life of an unborn child.

When the culture and politicians see that the Christian conservative movement has taken a principled, wide-reaching stance supporting life over death in all areas, the righteousness of our cause will compel them to listen and follow. This issue offers one of the major openings for our movement to lead the cultural debate with moral authority, love, and compassion.

Prayer Points

▸ Thank the Lord for staying the hand of governing officials who want to allow stem cell research on human embryos. Praise Him for every scientist who questions the morality of cloning, whether therapeutic or not (Rom. 13:4).

▸ Repent for the genocide that America has perpetrated against the unborn. Ask for forgiveness for the millions of babies of every race who will not walk among the living on this earth.

▸ Ask God to bring to light every pedophile, child abuser, sex trafficker, or child pornographer. Beseech Him to help criminal investigators to identify these people and arrest them and our courts to appropriately prosecute them (Acts 26:18).

Chapter 5

CORE VALUE #2: IMMIGRATION

THE NEW SLAVERY

During the acrimonious debate over the 2007 immigration bill, Harry got a call from *The O'Reilly Factor* staff asking him to come on the program to talk about immigration. The producer explained that a group of American pastors belonging to the so-called "Sanctuary Movement" had vowed to give sanctuary to illegal aliens in their churches. The participating churches allowed illegal families a way to avoid deportation, but in so doing, the churches and their ministers were committing an illegal act. Harry and his wife had watched one of the leaders of the Sanctuary Movement on *The O'Reilly Factor* the night before. She had argued that Jesus's love compelled her to take care of these immigrants because the welfare of children was involved. The interview had been compelling, but Harry still felt that this movement was nothing more than a sophisticated PR campaign.

As Harry prepared for the interview, he remembered how one of his volunteer workers, Ruth, had spent thousands of dollars and several years attempting to fulfill the Immigration and Naturalization Service (INS, now known as ICE—Immigration and Customs Enforcement) requirements. As a first-generation immigrant, she did not have firsthand knowledge of how to interact with our government. One afternoon, the INS actually called Harry to inquire about her case. But based on a technicality with her temporary visa, Ruth had been caught in an unproductive crossfire of rules and regulations. Her deportation prevented her from returning to our country. Ruth has remained in her homeland for nearly ten years.

Harry also thought about Roberto, who had spent nearly four thousand dollars in 1995 to correct his status—to no avail. A father of three children who were born in the United States and an owner of a legal company, Roberto appeared on the surface to be the "salt of the earth." After all, he was a twenty-year American resident and a tax-paying business owner and a faithful church attendee. In fact, he viewed Harry as a father figure, and the two of them had grown quite close over many years.

Roberto left Harry's church because the elders refused to promote him to lead a major outreach ministry until he cleaned up his immigration status issues. Their decision broke Roberto's heart and alienated many Hispanic members of Harry's church. The leaders felt that Roberto had only made halfhearted attempts to get legal paperwork. The leadership of Harry's church acknowledged that Roberto's "crime" was different from that of a fugitive, bank robber, or murderer—yet they were concerned about sending the wrong message to the rest of the church. They thought that promoting Roberto would have said to everyone that it's OK for the pastor's friends to break the law, but it is not OK for others to do the same.

Another of Harry's friends had a nineteen-year-old client who was an illegal alien. She had seen her family slaughtered in Sierra Leone. She came to the United States to seek asylum. She was placed in the county jail in Salisbury, Maryland, for about three months. When she was released, she went to nursing school. She was told she could not get a green card for six years. But though she was ill-treated and came under intense immigration scrutiny, she ended up becoming a strong contributor to our society.

All three experiences were in Harry's mind as O'Reilly opened the interview. Harry felt that he had no choice but to speak out against the Sanctuary Movement because it does not address the long-term problems that our nation faces with immigration. Those who are here illegally as well as those who benefit from illegal labor must be held accountable, and there has to be substantive reform in our immigration policies. Harry told O'Reilly's audience that the movement was more political than substantive, and it encouraged disobedience to the laws of the land without even having full knowledge of the individuals they were sheltering. Harry quoted Romans chapter 13, which says we need to obey the civil authorities, and he rejected the idea that the immigration debate of today is in any way similar to the struggle of the black civil rights movement of the past.

As we get God's heart for the immigrant, we can discuss public policy with greater wisdom and insight. There is a rational reason for changing immigration policy from time to time based upon the interest of the nation. Issues like national security should be considered in our immigration policy.

Part of the problem with immigration policy today is that we have not had a consistent, coherent philosophy of immigration in the past. To prove this point, let's look at a couple of key dates in history. The policies below do not reflect a national bias against any one race or culture.

- In 1882 the United States established the Chinese Exclusion Act.[1]

- In 1917, the same year the United States entered World War I, Congress made literacy a requirement for immigration.[2]

- In 1924 the Johnson-Reed Act established a quota for immigration that gave privileges to Europeans. This act, along with the Oriental Exclusion Act, severely curtailed Asian entry into the nation.[3]

- From 1882 to 1924 none of these measures applied to the United States–Mexican border.

- After World War II Congress created legislation that distinguished between immigrants and refugees.[4]

- Then, the Immigration and Nationality Act of 1952 was passed. This is the basis for immigration law today.[5]

- In 1965 the quotas established in 1924 were lifted.[6]

- In 1986 the Immigration Reform and Control Act (IRCA) was developed to control the influx of foreigners that occurred in response to the 1965 legislation.[7]

- Next, the Immigration Act of 1990 became a massive amnesty program for illegal immigrants in the country and temporarily raised the ceiling on the number of immigrants who could enter the country.[8]

▸ In the 1990s, the U.S. administration forced Mexico to devalue its currency. Massive Mexican immigration was the ultimate result.[9]

▸ In 1992 the North American Free Trade Agreement (NAFTA) doubled the number of immigrants entering the country. This was mostly due to the increase of available cheap labor from Mexico.[10]

▸ In 1996 Congress strangthened border enforcement to curb illegal immigration. Congress also approved a program to check the immigration status of those applying for jobs within the United States.[11]

▸ Also in 1996 President Clinton signed the Personal Responsibility and Work Opportunity Act, which cut many of the social welfare programs for legal immigrants. It also curtailed all federal and state benefits for illegal immigrants with the exception of emergency medical care and immunization, as well as disaster relief.[12]

▸ In 2003, when the Department of Homeland Security was created, it absorbed the INS and divided it into three units: the Bureaus of Customs and Border Protection, Immigration and Customs Enforcement (ICE), and Citizenship and Immigration Services (CIS). These units were established within the new Department of Homeland Security as its largest investigative arm.[13]

This unclear, back-and-forth government policy has created national disunity, a shadow economy, and broken families.

The nation remains divided over our immigration policy. Many Americans feel that our country is being overrun by illegal immigrants and that our government is standing idly by. When you go into a fast-food restaurant or convenience store and have trouble communicating with the employees because they don't speak English, it's easy to feel that the bonds of national unity are slipping. Tony was recently speaking at an event in Atlanta and was staying in one of the city's many hotels. Prior to taking a shower, he discovered there was no hair dryer in the bathroom. He called down to the front desk to request one. With great promptness there was soon a knock on the door. Tony opened the door, and there was a hotel worker of Hispanic origins holding a plunger. Through hand motions Tony was able to quickly communicate that a plunger wouldn't work. Experiences like this have left many Americans asking, "Who are we?"

Many others, like Harry, have experienced the pain of inconsistent immigration policies personally, as noted above. People on both sides of this issue are being hurt by the current situation. Despite the importance of this issue and how deeply it affects our national character, the evangelical community has been eerily quiet. There's an adage that says, "A pastor is 'down' on things he is not 'up' on." That's not just a cute turn of a phrase. When Christian leaders avoid issues like this, they rob society of clear biblical keys for action. Many evangelical leaders are paralyzed because of the competing claims of morality on either side of the illegal immigration debate. How, then, do we move ahead in a biblical way on this issue?

This is another issue where the religious Right can unite the country by taking a strong, morally based stand that favors law and order but at the same time also shows compassion and empathy toward those who are seeking a better life for themselves and their families. We believe that our public policy, guided by our private faith, can bring conservative Christians together on the issue of immigration and move the nation toward a long-term solution.

The Bible on Immigration

The Bible is straightforward concerning immigration. Consider the following passages:

> He executes justice for the orphan and the widow, and shows His love for the alien by giving him food and clothing. So show your love for the alien, for you were aliens in the land of Egypt.
> —Deuteronomy 10:18–19, NAS

> Nor shall you glean your vineyard, nor shall you gather the fallen fruit of your vineyard; you shall leave them for the needy and for the stranger. I am the LORD your God.
> —Leviticus 19:10, NAS

When a stranger resides with you in your land, you shall not do him
wrong. The stranger who resides with you shall be to you as the native
among you, and you shall love him as yourself; for you were aliens in
the land of Egypt: I am the LORD your God.

—LEVITICUS 19:33–34, NAS

You shall not pervert the justice due an alien or an orphan, nor take a
widow's garment in pledge.

—DEUTERONOMY 24:17, NAS

When you reap your harvest in your field and have forgotten a sheaf
in the field, you shall not go back to get it; it shall be for the alien, for
the orphan, and for the widow, in order that the LORD your God may
bless you in all the work of your hands. When you beat your olive tree,
you shall not go over the boughs again; it shall be for the alien, for the
orphan, and for the widow. When you gather the grapes of your vine-
yard, you shall not go over it again; it shall be for the alien, for the
orphan, and for the widow.

—DEUTERONOMY 24:19–21, NAS

"Cursed is he who distorts the justice due an alien, orphan, and
widow." And all the people shall say, "Amen."

—DEUTERONOMY 27:19, NAS

The scriptures that speak of the plight of immigrants often address how
the domestic poor should be treated as well, implying that both groups
often lack the means to defend themselves from exploitation. The scriptures presuppose that aliens often migrate to a foreign land under financial
duress. In addition, the Lord appeals to the people of Israel to remember
what it was like to be immigrants in Egypt.

What is it like to be an illegal immigrant in America today? It often
involves working in a shadow economy that provides fewer protections
and benefits than legal American workers receive. It means dealing in
cash, because most banks won't serve you. It means living in substandard
housing and not having access to medical care. It means not being able to
drive legally. It means family separation, often with the rest of your family
in the country of origin and no way for you to visit them without fear of
being detained and deported upon reentry.

Harry has spoken of "the new slavery" in America, where illegal aliens
work for companies or factories but have no legal standing to avail

themselves of workers' rights. In many cases, the workers are "slaves" of their employers.

Why would an illegal immigrant put himself in such a situation? Because, as the Bible recognized thousands of years ago, they are desperate or see no other options to better their lives. It is possible for us to understand and sympathize with the plight of the immigrant while still supporting strong border policies. For this reason, Tony went to Los Angeles in April 2006 during the height of the immigration debate and with the assistance of a pastor friend, Daniel DeLeon, to meet with a group of Hispanic pastors who represented several dozen churches. For about an hour he listened to them to hear what they had to say about the issue of immigration. To his surprise, most of them were not for amnesty programs, and all were opposed to illegal immigration. But they also bristled at all the talk of building a huge fence along the southern border because the rhetoric so often came across as thinly veiled anti-Hispanic sentiment. For example, few people have advocated putting a huge fence along the border with Canada, even though terrorists have entered our country across that border, not through our southern border.

These pastors also felt that the average voter does not understand the features of immigration policy that do more harm than good. For example, they said there was a seven-year or greater waiting period to become legal, and that if you leave this country during the process of obtaining authorization to see your family, you get pushed to the back of the line. If a person is caught here illegally for a few years, they cannot come back in some cases for ten years. A waiver is available if the person has an immediate relative who is a U.S. citizen. Nonetheless, the process is arduous. This terrible policy divides families and encourages immigrants to choose to come here illegally rather than go the legal route and remain separated.

As Christians, we must separate our support for strong borders from our personal and corporate approach to the immigrants among us, be they legal or illegal. We should seek above all to be compassionate to the plight of illegal immigrants by aiding them in immediate, unavoidable emergencies, but once the initial need is met, we must assist them in keeping the law as well. FRC has opposed efforts to penalize charities that give help to illegal immigrants, because giving such aid is part of our biblical mandate. Churches should not be put in a position to ask for a green card before they minister to the immediate needs of immigrants, be they legal or illegal. However, once it is known that someone is in this country illegally, the church should assist them in conducting themselves according to the law. Just because we oppose illegal immigration does not mean we value the spiritual or material needs of an illegal immigrant any less. We believe the church should do all it can to minister to the needs of immigrants, seeing it as an opportunity, as the pastors emphasized to Tony, to reach these people with the gospel.

Churches need to reach out to legal immigrants. In addition to sharing the gospel with them, we must insure that their families are supported and receive the legal assistance that they need. This is already happening, particularly among so-called "immigrant churches" here in the United States that reach out to people of their own culture. Many of these churches offer English courses, free access to immigration attorneys, free health-care clinics, food, and the intangible resources of a congregation that can help new immigrants navigate the often-Byzantine nature of American society.

But these efforts need to be made by all churches. The African American church is particularly well placed to help immigrants, and yet few black churches have Hispanic outreaches or immigrant outreaches of any kind. Black and Hispanic communities are often side by side in urban areas. What better way to promote racial unity than by stepping out of your own culture to help others? It presents a terrific opportunity for churches of all colors and backgrounds.

When illegal immigrants become part of the body of a church, and as they grow in their faith, it will become appropriate to encourage them to obey the law they originally violated to be here. The church is then there to walk through the process with them. The goal is to help them become legal. We can't think of a better support structure than a loving church body to help families through the difficulties of righting their past wrong.

As believers, we may support the rule of law concerning immigration, but we must also pray and get God's heart for the immigrant. If we do that, it will help us find new ways to assist the "strangers" among us. Here is the comprehensive approach we recommend, involving seven major facets of immigration reform:[14]

1. Enforcing security at our borders
2. Facilitating assimilation
3. Recommending source country reform
4. Establishing a "families-first" approach and permanent anchor baby reform
5. Curtailing chain migration

6. Sponsoring guest workers
7. Negotiating third-country resettlement

Let's take a look at these issues one by one.

Enforcing security at our borders

Our nation has provisions for those who are fleeing persecution and for immigration by people who follow legitimate processes. But there is no legal way to justify the brazen, dangerous act of violating our country's borders. When illegal immigrants choose to break the law, they suffer from the self-inflicted wounds of legal uncertainty, family breakdown, and more. We are convinced that these risks are largely an expression of personal desperation. When faced with the question of whether a family should be deported and kids who have only known residency in the United States should be forced to leave, our hearts break. Many of these aliens whom we have met seem to embody the noblest principles of hard work, honesty, and faith. They support our national vision. We also see the fact that the nation has waited so long to address this problem, in and of itself, as an immoral act. But it does not justify breaking our laws and violating our national sovereignty.

We need effective border security. The arrest of six Muslims charged with plotting to attack Fort Dix only underscores the importance of shoring up the borders. These men were not only Islamic extremists inspired by al Qaeda, but they were also illegal aliens who had broken many domestic laws. The fact that these men could move so freely in America ought to be of great concern to all of us. In fact, people like those in the Sanctuary Movement could eventually harbor these kinds of ideological warriors in their churches. When misguided compassion of liberal churches defies the law of the land without understanding the cost to our nation, they feel good about their acts of kindness, but they may create more damage.

Much of the legislation concerning immigration needs to be given more teeth—stiffer penalties and swifter punishment. In addition, we need to take away one of the major reasons for illegal immigration—the ability to send large sums of money back home to family and loved ones. We believe that foreign currency transfers, including automatic teller withdrawals, should be limited to legal residents or people with valid guest-worker visas. There is currently an entire "subindustry" based upon facilitating currency transfers to foreign nations in every major metropolitan area. Interestingly, swings in the value of American currency have recently begun to impact the national economy of several nations.

Facilitating assimilation

There is another side to what the Bible says about immigrants. It addresses the immigrant's responsibility to his new nation.

> And when a *stranger* shall sojourn with thee, and will keep the Passover to the LORD, let all his males be circumcised, and then let him come near and keep it; and he shall be as one that is born in the land: for no uncircumcised person shall eat thereof.
> —EXODUS 12:48, EMPHASIS ADDED

Here, the Bible calls upon immigrants to keep the laws of the land they now inhabit. They are to live by the customs and the norms of their adopted home. That is called assimilation, and it is the bedrock of successful immigration policy. We should never be anti-immigration or anti- any race or color. We should welcome those who want to come, live by the laws of our land, and become part of the fabric of the American family. But those who come here to take part in the American dream must participate in the whole dream. They must become part of the American family, and to do that they must actively assimilate. Theodore Roosevelt said:

> In the first place, we should insist that if the immigrant who comes here in good faith becomes an American and assimilates himself to us, he shall be treated on an exact equality with everyone else, for it is an outrage to discriminate against any such man because of creed, or birthplace, or origin. But this is predicated upon the person's becoming in every facet an American, and nothing but an American. . . . There can be no divided allegiance here. Any man who says he is an American, but something else also, isn't an American at all. We have room for but one flag, the American flag. . . . We have room for but one language here, and that is the English language . . . and we have room for but one sole loyalty and that is a loyalty to the American people.[15]

We believe that speaking English is a fundamental indicator of our national identity and history. We do not feel that requiring all American immigrants to speak English is cultural superiority. It is simply about unity. Most people do not realize that basic competency in English is a requirement for citizenship, requiring green-card holders (permanent residents) to become functional parts of American society in business, education, and democratic processes. Mastering basic English simply makes sense. Therefore, we should support legislation that reinforces the primary use of English in the public square. We should also support initiatives that restore a core of curriculum in both lower and higher education, emphasizing early American history and how our nation has developed. These initiatives also offer great opportunities for churches to teach English as a second language and even give courses about our country's history. This will both educate and assimilate immigrants into our culture. Faith-based organizations should also see their involvement as part of an outreach process that can help families train their children so that they might become contributors to our society.

Tony recently had a guest named Eduardo Verastegui on his radio program. Eduardo is a famous actor from Mexico and can be seen on shows on Univision, a Spanish-language television network here in the United States. He came to the States and met a movie producer on an airplane. The producer asked him to try out for a part, even though Eduardo didn't speak any English. Eduardo memorized his lines in English and got the part. Suddenly, he had to learn a new language! He hired a tutor who happened to be a Christian. The tutor talked to him about the Lord in the course of teaching him English. Eduardo felt true repentance for the roles he had played in racy soap operas in Mexico, and he felt he had wasted his life so far and was leading people down the wrong path. Now he has committed to live for the Lord, founded a company with two partners, and recently starred in the movie *Bella*. That's just one example of how something as simple as teaching English can change lives and change the world. Imagine if most evangelical churches were to offer tutoring services in English. Just think of the number of people we could lead to the Lord!

Recommending source country reform

In an ideal world, permanent and temporary visas should be issued on the basis of a preferred country or "favored nation" status, based on specific reforms within the source countries. These reforms would include fiscal policy and entrepreneurial incentives that seek to remedy poverty, the root cause of illegal immigration to the United States. To do this effectively, new legislation would be necessary that includes specific bilateral agreements that go beyond existing trade pacts. This may be hard to negotiate, but we should move in this direction.

The United States should not enter into treaties and trade agreements that do not require the above reforms. We should look to how our trade benefits the country's overall population and not just the ruling class.

Establishing a "families-first" approach that includes permanent anchor baby reform

It is no secret that the current immigration laws can separate families. The story of the little Cuban boy whose mother died in their attempt to come to the United States became national news a few years ago. Elian Gonzalez had to return to Cuba to live with his birth father despite the vision and efforts of his deceased mother. This was a hotly contested case. Some people argued that the boy should have stayed in the United States because of his future possibilities. Others believed that his broken family was where he belonged. Regardless of where you came out on that case, it is incumbent upon us as a nation to plan for the future and create policies that do not destroy families. Our anchor baby policies and chain migration laws both have a tremendous impact on families. Let us explain our approach, which is biblical and compassionate.

Congress should act to correct or reform an unchallenged application of the fourteenth amendment to the U.S. Constitution that has created the "anchor baby" policy. Anchor babies are babies born to illegal immigrants; these babies automatically become American citizens. A growing number of mothers will cross the border as their due date approaches in order to give birth to an American citizen who can then become a foothold for their own future citizenship. Decades ago, as soon as an immigrant family had a baby in the United States, the parents immediately received the benefit of that child's citizenship. Some people remember when expectant mothers would cross the border and chain themselves in a bus station until their babies were born. However, the current law does not allow a person under twenty-one years old to be the basis for parents to obtain residency. Babies born to people here illegally should not automatically be citizens. There is no evidence to suggest that the framers of the Constitution envisioned automatic citizenship for children born to individuals who are in this country illegally. Congress should pass a law and force courts to reinterpret this policy. As it is, the policy creates a moral dilemma. Do we deport the parents? That's no answer. Do we make the child a ward of the state? That's clearly not the compassionate thing to do. Rather, let's not put ourselves in this position in the first place.

Curtailing chain migration

Chain migration is the means by which aliens are permitted to immigrate because previous adult immigrants who now have gained citizenship send for their adult relatives. This means is most often used by immigrants who seek economic opportunity within the United States. Chain immigration became policy based on the principle of family reunification. The law was changed in 1965 to create the family reunification system. This resulted in a steady increase of sponsorship for family members every year. The rate nearly doubled in the first five years—from 1965 to 1970. It tripled in 1975, and in 2001 was thirteen times higher than before the law was changed.[16]

Congress granted illegal aliens amnesty in 1986. This fueled naturalization applications as these aliens then sponsored their family members to come to the United States. The U.S. Commission of Immigration Reform (USCIR) made a study of chain migration and proposed returning to the pre-1965 policies of sponsorship, which included spouses, children, and parents. Congress has ignored the USCIR's recommendations and has not eliminated the immigrant backlog or changed the system that is creating it.[17]

We must create legislation that minimizes chain migration. Chain migration is obviously aimed at helping the family of legal immigrants coming into the nation. The alternative to this would be to simply offer renewable, temporary visas to parents of U.S. citizens. These would need to be given with the condition that the U.S. citizen post some sort of guaranty or bond for the immigrant parent's health insurance costs.

Sponsoring guest workers

We believe that the nation should continue to offer temporary guest-worker programs based on employer sponsorship. This makes the temporary work visa predictable and based on the expectation of repatriation to their source country. However, such guest-worker programs should be nonrenewable and nonadjustable, confined to a period of two years. A third-year extension could be considered upon the employer's request.

Guest workers should be citizens of countries in the Western Hemisphere that have a regional trade pact with the United States and have earned the "favored nation" status under the specific bilateral agreement mentioned above.

Negotiating third-country resettlement

An innovative concept that several policy analysts have proposed is third-country settlement. Here is the idea. For those illegal residents who are currently in the United States, legislation and diplomatic initiatives should be created to negotiate third-country settlement. This would only benefit these illegal immigrants if they register with the designated authority and return to the source country while awaiting a third-country visa.

As we enforce the laws that are already on the books, we must speed up the applications process. There is too long of a wait for people to become citizens. There needs to be more people processing the applications, which would mean investing in departmental infrastructure. Critics of this approach feel that it is impractical and will be difficult to implement. They ask the question, "What country is willing to take illegal aliens from the United States?" Despite these issues, this concept may work in special cases.

Parting Thoughts

The religious Right and the church must take an active role in the immigration solution. We also must never forget that we are often dealing with needy people whose foremost need is to receive Jesus Christ as their Savior. Any Christian approach to immigration that does not acknowledge our need to preach the gospel to these diverse communities will fall short. What we have proposed in this chapter are solid ideas and policy initiatives that, if implemented, can enable our society to address the issue of immigration in a way that upholds justice and the rule of law, and displays Christian compassion to those seeking to be a part of the American family.

Prayer Points

▸ Thank the Lord that He has preserved America as a place where so many people want to come to experience freedom and a dream of a better tomorrow. Praise Him for every soul who is here legally, who has stepped out of another culture and joined us in our quest (Exod. 12:49).

▸ Repent on behalf of every immigrant who has been exploited
  for material gain by corporations or organizations. Ask for
  forgiveness that the United States has not been clear on
  what to do and how to handle immigrants who desire to live
  and work within our borders (Prov. 22:22).

▸ Pray that churches will become involved with immigrants,
  not to harbor illegal aliens, but to serve legal immigrants
  in assimilating into our society. Ask the Lord to prick the
  hearts of church leaders to embrace the immigrants within
  their communities in practical ways.

Chapter 6

CORE VALUE #3: POVERTY AND JUSTICE (PART 1)

SLASHING POVERTY

I n 1998, Harry preached the gospel message in a ghetto area of Capetown, South Africa. Hundreds of people came forward to receive Christ that night and each of the eight days of the crusade. During the course of the campaign, more than four thousand people came to Christ. What made this crusade different was that the services were conducted right in the middle of the most dangerous part of the city, Mannenberg. Under a ten-thousand-seat gospel tent, complete with JumboTrons, the crowds reached eighteen thousand nightly. Before each service the atmosphere brimmed with excitement. People from every religious background were there. At one point Harry saw young, pistol-toting gang members sitting near a group of people in traditional Muslim dress flanked by a group of pastors wearing suits and clerical collars. Talk about diversity!

Many unchurched people came because there had been several weeks of intense promotion before the crusade began. But the promotion was more than radio and television ads. It included feeding the poor at the preaching site weeks before the lights, cameras, or music were there. Medical care was given to the sick by a team of volunteers, and Jesus was presented as the ultimate answer to all of the problems of this needy community. Practical help and peace for the soul were offered by a well-organized, indigenous South African team.

Everything was paid for by a wealthy businessman named Jerome Liberty. Born under apartheid, this South African "colored" had built a tremendous business from scratch. The crusade was his gift to the community, an expression of his thanks to the Lord for his own salvation and deliverance. Jerome wrote a check to pay for the first event in its entirety. Through offerings received during the eight-day crusade, and through support from local businessmen who were moved to help, the community raised enough to finance another crusade. Using this approach, three to four crusades a year were conducted for two years prior to Jerome starting a church in the Nelson Mandela Metroplex under Harry's leadership.

Jerome's outreaches at the central church now include feeding the poor daily at several sites around the region, preaching the gospel in prisons, and sending an eighteen-wheel mobile health clinic on a specific route six days a week. GED-like classes are offered in the evenings for people attempting to lift themselves out of poverty. All of these things happen in addition to Sunday services. The work could not happen without the help and support of the government and business leaders. The government pays for the doctors and nurses who assist the staff at the mobile clinic. In addition, successful businessmen give large contributions and help employ needy people as a form of Christian discipleship and life development.

A Public Relations Problem

Jerome Liberty is winning both public opinion and souls in South Africa in a way that few churches in the United States are. Why? Not because American churches are callous toward the poor (though some Christians are). Rather, the church and therefore the religious Right in America have a PR problem when it comes to poverty. We have been labeled as those who blame the poor and ignore the economic plight of minorities because of the policy initiatives we advocate. We have done little to counter those charges since we are rarely seen serving our communities. We've made our policy platform highly public, but we have kept our works of compassion under a bushel basket, sometimes out of a belief that we should not publicize our good works. As a result, the casual observer perceives that we have forgotten to serve "the least of these." Some of the anti-Christian rhetoric in the public square is a result of the world *hearing* us more than *seeing* us. And if the church is not visibly seen serving the poor of our communities, we will become irrelevant to the next generation.

The religious Right can regain unchurched America's attention and reestablish the trust of the average person by reasserting our mission to help the poor. We must lead the way in helping orphans, widows, and the destitute to find personal, spiritual, and financial refuge. We must also let the world know that this is, and always has been, primary to our mission.

We believe that on this issue, perhaps above all others, the religious Right can find common ground with potential partners and even opponents of our movement. We also believe that the church can do an even better job of lifting the working poor out of the rut of generational poverty by understanding more fully its biblical responsibility to the poor. We will discuss this and make some specific recommendations about how we can work together to improve both the spiritual and material life of all Americans, but first we want to debunk a few myths about the so-called uncaring cheapskates who make up the religious Right.

Who Gives?

More than any other group, conservative Christians are portrayed as heartless Scrooges when it comes to the poor. The overwhelming popular perception is that liberals care about the poor and values voters do not. Bible-believing Christians in particular are often singled out and accused of gross insensitivity to the poor and outright ungodly selfishness.

This is not just a mischaracterization; it is totally untrue. In his book *Who Really Cares*, Arthur C. Brooks, professor of public administration at Syracuse University, dispels the false claim that conservatives don't give to the poor, and he negates the claim that liberals really care—or at least care enough to give. Using Internal Revenue Service data as the basis for his research, Brooks finds that a person is most likely to give if he or she is religious, conservative, and married with children in an intact home, religion being the strongest factor. "People saying they devote a 'great deal of effort' to their spiritual lives are 42 points more likely to give money to charity than people who never pray," Brooks concludes.[1]

This giving is not based upon income. According to Brooks, the working poor include some of "the most charitable members of our society," giving a much greater percentage of their income to charity than wealthy liberals. Interestingly, this generosity at the lower economic level of society is related to the source of the income. Low-income individuals who earned their income gave. Low-income individuals who received government redistribution of wealth through welfare or other payments were among the least charitable.

Brooks actually found that those who build their political and social platforms on the issue of poverty are among the most uncharitable. How can this be? In their minds, they are not uncharitable. According to Brooks, liberals see themselves as "charitable because they advocate government redistribution of money in the name of social justice..."[2] In short, the purveyors of the poverty programs do want to help the poor— with someone else's money.

Why do Bible-believing Christians give at the highest rate? It is probably simple obedience to God. The Scriptures teach us to give generously. Passages like Proverbs 11:25 tell us, "The generous soul will be made rich, and he who waters will also be watered himself" (NKJV). Therefore they give of their money, their time, and, according to Brooks, they even give their blood to help those in need and in accordance with God's desires. We believe America is a blessed nation because it is a giving nation.

Even knowing that Christians and many Americans are generous, we believe the church is not yet doing all it can to help those in poverty. The heart of God is moved by the cries of the poor and disadvantaged. As people who desire to reflect the glory of God in the earth, we must try new approaches, make new alliances, and work toward social reform that reduces poverty. The cries of the poor must reach our ears and our hearts like they reach God's, and then we must act. While we are not to do such acts of compassion for the praise or recognition of other men, we must not be bashful about being seen serving those in need.

What Does the Bible Say About Poverty?

According to the federal government's poverty guidelines, in 2007 a family of four with an income of less than $20,650 is in poverty. How did the federal government settle on this figure? By drawing a "poverty line" that includes incomes that are less than three times a low-cost food budget. Anyone falling below this line is defined as poor.

We should mention right up front that, according to sociologists, "this official measure of poverty is grossly inadequate" and overestimates the number of poor in America.[3] In fact, according to a 2004 Heritage Foundation study titled "Understanding Poverty in America," "Relatively few of the 35 million people identified as being 'in poverty' by the Census Bureau could be characterized as poor."[4] According to this study:

Overall, the typical American defined as poor by the government has a car, air conditioning, a refrigerator, a stove, a clothes washer and dryer, and a microwave. He has two color televisions, cable or satellite TV reception, a VCR or DVD player, and a stereo. He is able to obtain medical care. His home is in good repair and is not overcrowded. By his own report, his family is not hungry, and he had sufficient funds in the past year to meet his family's essential needs. While this individual's life is not opulent, it is equally far from the popular images of dire poverty conveyed by the press, liberal activists, and politicians.[5]

Are we then suggesting that we should not be concerned with those who fall within the government's definition of poverty? No. As Christians and as a nation we should not want to see anyone locked into a cycle of poverty. Rather, we should take individual and collective actions to address their needs from a biblical perspective.

The Bible makes clear that the Christian's responsibility to address the plight of the poor is fundamental to having faith. From beginning to end, the Bible tells us that God hears the cry of the poor. He takes the treatment of the poor personally. See what He says in Matthew 25:40: "And the King will answer and say to them, 'Assuredly, I say to you, in as much as you did it to one of the least of these My brethren, you did it to Me'" (NKJV).

Even Israel's deliverance from Egypt is a powerful example of God's justice on behalf of the needy (Exod. 2:23–24; Ps. 68:8–10). Old Testament Law structured the life of Israel so that the poor could be helped. Privileges such as restrictions on loans and collateral were given to the landless poor in the Old Testament. Every seventh year, the law said, whatever grew on the land was for "the poor...[that he] may eat" (Exod. 23:11). In the seventh year, creditors were instructed to cancel the debt of their neighbors (Deut. 15:2). This concept has made its way into American bankruptcy law. Every seven years our credit mistakes can be erased.

Proverbs 28:27 states boldly, "He who gives to the poor will lack nothing..." yet the verse doesn't stop there. It promises a penalty to those who overlook the needy in their world, "...but he who closes his eyes to them receives many curses" (NIV). Proverbs 19:17 says, "He who is kind to the poor lends to the LORD, and he will reward him for what he has done" (NIV).

Poverty is an issue that we should be concerned with, because God Himself is concerned with it. The Scripture speaks to material poverty more than two hundred fifty times in the Old and New Testaments. In fact, God is very clear about how the poor should be treated. Following the Babylonian captivity, God explained through the prophet Zechariah (in chapter 7 of that book) how Israel's perfunctory religious observation did not prevent their downfall and judgment. God was interested in His people obeying His words, in particular that justice, mercy, and compassion were shown to the widow, the fatherless, the stranger, and the poor (vv. 9–10). The vehicle for this act is found in verse 9: "everyone to his brother."

But the Bible also distinguishes between different types of poverty. The New Testament speaks of three economic classes:

1. *Plousios (ploo'see'os)*—people who need not work to survive or even thrive, but live on the earnings of their investments

2. *Penes (pen'-ace)*—people whose focus is upon meeting the physical needs of each day

3. *Ptochos (pto-khos')*—people who cannot sustain themselves because they are too old, too young, or too handicapped to work

The categories of *penes* and *ptochos* are those in poverty. *Penes* does not indicate extreme poverty, but rather connotes a condition that present-day observers would call being a member of the working poor. This is the word that is used to describe the widow in Luke 21:2 who Jesus said contributed her entire living to ministry. She was not completely destitute, but she gave her meager earnings to God. We can translate this into a modern-day image of a grandmother who lives on a fixed income or pension, yet she gives to Christian causes. This word *penes* could also speak of someone who is employed but lives hand to mouth. This kind of poverty is similar to those in America who live near or beneath our poverty line. Most Americans are not absolutely destitute. Many are, however, unable to escape the repeating cycle of need, and their children face major challenges in rising to a higher economic level.

Interestingly, the New Testament implies that there will be a specific blessing given to those who help the working poor overcome their problems. Second Corinthians 9:9 uses this term when it says, "As it is written: 'He has scattered abroad his gifts to the poor; his righteousness endures forever" (NIV).

The other word for poverty is *ptochos*, which indicates abject poverty that often leads to begging. The story of Lazarus who was laid at the gate of the rich man's palace (Luke 16:20–21) shows this kind of poverty. This word is used more than thirty times in the New Testament to describe material need and also the abject spiritual poverty that man faces and is unable to deliver himself from.

What we take from these scriptures is the fact that there are at least two different types of poor people. The first are the working poor who need to be directed into life skills, values, and practices that will help them escape the intergenerational trap of lack. The second group is the abjectly poor who are poor because of some handicap or traumatic event. They need immediate help and in some cases long-term help.

For Christians, alleviating poverty is to be a way of life, not a government program. It is primarily our responsibility as individuals, families, and churches to care for the poor. Tony has actually made the case that our nation's welfare system, as costly and ineffective as it is, may have prevented the type of judgment upon this nation that Israel saw in the Old Testament. However, he quickly points out that it has come at a very high price. Allowing the civil government to assume the responsibility for caring for the poor has led to the expansion of the term "poor," and it comes with no accountability for genuine need and discretion in the way it is met.

Jesus declared, "The poor you will always have with you" (Matt. 26:11, NIV). This was not a cynical assessment or denunciation of the poor. Rather, Jesus was quoting Deuteronomy 15:11, "The poor shall never cease out of the land: therefore I command thee, saying, Thou shalt open thine hand wide unto thy brother, to thy poor, and to thy needy, in thy land." Jesus knew the hardness of the heart of man. His words reflected His recognition of the choices of men and society that would lead people into poverty. In contrast to man's priorities, God exhorts us to be generous, reflecting His heart. If our generation becomes serious about reaching the poor and needy, the widows and orphans of our generation, we will see an amazing release of God's power backing our efforts.

Causes of Poverty

Any good doctor begins his work by diagnosing the cause of a problem before he gives a prescription. America is full of pundits, politicians, and even preachers who have their own ideas on the causes and cure for poverty. But we think the best diagnosis and prescription come from the Bible. In the Bible we find these main causes for poverty:

▶ Economic depression, natural disasters, and wars
▶ Government corruption and oppressive policy
▶ Banking or lender abuse
▶ Persecution
▶ Family breakdown
▶ Addictive personal behavior
▶ Laziness

Let's take a look at them one by one.

Economic depression, natural disasters, and wars
Throughout history, these three types of calamity have thrown countless people and nations into poverty. For instance, *Unger's Bible Dictionary* records the following instances of famine in the Bible:[6]

▶ In the time of Abraham (Gen. 12:10)
▶ In the time of Isaac (Gen. 26:1)
▶ In the time of Joseph (Gen. 41:53–56)
▶ In the time of the judges (Ruth 1:1)
▶ In the time of David (2 Sam. 21:1)
▶ In the time of Ahab (1 Kings 17:1; 18:2)
▶ In the time of Elisha (2 Kings 4:38)
▶ During the siege of Samaria (2 Kings 6:25)
▶ In the time of Jeremiah (Jer. 14:1–6)
▶ During the siege of Jerusalem (2 Kings 25:3)
▶ After the captivity (Neh. 5:3)
▶ In the reign of Claudius Caesar (Acts 11:28)
▶ Before the destruction of Jerusalem (Matt. 24:7)

In each one of these famines, emergency measures had to be employed to bring people through the crisis. Storms, plagues, droughts, fires, and wars were often at the root of the famines recorded in the Bible. Today, those same factors play an enormous role in creating poverty. Much of the world's population is still ruled by the economic pressures, conflicts, and destructive natural cycles seen so clearly in the Bible.

America and other Western societies are far from immune. In terms of war, the twentieth century was the bloodiest in history, killing, displacing, and impoverishing millions. The Great Depression of the 1930s is another example of a national calamity as challenging as many biblical famines.

In 2005, we all saw that the weather can still cause poverty. There were twelve major tropical storms and hurricanes in that year alone. It was the only season to have two hurricanes reach Category 4 before the end of July. It had the most storms form during the month of July (five) and had the strongest storm on record before August. Hurricane Katrina ranked as the third most intense hurricane to ever strike the U.S. mainland. Louisiana and Mississippi are still dealing with damaged infrastructure and economies.

Government corruption, oppressive policy, and persecution

Isaiah's writings point out another cause of poverty as he describes the oppression of the people by their own rulers. In the first twelve chapters of the Book of Isaiah, he enumerates Judah's social sins (chapters 1–6) and her political entanglements (chapters 7–12). Consider the following scripture from Isaiah 10:1–2 (NIV):

> Woe to those who make unjust laws, to those who issue oppressive decrees, to deprive the poor of their rights and withhold justice from the oppressed of my people, making widows their prey and robbing the fatherless.

Persecution and improper government policies can be just as harmful to the economic well-being of citizens as a severe natural disaster. Sudan and Rwanda are two recent, tragic examples where persecution has led to total poverty of the nation. Partial justice (Job 24:1–12; Isa. 1:21, 23) gives advantages to the wealthy or to the poor. Oppressive taxation hinders economic growth of both individuals and of society as a whole by discouraging work and productivity.

Other more obscure government policies dampen opportunity and the creation of wealth. Laws and ordinances that restrict entry into a particular field or business are one such cause of poverty. As a legislator, Tony often saw how existing businesses enlisted the aid of government to create licenses for certain professions and the accompanying boards and commissions who would determine who could enter that particular profession. While there is certainly a case to be made for states to regulate who practices medicine or to establish certain criteria for those who build skyscrapers, there is a much less compelling case to be made for why the state should license and regulate interior decorators or taxi services. What is most egregious in this process is that the regulatory boards that set the standards of entry are made up of individuals who are established in the particular business. It becomes a vehicle to block people from entering the field.

Consider the obstacles that the government erects in the taxicab industry in New York City. To enter the business you have obtain a medallion and be approved by the New York City Taxi and Limousine Commission (TLC). The TLC controls the number of medallions, which drives up the value of medallions, which are auctioned off. One medallion sold for $600,000 in 2007.[7] The limited number of medallions limits competition and makes it very difficult for someone to enter the taxi business. While the cost of a taxicab medallion is an extreme example, the principle is the same. If the price of admission into the economic arena is too high, many people are left outside to contend with poverty.

Similar effects can be seen with other government ordinances and policies that are designed to help the poor but actually hurt them. Rent control policies appear to make housing more affordable, but the outcome is that fewer units are available and the quality is much lower. Why? Because landlords are not going to make capital expenditures that they cannot recoup. Minimum wage laws are also designed to benefit the poor. The reality is that while they increase the income of those who have the jobs, they decrease the income of those who are then excluded from the workforce because of the government-imposed increase. Teenagers and lower-end minority candidates seeking their entry in the job market are disproportionately impacted by the loss of jobs resulting from increases in the minimum wage. Additionally, an increase in the minimum wage often creates inflationary pressure, which generally drives up the costs of goods and services. Tony saw this firsthand on a recent Saturday afternoon as he stopped in at a local McDonald's with one of his children. A sign posted on the door read, "Notice: Prices have increased to cover the costs of the recent federally mandated minimum wage increase."

Banking or lender abuse

The problem of mortgaging lands at exorbitant interest developed within the Jewish community during the captivity. This was in direct violation of the Old Testament law (Lev. 25:36; Ezek. 18:8, 13, 17). As part of a massive social reform in Nehemiah's day, the nation discontinued its practice of charging excessive interest (Neh. 5:3–13).

In the New Testament, Jesus denounced all extortion and proclaimed a new law of love and forbearance (Luke 6:30, 35).

How does all of this apply to us? Bank regulations have a moral dimension. The practices of redlining a neighborhood and predatory lending are not moral from a biblical standpoint. On almost any commercial city block today you will find a payday loan establishment that makes money by lending money, primarily to the working poor, until the next payday. The interest rates on these short-term loans can reach 782.14 percent for a fourteen-day loan.[8] Some argue these lending companies are nothing more than legal loan sharks. Others argue that they provide a needed service to people who cannot obtain a loan anywhere else. Reality is probably somewhere in between.

Increasingly, state and local governments are regulating the interest rates these businesses can charge, as they often tend to facilitate a lack of fiscal discipline and only exacerbate the financial woes of the poor. There can be good lenders in this field providing a needed service, but the ideal situation would be for communities to help the working poor gain the life management skills that in many cases would make payday loans unnecessary.

Family breakdown

During his time as a police officer, Tony witnessed the effects of the breakdown of family. One time he was dispatched to a home in an inner-city black neighborhood on a report that a young woman was not answering her phone or the door and a toddler was seen in the house by neighbors looking through the window. The report was correct, and Tony had to break down the door of the house to retrieve the toddler, who had been sitting for hours in the house next to her single mother who had overdosed on drugs.

Since President Lyndon B. Johnson launched the war on poverty with his "Great Society" speech in May of 1964, the federal government has spent close to $7 trillion, an amount more than double what the United States spent in World War II to defeat both Germany and Japan (this is after adjustments for inflation). But studies indicate that the number of children in poverty has actually increased.[9] Had the Johnson-era strategies been based on a more scriptural approach—maybe even providing certain incentives for intact families—the rate of family breakdown might have slowed rather than accelerated.

Consider the following:

▶ From the fact that 5 percent of births were out of wedlock at the time the war on poverty was launched to now where the percentage of out-of-wedlock births is 38.5 percent, we see that there has been an increase of single-parent families.[10]

▶ Single-parent homes are a leading cause of child poverty. Single mothers are nine times more likely to live in "deep poverty" with incomes less than half the official poverty level.[11]

▶ Beyond income, children in single-parent homes fare poorly in many areas when compared with their counterparts in intact families. Areas such as conduct, educational achievement, occupational achievement, psychological adjustment, self-esteem, and marital stability are all affected by family poverty.[12] The problem of poverty does not just affect the poor; we all pay for their unrealized potential.

▶ A 1990 study conducted by the Progressive Policy Institute, the research arm of the Democratic Leadership Council, explains that the "relationship between crime and one-parent families" is "so strong that controlling for family configuration erases the relationship between race and crime and between low income and crime. This conclusion shows up time and again in the literature."[13] The growing cost of corrections is one of the largest expenditures in state government budgets today.

We understand that all children in single-parent homes are not born out of wedlock. Many end up in single-parent homes as a result of divorce and even death of a parent. However, the breakdown of a family unit as a result of any of these causes makes it difficult for people to not fall victim to poverty.

Addictive personal behavior

Both gluttony and drunkenness are clearly shown in Scripture to be habits that lead to poverty and personal destruction. Consider these words:

> Listen, my son, and be wise,
>   and keep your heart on the right path.
> Do not join those who drink too much wine
>   or gorge themselves on meat,
> for drunkards and gluttons become poor,
>   and drowsiness clothes them in rags.
>   —Proverbs 23:19–21, NIV

In our overweight and self-medicated society, few things steal both our health and resources more than these two things. The drunkenness of the Bible can be applied to both legal and illegal drugs. Harry believes that one of the major causes of health and financial challenges in his family line has been these twin sisters of disaster. Most of the men in Harry's family were quite heavy in their younger years. As they aged, even dramatic weight losses and stopping their weekend alcohol binges did not purchase long life for them.

These are truths that should be taught to our young people. In addition, practices such as proper diet and exercise should be passed on to each succeeding generation.

Laziness

Laziness has an obvious relationship, and a not-so-obvious relationship, to poverty, making it a deceptive problem. The first aspect is the refusal to work hard. There can be many reasons for this lack of follow-through, including poor role models and a lack of understanding concerning the cycles, seasons, and rewards of a particular job. Christianity endorses a strong work ethic, which we are to perform as unto the Lord (Col. 3:23–24; 2 Thess. 3:10).

The second, much more subtle reason for laziness deals with the thought life. Some people are afraid of things that will never happen, while others expect help that will never come. Proverbs 26:13 says, "The slothful man saith, There is a lion in the way; a lion is in the streets." Proverbs 28:19–20 says, "He who works his land will have abundant food, but the one who chases fantasies will have his fill of poverty" (NIV).

Either way, unrealistic expectations can mentally cripple an able-bodied man. Over the years Harry has counseled many men with these mind-sets. They are either paralyzed with fear or do not put in the diligence necessary to have true success.

Pushing Back Poverty

What then should be our response to poverty in our midst? The solution requires four partners to work together to reflect God's heart of compassion toward America's poor:

1. Individual philanthropy
2. Government
3. Churches
4. Businesses

The role of the individual

Let's start with the first line of responsibility for helping the truly poor. Both the Old and New Testaments make clear that as believers we each have a personal responsibility to care for the poor. God laid out specific instructions in Deuteronomy 15 for the responsibility that the children of Israel had individually and collectively to care for the poor when He instructed them to have an "open hand" to the needy. In the New Testament Jesus confirmed the priority that individuals should place on caring for the poor (*ptochos*) when He told the young man who apparently saw himself as perfect in the eyes of the biblical law to sell all that he had and give it to the poor.

The average American citizen has allowed the government to crowd out his participation in helping the poor. This is exactly what Arthur Brooks points to in his book about charitable giving. Many people, especially liberals, see tax-funded poverty programs as their contribution. But it is not! We are to address and alleviate poverty personally and individually.

Despite how biblical conservatives are portrayed, we are very much hands-on when it comes to poverty. Both of us have worked with the homeless and families in financial crisis. Tony has been working with the homeless for nearly two decades. His involvement has gone beyond financial support of homeless ministries to providing temporary housing, sharing meals with the homeless, and mentoring homeless men to help them address the root causes of their property.

Harry has given a great deal of money to individuals in danger of losing their homes and the like through an outreach of his church called the Jeremiah Ministry. This approach guarantees that people do not give on the basis of emotion alone. Jeremiah Ministry screens people who request food or housing aid from the church. The ministry attempts to help them with major transitions but will not carry anyone long term. Folks who don't make major strides toward personal financial independence will not get Jeremiah support for long.

We encourage you to pray for opportunities to minister to those in need. We also exhort you to start solving poverty within your own family. You may have a relative who is elderly or incapable of working. Care for those closest to you first, and then work outward. Consider those in your local church. We have found numerous opportunities to help those who are in need because of sickness or economic setback.

When that base is covered, support a local church-based outreach to the poor or homeless. Not only are these ministries able to meet the short-term physical need, they are often able to meet the greater needs that lead to poverty situations. Consider volunteering at one of these ministries to the poor. Tony's family is part of a group of families that prepares and serves dinner and shares the gospel with homeless men once a month at a local shelter operated by the Catholic diocese.

If your community does not have sufficient outreaches to the poor, encourage your church to consider partnering with an existing ministry to expand their outreach, or consider starting one in your church. These can be as simple as a food pantry that is open once a week.

Start a scholarship

One of the best ways to get rid of poverty in your family or community is to help others get an education. Harry grew up in an inner-city black home. His grandfather, Simmie Jackson, had moved to Cincinnati from Georgia in the early 1940s. With only a second-grade education, he had few marketable skills. Simmie had one more strike against him: his thick West Indian accent. He was one of a group of blacks, called the Gullah or Guichee people, who settled in North and South Carolina. The Gullah are known for preserving more of their African linguistic and cultural heritage than any other black community in the United States. They speak an English-based Creole language containing many African loan words.[14] As a Southerner relocating to the North, he had even more difficulty landing a good job, even in the areas normally reserved for blacks.

Yet in one generation Simmie started a thriving construction business, helped both of his sons attend college, and purchased a lovely home in the suburbs. Harry's uncle Booker fought in World War II as a lieutenant in the army before pursuing a lucrative construction career. In addition to a stint in the navy in World War II, Simmie's youngest son (Harry Sr.) became the director of personnel for the Bureau of Engraving and Printing in Washington DC before his death in 1975.

Not only did Simmie's children accomplish a great deal, but also his great-grandchildren have all started life at a higher economic plane than he could have ever imagined. This kind of testimony is what God wants for every family living in poverty in America. It is the kind of generational breakthrough that America needs.

A big part of Simmie's story is education. Each one of us can encourage those around us to pursue an education. Statistics clearly show that education can be an avenue out of poverty. Consider the following numbers from the U.S. Census Bureau:[15]

Average Earnings of Blacks and Whites With Bachelor's Degrees	
Blacks	$37,103
Whites	$40,798
Blacks and Whites With Master's Degrees	
Blacks	$49,716
Whites	$50,708
Blacks and Whites With Doctorates	
Blacks	$74, 207
Whites	$73,993

These statistics confirm the powerful economic advantage that accrues to anyone who holds a four-year college degree or higher. Education even erases the racial difference. Blacks with a doctorate actually have higher incomes than similarly educated non-Hispanic whites.

When Harry was a youngster, his mother and father emphasized that education was "the great equalizer." Their intuitive desire for education was a good investment of time and energy. You too can help people pursue an education at any number of levels, from community college to an Ivy League university, by helping them with tuition, books, or setting up a long-term scholarship. Again, start with family and work outward. Even a small investment can change a life.

As Christians, all of us are frontline warriors against poverty. We have a responsibility, individually and corporately, to address the needs of the truly poor. The more we attempt to shift the responsibility to the government, the more costly and ineffective the effort will be in meeting the genuine needs of the poor. If we approach this problem personally, with the wisdom of the Scriptures, we can win souls, reduce poverty, and transform the nation as well.

The role of government
Another partner in remediating poverty is the government. But we don't advocate more welfare benefits or direct aid. While some may see government aid as an act of compassion, it is short-changed compassion. The research shows that government redistribution of wealth stymies charity. When the government takes on the role of Robin Hood, people privately give less to charitable causes. Government spending displaces private dollars. This not only affects the charity, but it also robs the potential giver of all the associated benefits that accompany charitable giving, such as prosperity, health, and happiness.

Instead of breaking the cycle of poverty by addressing the root causes, government programs actually extend the cycle of poverty by medicating the recipient with short-term fixes. Government aid can be addictive. The Scriptures clearly say that if a man will not work, he should not eat. Short-term financial assistance should be like using crutches when your leg is broken. The crutches should be leaned on for a period, but after healing has occurred they become an unnecessary nuisance. The liberal approach to poverty, unfortunately, gives people crutches, if not a wheelchair, for a lifetime. This threatens not only the economic well-being of the poor but also that of the entire nation.

But government can reduce poverty in important ways. First, it must avoid corruption, because corruption brings the judgment of God on a nation. When most people hear the words *government corruption*, their minds immediately may think of third world countries, but America is not free of government corruption. In September 1998, Tony testified before the National Gambling Impact Study Commission about how legalized gambling had "corrupted Louisiana's government, preyed on the poor, and racked up billions of dollars in social costs."[16] The spread of gambling in

Louisiana had been a catalytic issue in prompting Tony to successfully run for public office in 1995.

In rapid succession Louisiana created a state lottery in 1990; legalized riverboat gambling and video poker at bars, restaurants, and truck stops in 1991; and opened a large casino in the heart of New Orleans in 1992. Shortly after video poker was legalized, Louisiana became the site of one of the largest corruption probes in the history of the FBI. Organized crime set up shop in Louisiana, skimming millions from gambling operations. However, the mob found they had competition in the form of government officials.

As a result of the federal investigations, dozens of indictments were issued between 1995 and 1996. Among the many people indicted were a state representative, three state senators, and one governor. Of the elected officials indicted, one senator and the governor were convicted. Former governor Edwin Edwards remains in prison.

How does this corruption relate to poverty? Gambling, corruption, and poverty always go hand in hand. During this time, government officials were looking for easy revenue through decriminalized gambling instead of making the difficult decisions to cut spending or raise the necessary revenue. As gambling grew in Louisiana, so did bankruptcies. Statewide bankruptcy filings increased 17.63 percent in 1995, one year after the casinos became operational. In 1996 there was a 38.7 percent increase. It should be noted that these increases in bankruptcy, which resulted in the construction of a new bankruptcy court to handle the increased volume, came at a time when Louisiana and the rest of the nation were enjoying economic growth.[17]

A nationwide study in 1997 found that the bankruptcy rate in counties with at least one gambling establishment was 18 percent higher than for those counties without gambling. The rate was 35 percent higher for counties with five or more gambling facilities, drawing a direct link between the increase in legalized gambling and increased bankruptcies.[18]

The very officials who were supposed to protect the citizens of the state looked the other way while others enriched themselves by exploiting the poor and the unwitting. The government helps poverty most by standing for justice and not overregulating or overtaxing the population.

The role of the church

Churches should be much more directly involved in solving poverty than the government. It is our task first, not the government's.

Evidence suggests that African American churches and racially mixed nondenominational churches have done the best job of integrating practical community services with preaching the gospel. Greater Exodus Baptist Church in downtown Philadelphia, with Dr. Herb Lusk, is an example of the type of church that Harry and George Barna wrote about in their book titled *High Impact African-American Churches*. His church is revitalizing a depressed portion of Philadelphia. Through the church's social service arm, People for People, Herb took a condemned vacant building and turned it into a community service center with a charter school, computer lab, food bank, and a savings and loan office to help people become homeowners. The church has grown from about two dozen attendees to over fifteen hundred.

The Greater Allen A.M.E. Cathedral of New York City is another example of what a church can accomplish within the urban ghetto. Located in notoriously rundown Jamaica, Queens, pastor Floyd Flake has taken his parishioners on a journey to create justice among hopeless people. One ministry is the "Annual Feeding of the Five Thousand," which has grown to provide close to nine thousand meals to needy neighbors. Another ministry is the soup kitchen and clothing closet. This outreach distributes dry and canned food, clothing, and hot, nutritious meals to over twenty-five hundred clients monthly. In 2004, fifty-four thousand people were served through this ministry. The church is so committed to changing the face of the community that it buys every piece of real estate within twenty-seven blocks of the cathedral to turn it into good-quality, low-income housing, small businesses, and safe educational and recreational facilities.

In California, we can also cite the ministry of social justice being carried out by West Angeles Church of God in Christ. Bishop Charles E. Blake has led a team of ministry that includes everyone from street people to notables such as Denzel Washington, Stevie Wonder, Angela Bassett, and Magic Johnson. West Angeles has approximately eighty specialty ministries and support groups. For example, the church's Community Development Corporation (CDC) receives grants and funds from foundations and businesses, dispersing these to its faith-based social services. West Angeles's CDC has been recognized as one of the most productive in California in terms of food services and emergency relief. Over five thousand meals are given to homeless and disadvantaged people through its skid row ministry. The CDC has also partnered with Pepperdine University Law School to provide legal services for people with moderate incomes who do not qualify for legal aid.

West Angeles also has created Individual Development Accounts (IDA) to help low- and middle-income people move out of poverty and achieve self-sufficiency through home ownership. The person's existing assets are supplemented on a three-to-one basis and placed in the IDA account. These savings are used for home purchase or to initiate or expand a business venture. The funds can also be used for postsecondary education tuition costs. The first black banks and savings and loans came out of the church.

These churches are forerunners that have developed working models that can serve churches of any racial makeup.

The role of business

Business is a critical partner in community renewal and poverty alleviation, but businesses should not work in a vacuum. They should be part of a team that includes churches and ministries. Some of the most successful economic development models used to revitalize African American communities combine business interests with black churches as the foundation for community renewal. This cooperation is part of a new kingdom mind-set in the church. What the black church has done regionally in an isolated way can be adopted by the entire church—black, white, Hispanic, and Asian—to produce real results.

Successful businesspeople can choose to mentor others, using their business as a place to disciple and develop people for God's purposes. They can also invest far more money in the kingdom than most of us. The story of Jerome Liberty's vision to impact his nation should encourage every businessperson. Motivated companies can take on causes that individuals and churches cannot tackle alone.

Businesses can create wealth in troubled regions without giving handouts. This is what the black church did during the Reconstruction period just after the Civil War. Mutual help societies became the source of funding for people in crisis and working capital for starting small businesses.

Microfinancing is another way businesses can pave the way to a new future for the poor. Small, incremental loans can teach a person how to fish instead of just giving them a fish. Microfinancing can be an on-ramp to the mainstream financial system for a great number of forgotten people in America and around the world.

In Bangladesh, Muhammad Yunus did just that. He established a bank in 1983. In 2006 he received the Nobel Peace Prize for his microfinancing efforts. The idea was birthed in Yunus's heart in 1976 when this American-trained Fulbright scholar loaned $27 of his own money to a group of forty-two stool makers. The workers were all women. This seed money allowed them to purchase materials that led to enough profit to get them out of a cycle of poverty. The Grameen Bank that he founded has loaned $3.8 billion to 2.4 million families in rural Bangladesh. Yunus and his bank are at the forefront of a movement, called the microlending movement, to eradicate poverty.

Yunus records his journey in his book, *Banker to the Poor*, and says:

> I made sure that the real borrowers, the ones I call the "banking untouchables," never had to suffer the indignity and demeaning harassment of actually going to a bank....I had no intention of lending money to anyone. All I really wanted was to solve an immediate problem.... To my great surprise, the repayment of loans by people who borrow without collateral has proven to be much better than those whose borrowings are secured by assets. Indeed, more than 98 percent of our loans are repaid. The poor know that this credit is their only opportunity to break out of poverty.[19]

Microfinancing is active in over one hundred countries by two hundred fifty institutions. Some nations give foreign aid to developing countries by offering micro-credit programs that go directly to needy entrepreneurs. This avoids the potential corruption when foreign aid dollars are siphoned away into the Swiss bank accounts of despotic leaders.

It's Time to Serve

The Lord is watching how we take care of the needy in this world. Jesus wants to be able to commend the church in America, whether we are Democrats or Republicans, black or white, Southern or Northern, liberal or conservative. Serving the poor is part of our personal responsibility to help those less fortunate than ourselves. It is also part of our corporate calling as churches, and our public policy objectives should support and encourage this personal and corporate duty to the poor. The Lord's concern for justice requires that we assist in creating public policy that will demonstrate His love and mercy in tangible ways.

The Lord desires to say to us one day:

Come, you who are blessed by my Father; take your inheritance, the kingdom prepared for you since the creation of the world. For I was hungry and you gave me something to eat, I was thirsty and you gave me something to drink, I was a stranger and you invited me in, I needed clothes and you clothed me, I was sick and you looked after me, I was in prison and you came to visit me.

—MATTHEW 25:34–36, NIV

Let us honor Christ now more than ever by serving the poor.

Prayer Points

▶ Give thanks that God has supplied your daily bread. Praise God for His bounty and His faithfulness to you, your family, and our nation.

▶ Ask that God the Father would bring protection to the poor and needy of our land and the world beyond our borders. Ask Him to bring the government, businesses, and church together in creative ways to end poverty in America (Matt. 6:11).

▶ Seek the Lord's direction in how He would have you, your family, your church, and possibly your business help address poverty in America (Acts 10:4).

Chapter 7

CORE VALUE #3: POVERTY AND JUSTICE (PART 2)

HEALTH-CARE REFORM

n August 2005, Harry and his wife, Michele, sat in the office of world-famous surgeon Dr. Stephen Yang of Johns Hopkins Hospital. Saturday struck them as an unusual time to meet with such a prestigious doctor. The hospital looked like a ghost town—darkened hallways, empty offices, and a skeleton staff at the main entrances for security. Dr. Yang appeared without the traditional entourage of receptionists and assistants. Chipper and buoyant as always, he greeted them with a smile.

As Harry stared into the face of this sharp, young physician, he felt inspired and hopeful. Harry's primary-care physician had refused to refer him to any of the other institutions in their region, believing that Hopkins was the best hospital in the country. The reasons for the Jacksons' visit was that the doctors had found cancerous cells. But nobody had yet answered the question, "How bad is it?"

Despite his cheerful demeanor, Dr. Yang delivered an ominous message. He thought that Harry had a 15 percent chance of surviving esophageal cancer if they followed the traditional approach to treatment. He went on to say that a special treatment protocol developed by Dr. Arlene Forestiere and the Johns Hopkins Hospital staff could actually quadruple Harry's chances of survival. Naturally, he could not guarantee that the innovative, treatment protocol would work.

A few days later, additional tests showed that Harry had a stage-three cancerous tumor about the size of a golf ball at the opening of his esophagus. "This cannot be happening to us," Harry and his wife thought. Harry had served faithfully in ministry for more than twenty-five years. In addition, they felt that Harry's national work had just begun. So they prayed intensely and believed that God would somehow deliver them.

The treatment required massive doses of chemotherapy, radiation, multiple surgeries, and postsurgical chemotherapy. Hopkins assigned a team of five doctors to manage his case because of the danger and the complications that ensued. The labyrinth of tests, procedures, and protocols was almost as daunting as the diagnosis of cancer.

But just as daunting were the costs. The preliminary treatments racked up nearly $10,000 in bills in less than two weeks. There was a constant tug-of-war between the Jacksons and their insurance company. The insurance company preferred local doctors and local tests. As a result of their threat to discontinue payments for his treatment, Harry paid special attention to every request for insurance verification; he also sought preapprovals for every aspect of his treatment plans. It seemed to the Jacksons that more hours were spent working on the intricacies of the insurance puzzle than were spent treating Harry.

Eventually, the insurance company relented, and the healing effects of medicine and prayer began to work. Today, Harry is cancer free. He and Michele are expecting that he will live a long and meaningful life. But the costs were high. Beyond the medical costs, the cost of this new lease on life was approximately $100,000 in unexpected personal costs including special food, clothing, and preventive health treatments. These numbers don't begin to reflect the loss of income that the disease inflicted upon them. After fighting off cancer and fighting many an emotional battle, the Jacksons had to fight to get their financial lives back.

We believe that Harry's experience points out three problems in America's health-care system:

1. The lack of access to the best health care for all Americans
2. The high costs of treatment
3. The need for people to take personal responsibility to prevent sicknesses and health problems

Let's turn first to the specific biblical approach to health, healing, and national health.

Biblical Health Care

The Old Testament is much more direct in terms of health mandates and ordinances than the New Testament. The Jewish dietary code was aimed at sustaining health. Other health rules were meant to prevent disease and stop the spread of plagues. Dr. Michael Jacobsen, author of *The Word on Health,* observed that in A.D. 1348, approximately 100 million people inhabited Europe, Africa, and the Middle East. The next year 25 million people, or one quarter of the world's population, died of the bubonic plague.[1] This cyclical plague also claimed 23 percent of the population of London in 1603. Consider his analysis of why the Jewish population of those ancient times was not affected:

> The truth is that, hundreds of years prior to the discovery of bacteria, the Jews were protecting themselves from the deadly *Yersinia pestis* microbe by practicing cleanliness and good hygiene. Why? Because more than three thousand years before man discovered bacteria, the Creator had given instructions that, if followed, would prevent the spread of such a communicable disease.[2]

In the Old Testament, God's message was that those who followed the rules would not experience the diseases of the Egyptians. Deuteronomy 7:15 states, "The LORD will keep you free from every disease. He will not inflict on you the horrible diseases you knew in Egypt, but he will inflict them on all who hate you" (NIV). By the time of the New Testament, doctors were recognized professionals. Luke, the writer of the Gospel of Luke, was called by Paul "the beloved physician" (Col. 4:14). Most scholars think that Luke was Paul's medical advisor and probably prolonged his life by treating him for several serious illnesses. Luke may well have been the first "medical missionary." Interestingly, he wrote more than one-fourth of the New Testament, but he did not once mention himself by name, perhaps indicating that his focus was on the well-being of others. The Gospel of Luke reveals his concern for the poor, social outcasts, and, naturally, the sick.

The *Encyclopedia Britannica* tells us that:

> The modern concept of a hospital dates from AD 331 when Constantine, having been converted to Christianity, abolished all pagan hospitals and thus created the opportunity for a new start. Until that time disease had isolated the sufferer from the community. The Christian tradition emphasized the close relationship of the sufferer to his

fellow man, upon whom rested the obligation for care. Illness thus became a matter for the Christian church.[3]

Europe's first medical schools came out of the church. Most cities still have hospitals that are attached to the faith community. The involvement of people of faith in this arena is both historic and pervasive.

The development of hospitals in America followed a very similar path as the Christian community helped establish infirmaries that developed into hospitals. What biblical mandate was the church operating from? There is no real scriptural directive about modern health care. Still, we believe that concern about health care falls under the general principle of "loving your neighbor." When Jesus gave an admonition to a lawyer who attempted to trap Him in a tangle of questions concerning who his neighbor was, Jesus told the following story in Luke's Gospel:

> And Jesus answering said, A certain man went down from Jerusalem to Jericho, and fell among thieves, which stripped him of his raiment, and wounded him, and departed, leaving him half dead. And by chance there came down a certain priest that way: and when he saw him, he passed by on the other side. And likewise a Levite, when he was at the place, came and looked on him, and passed by on the other side. But a certain Samaritan, as he journeyed, came where he was: and when he saw him, he had compassion on him, and went to him, and bound up his wounds, pouring in oil and wine, and set him on his own beast, and brought him to an inn, and took care of him. And on the morrow when he departed, he took out two pence, and gave them to the host, and said unto him, Take care of him; and whatsoever thou spendest more, when I come again, I will repay thee.
>
> Which now of these three, thinkest thou, was neighbour unto him that fell among the thieves? And he said, He that shewed mercy on him. Then said Jesus unto him, Go, and do thou likewise.
>
> —Luke 10:30–37

This story emphasizes the brotherly care that a Samaritan man gave to someone in a crisis who could not care for himself and who was not of his race. In fact, there was deep-seated hostility between Jews and Samaritans. A needy stranger had fallen upon hard times. The "good Samaritan" had more compassion upon this man than both a priest and a Levite. It is important to grasp the fact that Jericho was an eighteen-mile journey from Jerusalem, and that Jericho was a city in which thousands of priests and Levites lived. This was the main thoroughfare between two religious centers. It was a religious area that had doctrine and dogma without the type of love that Christ encouraged. This highly used road would have had scores of religious leaders passing by this man if he had been lying there awhile. Ironically, the Old Testament law encouraged these people to treat a neighbor's animals better than these religious leaders were willing to treat a man who was outside of their social clique (Deut. 22:4; Exod. 23:4–5).

Jesus's story was designed to tell everyone listening that we should get out of our comfort zones and help needy people as one of the major aspects of contemporary faith. Historically, great Christians have used their medical training and health care as a gateway into foreign missions, just like Dr. Luke. For example, Dr. David Livingstone was a Scottish Presbyterian medical missionary who served with the London Missionary Society. His burden was for Africa, and he developed a heart to end the illegal slave trade in Africa during the 1840s and beyond. His motto was "Christianity, Commerce, and Civilization"—and these were the weapons he used to transform life in several parts of Africa.

Overlapping Livingstone's era, a young Christian woman named Florence Nightingale became the mother of modern nursing. She served on location as a nurse in the Crimean War, which took place in modern-day Ukraine. The British supported the Turkish army against the Russians, who occupied the principalities (modern Romania).[4] In this dread war, more soldiers were dying from diseases and infections contracted after they were wounded in the field than from actual combat. Nightingale's Christian witness was immortalized in secular songs during her lifetime and in medical history today. She, like Mother Teresa, became a cultural icon.

Each of these figures was a good Samaritan in their day who transformed their culture because they were not afraid to cross racial and cultural barriers to help a needy person whom they saw "bleeding on the Jericho road." We believe that the example of the good Samaritan is just as valid for us today as it was for Livingstone and Nightingale. Christians may need to invest a little money to help needy people afflicted by sickness, who perhaps have been stripped by an impersonal health-care industry and ignored by people who had vowed to serve both God and their fellow man. But in doing so, we can follow the heart of God.

Today's Health Options

We desire to serve the most vulnerable members of society, but that does not mean we want to waste resources, nor does it mean that individuals bear no responsibility for bad decisions and/or lifestyle choices, expecting the rest of society to pay. We must use our brains and our hearts to accomplish our goals to help transform America's health-care system. We also believe that this is not a problem to be solved by government alone. The best health-care plan will be a public/private commitment based upon biblical values that is neither Republican nor Democrat, liberal nor conservative. The historical record shows that in addition to faith-based hospitals here in the United States, hospitals have been a private-public partnership.

The first hospital founded in the nation was in 1751 in Philadelphia. It was created by the legislature when Benjamin Franklin raised matching contributions. It is clear that America has the world's best health-care delivery system because of the commitments and contributions from both philanthropists and policy makers. Any viable solution to the present and pending health-care dilemma will require the participation of individuals, families, the public and private sectors, and the church.

Two trillion dollars a year is approximately the national budget for health care. This amounts to about 17 percent of our gross national product. The most other nations spend is 10 percent of their GNP.[5] In addition, we have around 47 million uninsured American residents.[6] Some researchers suggest that 18,000 uninsured people die every year, according to the Institute of Medicine.[7] It is hard to draw a one-to-one correlation between lack of insurance and premature death, but it seems logical to us that there is some connection.

What do these numbers mean to the average person? Each one of us contributes seven thousand dollars annually for this jigsaw puzzle of care. Despite this high "national overhead," half of U.S. bankruptcies are caused by medical expenses, even though two-thirds of bankruptcy filers had health insurance.[8] This means that there is a mismatch between what we think we are paying for and what we are actually getting when it comes to our medical insurance plans. The Jacksons were very lucky that they had enough financial resilience to handle their personal crisis. Most Americans are not that fortunate.

"Universal Health Care" is a catchphrase that some have used to describe a program that would guarantee access to health care for everyone. To conservatives it has socialist overtones. It is unfortunate that this term has been co-opted by people who advocate socialized medical care, because we Christians should also believe that everyone should have access to health care. The difference with our definition of "universal" is that we believe that there can be a unique combination of conservative and liberal concepts that will produce the best health-care system in the world.

As we have repeatedly alluded to throughout the pages of this book, too many people think about America's problems in terms of political ideologies (coming from the Left or Right) instead of in terms of scriptural concepts. In the delicate area of health care, compassion and common sense must intersect to bring us to a place where we help hurting people, create an atmosphere of fairness for physicians, give profit to the insurance companies, and protect generations to come from exploitation and a myriad of shortcomings.

Let's start on the Left side of this issue with the health-care plan of John Edwards, which became the benchmark, or starting point, for all the Democratic health-care plans offered in the Democratic presidential primary. The other candidates mostly copied his analysis and priorities with a few minor adjustments. Edwards made the following statement during his primary race for president in 2007: "We have to stop using words like 'access to health care' when we know with certainty those words mean something less than universal care. Who are you willing to leave behind without the care he needs? Which family? Which child? We need a truly universal solution, and we need it now."[9] We think we know what Edwards meant, but we disagree with the implied strategic direction of the solution. He set forth several noble goals that we agree with:

- Families without insurance will get coverage at an affordable price.
- Families with insurance will pay less and get more security and choices.
- Businesses and other employers will find it cheaper and easier to insure their workers.[10]

We are convinced that where Edwards's approach falls down is that he wants to replicate universal health care as administered in Europe— a system that is broken. A personal illustration will best explain our concerns. Recently, a woman at Harry's health club stopped him to inquire about his doctors and the treatment he had received. Her father, who lives in England under universal health care, had the same type of cancer but was essentially sent home to die. They did not allow the advanced treatment protocol Harry had received. She attempted to get Harry's doctor to consult with her father's physicians overseas.

This incident brought back to Harry's mind that every day in the cancer clinic he saw people from South America, the Middle East, Europe, and numerous domestic states patiently waiting for treatment. Many of them were wealthy people who were willing to pay any price to regain their health. The knowledge and experience of the Hopkins doctors made them a critical resource for these beleaguered travelers.

Americans have the world's finest doctors and best hospitals. Our national conundrum is how we help each individual get the care he or she needs. Under universal health care in other nations there are three major problems:

1. Endless lines to see physicians

2. Large numbers of underprepared "cheap doctors" and less qualified nurses and support staff

3. Fewer innovations in substantive techniques and practices

Thomas Sowell wrote an interesting article titled "No Health Insurance" on September 4, 2007, that summarized the problems with universal health care in an anecdotal style:

> Few people show the slightest interest in what has actually happened in countries with government-controlled medical care. We are apparently supposed to follow those countries' example without asking about the months that people in those countries spend on waiting lists for medical treatments that Americans get just by picking up a phone and making an appointment. It is amazing how many people seem uninterested in such things as why so many doctors in Britain are from Third World countries with lower medical standards— or why people from Canada come to the United States for medical treatment that they could get cheaper at home.[11]

Sowell's statement certainly describes our experience and perspective. Yet we still believe there needs to be a "universal" option for destitute people, who may be widows and orphans. There must be a place where the "least of these" (Matt. 25:40, 45) are given special care. Perhaps some sort of free-market system could alleviate some of the variables in our system that make health care so expensive. Through this the needy participants could be challenged to sign up only for what they are actually going to use.

On the Republican side, Senator Sam Brownback, a cancer survivor, laid out an approach to solving the system's woes. Brownback's plan calls for incentives for individuals or businesses to address the waste in the health-care system. Brownback said:

> Our health-care system will thrive with increased consumer choice, consumer control and real competition. I believe it is important that we have price transparency within our health-care system. This offers consumers, who are either enrolled in high-deductible health plans or who pay out-of-pocket, the ability to shop around for the best prices and plan for health-care expenditures. Also, the existing health insurance market forces consumers to pay for extra benefits in their premiums.[12]

Similarly, in September 2007, former mayor and 2008 presidential candidate Rudy Giuliani made this statement:

> America is at a crossroads when it comes to our health care. All Americans want to increase the quality, affordability and portability of health care.... I believe we can reduce costs and improve the quality of care by increasing competition. We can do it through tax cuts, not tax hikes. We can do it by empowering patients and their doctors, not government bureaucrats. That's the American way to reform health care.[13]

We lean toward a free-market approach, but we acknowledge that given the complexity of today's health-care delivery system, which is a hybrid of both public and private, solving our nation's health-care challenge is going to require more than tax credits alone. For example, tax credits do not acknowledge that there are hidden personal costs associated with catastrophic illness. People at the lowest rungs of the health-care chain may need temporary financial help and cannot wait for an end-of-the-year refund. In addition, the loss of potential income through physical or emotional trauma is difficult to measure. None of the plans we have read to date adequately protect victims of catastrophic illness from financial collapse. We believe that special bankruptcy provisions may need to be developed so that people don't lose their homes or businesses because of unavoidable illnesses.

So what do we do about this problem? As we mentioned, Christians and churches have been a part of the delivery of health care in the country. While some would argue the public sector has crowded out the church, we must be a part of this important discussion that controls nearly one-fifth of our nation's GDP. We must come to this discussion not only with passion but also with potential solutions. Our goal should be access to affordable health care for all Americans within the next decade.

True reform must start with individual responsibility. We must encourage good personal choices not only about individual health, which we will discuss in a moment, but also about securing health-care coverage. Personal responsibility will be a component of any successful reform effort. Secondly, there is no question that Congress, and to a lesser extent state legislatures, will play a key role in making health care accessible to all Americans. There is evidence that suggests that employer-based health care is going the way of employer-based retirement systems, reverting health-care coverage back to the individual. Congress can help by making health care more portable so insurance follows the individuals regardless of their employer. Allowing health-care coverage to be purchased across state lines will help small businesses continue to provide health care by increasing the size of the pool of insureds, creating stronger competition among insurance companies, which will lower costs to the consumer.

For low-income Americans who do not have insurance and cannot obtain it, a health-care tax rebate program that allows withholding to be adjusted for health-care expenses should be developed. A similar approach should be taken for those Americans who cannot obtain coverage privately or through their employer.

There is no question that government has been, is, and will continue to be a significant part of America's health-care system. With that said, the church should make health care a priority issue by expanding voter guides to show voting records on health care and platform positions. Further, we should develop a National Church Health Care day and offer free testing for things like HIV/AIDS and high blood pressure, and offer healthy cooking contests and nutrition instruction. We should even develop a health curriculum for churches that would include both Christian and secular materials. We should also encourage national Christian media ministries and networks to promote physical stewardship and health-care reform.

We must cross the political aisles to create new solutions. In addition, the stakeholders—insurance companies, doctors, nurses, HMOs, hospitals—must be brought to the table to discuss the pressing problems of the day. We believe a combination of free-market solutions and a plan to give access to people with low incomes will work best. The Scriptures are clear that we are responsible for the care and well-being of our families (1 Tim. 5:8). How far does this obligation go? We believe it extends at least to the community around us and to those who cannot protect themselves. Therefore health care has a social justice dimension. The question becomes, given the huge expenses of having proper health care, how much are we in America willing to help the needy?

This is a healthy debate for Christians to have, and we believe people of conscience can disagree in good faith about how to achieve universal access to health care. But on this we should be unified: it is our goal that all Americans have as much access to health care as they need. Our personal conviction is that government cannot do better than the private sector in providing health care efficiently and with excellence. But we do believe that one way or another, the poorest of society should have access to health care, even though they cannot always pay for it.

We see an opportunity here for conservatives and liberals to come together. We only disagree about the means, not the goal. Why not advocate for more health-care coverage together in the media and from our national platforms? What is preventing us from standing together for the poor and needy, and even the middle-class people who can't afford some of the coverage they need? Wouldn't this encourage more private action, such as national family ministries developing health-care arms? Wouldn't the private sector, and even insurance companies, feel inspired (or at least pressured) to make more health care available by seeing people across the political spectrum standing together and calling for a solution? Religious conservatives have successfully stopped irresponsible and arguably immoral efforts heralded as solutions to the health care challenges facing our nation. So-called universal health-care measures that seek to federalize America's health-care delivery system puts every American's health care at risk. Mandated coverage and taxpayer-funded services such as abortions, sex change operations, and other morally objectionable services simply ignore the moral complications and concerns that come with a government-run or -funded health-care system. A successful solution to the health-care challenge facing America will not only prevent taxpayers from funding morally questionable services, it will protect the moral consciences of the health-care providers as well.

Personal Accountability for All Christians

We also must lead by personal example. Each of the seven major issues we deal with in this book has a personal mandate. Health care is no exception. It is our personal responsibility to take care of our own health through proper diet, exercise, rest, and other preventive measures. Our bodies are physical temples God has given to us. As a veteran of the U.S. Marine Corps, Tony developed great exercise and physical health practices that he has maintained over the years—running, calisthenics, and weight training. In addition to these, he has recently starting eating better. Harry has done this as well, as a response to illness.

As committed believers, we should care for our temples by doing the following things:

1. Have regular physicals
2. Exercise daily
3. Drink lots of water
4. Get proper rest
5. Focus on eliminating chronic health problems
6. Fight the battle of the bulge by setting healthy weight goals for ourselves
7. Model proper eating, rest, and hygiene practices for our children
8. Engage a nutritionist if personal coaching is needed in order to overcome bad eating habits

Finally, there are three resources you might want to read on your journey toward better health. Harry's nutritionist, Dr. Oz Garcia, has written a great book that gives an overview of what's out there today in the health-care arena. The book is titled *Look and Feel Fabulous Forever*.[14] It discusses nutrition and health from a very broad perspective. It gives the most comprehensive approach to food, exercise, and nutrition of anything we have seen on the market today. Oz has coached Donna Karan, Hilary Swank, and a list of models and regular people with serious health problems. His work is clear, easy to read, and comprehensive. See his Web site at www.ozgarcia.com.

Second, Jordan Rubin, who developed the Maker's Diet, has written an excellent book titled *The Great Physician's Rx for Health & Wellness: Seven Keys to Unlock Your Health Potential*.[15] This book integrates faith with wellness techniques and is an easy read with lots of good take-aways. Learn more at www.jordanrubin.com.

Lastly is Don Colbert's *The Seven Pillars of Health: The Natural Way to Better Health for Life*, a great resource.[16] His book is set up as a fifty-day guide and is quite engaging. He believes that each one of us can add years to our lives by taking simple steps now to ensure good health in the future. One of the most interesting things about Dr. Colbert is that he personally treats some of the nation's best-known Christian ministers. His patient list reads like a who's who of popular ministry. Visit the good doctor at www.drcolbert.com.

By becoming healthy ourselves, we gain credibility to engage the culture on issues of health care, and we gain strength to fight the many other battles for our values. If you are personally attempting to be a better steward of the gift of life, it will reinforce your desire to help others in the nation. Not only that, but we also want to make sure that you are still around making a difference for Christ and the culture for many more years. Stay strong!

Prayer Points

▸ Praise the Lord for being our healer according to Isaiah 53:5. Give thanks for every medical breakthrough that has improved the quality and length of our lives.

▸ Pray that the church will rediscover its role in caring for the sick and needy. Ask forgiveness for any specific ways that you see the church has not stepped in to help families and individuals who need care.

▸ Ask God to speak to those who work in the health-care industry to bring righteousness to bear in their fees and depiction of new drugs and treatments. Pray that the nation will bring justice to bear for widows, orphans, and those who have catastrophic illnesses (James 1:27).

Chapter 8

CORE VALUE #4: RACIAL RECONCILIATION

MOVING TOGETHER

just want to know one thing," the angry voice on the call-in line shouted. "Who is giving you the money for this organization? You probably got a whole lot of that faith-based money!" This black radio listener was suggesting that Harry had sold out his race because of his 2004 support for George W. Bush. "I know your kind," the caller continued. "You wear $2,000 suits and drive a big car. Your kind never really helps the community."

Harry was suddenly part of one of the oldest traps that television and radio interviewers set for unsuspecting talk show guests. They prime their audiences for days, telling them that a certain "awful person" is coming and that the host is going to set them straight. Meanwhile, the producers and host almost beg the interviewee to be a part of their program. They tell him that he will get a chance to tell his whole story and imply that many of the listeners will agree with his point of view.

Having fallen into this trap before, we both know that during the first two minutes of the program, the hosts are all sweetness and honey. They sound open, engaging, and almost sympathetic. But once the host has lulled you into a sense that you're in a warm, welcoming environment, he turns on you. It typically starts with the host saying something like, "Our listeners have been waiting all week to talk to you. Our first caller is Sam from College Park. Sam, what do you think about what Bishop Jackson has just said?" Next, the callers and host double-team you and mount a rowdy,

132 Personal Faith, Public Policy

deafening assault on your position using accusations and ridicule. Finally, when you're safely off the line, the host follows up with a solo diatribe against you.

These kinds of media traps don't surprise us anymore. But they are especially difficult to handle when, as in the example above, they have to do with race relations. Perhaps the most daunting of all topics for Christians to discuss is race relations. Even though it has become more common for churches to develop racially mixed congregations, still no one has successfully bridged the racial divide in terms of social mobilization and public policy. It is the exception rather than the norm for black and white Christians to work together to solve local or national problems. But if we are to change the social climate of our nation, we have no choice; we must unite around a biblical worldview that can include all races, both genders, all classes, and all generations of Christians. Without this unity, our success will be limited at best.

The apostle Paul called for the body of Christ to live and work together. He named the three most significant social divisions of his day:

> You are all sons of God through faith in Christ Jesus, for all of you who were baptized into Christ have clothed yourselves with Christ. There is neither *Jew nor Greek, slave nor free, male nor female*, for you are all one in Christ Jesus. If you belong to Christ, then you are Abraham's seed, and heirs according to the promise.
> —GALATIANS 3:26–29, NIV, EMPHASIS ADDED

In Paul's world, the distrust between Jew and Greek was a deep root of division. The unity of the early church nearly ruptured because of the perceived inequity in the treatment of Christian widows with Jewish backgrounds compared to Christian widows of Greek descent. Once this rift was healed in Acts chapter 6, the hardest-to-reach nonbelievers—Jewish priests—were immediately converted to Christ. We strongly believe that the same spiritual transformation will begin to happen when black, white, and Hispanic Christians come together in spiritual unity today.

In our day, the black-white division is the most intense racial divide in America. It is freighted with bitterness and suspicion. Worse, it seems that anyone who attempts to create a sense of racial unity is attacked and labeled a sellout and puppet (if you're a black conservative) or liberal panderer seeking to soothe your moral conscience (if you're white).

How do we as Americans and Christians heal this division? We do well by learning the lesson from one of the great unifying books of the Bible, Paul's letter to the Galatians. *The Biblical Illustrator* points to three aspects of Galatians chapter 3 that we must remember:

1. True freedom comes from God.
2. Equality among believers comes from Jesus Christ.
3. True brotherhood is achieved only in Jesus Christ.[1]

These three statements are not meant to deny current social inequities. They simply help us as believers understand that there is a higher biblical concept of the unity of the Christian community. Spiritual unity should make us essentially a new ethnic group in terms of our heart, our worldview, and our allegiances. Blacks should not work with whites, or vice versa, out of a sense of obligation to right wrongs of the past or to advance personal or political agendas. We should work together because we are brothers and sisters in Christ Jesus and He has called us to be unified around a biblical agenda that advances all of society as Christ intended.

We can never achieve the unity we hope for by networking, public policy, or lobbying techniques. The unity that we are referring to must come from within us spiritually and then affect our approach to life, relationships, and politics. This true biblical fraternity and brotherhood is challenged by the forces of darkness. We do not think that this statement is an overspiritualization. The attacks and accusations that come politically against our unity are based upon a secular view of the world. Racial unity and joint public policy initiatives seem unnatural or contrived to nonbelievers or carnal Christians.

As a result, people who seek unity must work through constant accusations and questioning. The motives of Christian leaders who work toward a unified social and public policy agenda will continue to strongly be questioned. Harry has been called a "sellout" by some blacks. And though he is a registered Democrat, some have accused him of being "the GOP's boy" or a "House Negro for the white religious plantation owners." To set the record straight, Harry is not on the GOP payroll, has never received a faith-based initiative grant, and has no major donors encouraging him to take up specific agenda items.

On the other side of the debate, Tony has been falsely accused of being a Ku Klux Klan supporter and a direct operative of the Republican Party in an effort to drive African American leaders away from him. Again, neither accusation is true.

It's easy to say that we need to work together. It's another thing to actually develop a working unity that can transform the nation. It will take courage on the part of leaders and people in the pews to change the direction of the nation.

Black Evangelical History

Racism is one of America's original sins and one of the toughest problems to overcome. It has plagued the nation since before its independence. At the same time, African Americans have embraced Christ almost as long as they have been on this continent. Consider this excerpt from a book that Harry coauthored with evangelical leader George Barna:

> Despite the popularity of the idea that whites "seduced" blacks into joining their religion, this view of history has little, if any, basis in fact. On the contrary, "No Blacks Allowed" signs seemed to swing over the entrance of churches for at least the first 120 years of the slaves' presence in America. Even though early colonial Christians rejected blacks, many African-Americans made the choice to follow Jesus wholeheartedly. Their zeal for God and their soul-winning efforts were so fruitful that some people believe whites must have "brainwashed" the early African-American elders. Black Christians of that era were not passive recipients of the Word. Indeed, a true depiction of the evangelization of African-Americans is a story of black heroism, tenacity, and genuine faith.[2]

As we mentioned in chapter 2, African Americans first landed on American soil at Jamestown, Virginia, as slaves in 1619—one year before the *Mayflower* arrived with the Pilgrims who settled at Plymouth Colony in Massachusetts. Unfortunately, white American Christians from the beginning embraced the idea of the inferiority of blacks. This idea was fostered in the colonies in part to justify the chattel slave status of blacks there.

It was not until, and because of, the Great Awakening in America in the 1740s that evangelism of blacks was widely accepted. Many colonial Christians believed that it would be wrong to keep converted blacks in slavery; therefore, perversely, many slaveholders did not attempt to lead blacks to Christ. During the First Great Awakening, things shifted greatly, and evangelism of blacks and the concept of abolishing slavery came into the public conscience. The Christian community worked for the abolition of slavery for over one hundred years until the Civil War.

The Christian desire to abolish slavery was first expressed politically through the founding of the Republican Party. This is surprising to many because of the current antiblack reputation that Republicans have among some modern blacks. The party was actually founded to oppose slavery. In 1856 the party ran its first nominee for president, John C. Fremont. His political slogan was "Free soil, free labor, free speech, and free men." The party first showed strength in geographic regions where today it is very weak—New England, New York, and the northern Midwest. Historians tell us that Republicans had almost no support in the South. In 1860 they elected Abraham Lincoln, who led the nation through the Civil War and the abolition of slavery.

More blacks responded to the Christian message in the South than in the North. Churches became the anchor of the black community in the Reconstruction Era after the Civil War. Southern blacks formed their social networks around the church community, and the first buildings built by former slaves after the Civil War were churches. Early black voters were almost exclusively Republican. But Southern white Christians were influenced by the legacy of slavery and maintained views of black inferiority and segregation.

Space precludes a lengthy discussion of organizations like the Ku Klux Klan that mixed spirituality and racism. It is enough to mention that some Klan members seemed like God-fearing Christians by day but donned white hoods and robes by night and performed acts of terror upon blacks, Catholics, Jews, and other groups in the name of faith and country.

In the late 1940s, a political movement called the Dixiecrats emerged to oppose the post–World War II efforts of blacks to achieve civil rights. It is interesting to note that the Christian community that had helped blacks become extricated from slavery in the 1860s had by this time become unsympathetic to the black dilemma. One of the most painful aspects of the civil rights era was the fact that white Southern Christians often opposed the work of Martin Luther King Jr.

On April 16, 1963, Dr. King wrote a letter from a jail in Birmingham, Alabama, in response to a letter from white clergy that told him to stay out of their local affairs. The following excerpt from King's letter gives an understanding of the intersection of personal faith and public policy in the mind of one of our greatest Americans:

I am in Birmingham because injustice is here. Just as the prophets of the eighth century B.C. left their villages and carried their "thus saith the Lord" far beyond the boundaries of their home towns, and just as the Apostle Paul left his village of Tarsus and carried the gospel of Jesus Christ to the far corners of the Greco-Roman world, so am I compelled to carry the gospel of freedom beyond my own home town. Like Paul, I must constantly respond to the Macedonian call for aid.

Moreover, I am cognizant of the interrelatedness of all communities and states. I cannot sit idly by in Atlanta and not be concerned about what happens in Birmingham. Injustice anywhere is a threat to justice everywhere. We are caught in an inescapable network of mutuality, tied in a single garment of destiny. Whatever affects one directly, affects all indirectly. Never again can we afford to live with the narrow, provincial "outside agitator" idea. Anyone who lives inside the United States can never be considered an outsider anywhere within its bounds.[3]

As compelling as we may find this language now, on the whole, evangelicals failed to support blacks in their struggle for civil rights. This lack of support put a wedge between the strongest branches of the Christian movement. In retrospect we can see that God used the civil rights movement to free many blacks from second-class citizen status. But this war against integration continued in the South for many years. In the late 1960s many whites used the private school movement to avoid having their elementary and high school students educated with blacks.

Even as recently as 1982 the Supreme Court ruled that Bob Jones University and Goldsboro Christian Schools, Inc., had maintained racially discriminatory admissions policies based upon their interpretation of the Bible. Their theology led them to accept mostly Caucasian students and set up rules against interracial dating. The implications of this ruling were that these institutions were not entitled to federal tax-exempt status because of the racial policies they followed in the 1970s.[4]

Today Bob Jones University serves over five thousand students from the entire United States and forty-three nations. We are assured by our friends, some of whom are BJU graduates, that today the university has an excellent Christian atmosphere and continues to offer a great education to its students. The student body includes African Americans and carries none of the stigma of the past. Our point is not to blame BJU again, but to note that this great fundamentalist university drifted into errant waters by resisting equality for all men, which is at the heart of the gospel and the civil rights movement. In essence, the university, like many white Christians, was slow to respond to the manifestation of biblical truth and the truths of our declaration that were at the heart of the civil rights movement.

If we are to move forward together we must avoid both the white racism and the black militancy that have clouded efforts in the past. We must instead rally behind clear-thinking, visionary Christian leaders who desire to become architects of a new colorless, raceless, Christian manifesto for social change in the nation. The only chance for racial healing to occur in America will spring from the church.

The Price of Our Separation

On March 3, 1991, an amateur cameraman recorded one of the most significant segments of film recorded in the 1990s—the beating of Rodney King, a black man, by four white Los Angeles policemen. The video was straightforward and unadorned with commentary or interpretation. Despite its minimalist starkness, different interest groups read much into its images. A little more than a year after the incident, a California state court acquitted the four officers of wrongdoing. The verdict led to a major race riot that sent shock waves around Los Angeles and the world. Seven hundred million dollars of property damage, 13,212 arrests, 2,383 human injuries, and 54 deaths lay in the wake of this initial lower court verdict.

Is such a thing possible today? How would our nation handle things if such a devastating riot occurred again? With the current complications of growing black poverty, the tragic mishandling of Katrina victims, the immigration debates, and a litany of other mounting black woes, it is easy to imagine future riots if the substantive racial problems of the nation are not addressed. Remember that the L.A. riots happened less than twenty years ago, just thirty-seven years after the beginning of the civil rights movement—marked by the death of Emmett Till and the Montgomery Bus Boycott. Before the L.A. riots, many people would have rejoiced in how far black and white relations had come since the days of the "Mississippi Burning." But one video and a court decision later, and the very fabric of one of the nation's most powerful cities was torn asunder.

This kind of race riot could happen again if we do not address racism within the walls of the church. The next riot may be black-led, Hispanic-led, white-led, or incited by some combination of all three. As we are poised for dramatic social and political change and transition in the nation, it is time for the church to conduct a national intervention. Instead of just trying to prevent something bad, we should join together to do something good. Churches can be the place where the divided can be unified to advance our mutual cause as a nation. Imagine our combined efforts creating millions of dollars of assets; transferring thousands of ethnic prisoners back into the society as healthy contributors to their community; saving thousands from contracting AIDS, cancer, heart disease, or diabetes; and seeing thousands born again in the process. This is not a pipe dream—it's our calling! The church must be a proactive healing agent for race relations in this nation.

Where We Are Now

We are optimistic about healing the racial divide in the nation partly because of the partnership we already see developing across racial lines. Harry's personal experience argues that racial healing can occur. In 1981, he had the privilege of pioneering a predominantly white congregation in the Corning, New York, area. After nearly eight years there, he and his family began ministering in a congregation in the Washington DC area that was 70 percent black to 30 percent white. What a transition! Harry moved from the upper reaches of Appalachia to "chocolate city." Over the last twenty-five years, he has seen firsthand that black and white churches need each other desperately.

In 1992 Tony was a part of an effort to connect the men of a rural white church with an inner-city black church in his home state of Louisiana. During one of the initial events Tony spontaneously repented to one of the elders of the inner-city congregation for the racism of white evangelicals that had divided the body of Christ. The act was met with politeness but an obvious sense of skepticism. Tony recalled talking with the men of his church suggesting that before white evangelicals would be received by their black brothers, they would have to experience some of the same rejection that black Christians had endured from their white brothers. The daily suffering that marks the black experience in America is often never understood by whites. Black anger and mistrust are often the result of a sense of hopelessness about racial reconciliation that sets in after hundreds of subtle rejections in which blacks feel devalued or violated.

Despite ongoing politically motivated attacks from the Left that try to paint Tony as racist, which date back to Tony's campaign for the U.S. Senate, he continues to build personal and professional relationships with many black leaders.

Furthermore, we have both seen blacks and whites begin to unite over certain policy agendas. During the 2004 election, we both echoed the prediction of the Joint Center for Political and Economic Studies that double the number of blacks would vote for George W. Bush because of a redefinition of moral priorities. We spoke out on national television that the "new black church" carried more of the same concerns as its white counterpart than most of the nation had realized. Harry went so far as to write an article that appeared on the front page of the *New York Sun Times* on election day, November 2004. It was titled "New Black Church on Election Day."

What was the real impact of the efforts of black Christians on the election? Their vote helped to clinch the victory for Bush. Although the national percentage of blacks voting for Bush only increased by a few percentage points, the important swing states of Ohio and Florida reported a doubling of 2000's votes. Sixteen percent of black voters in Ohio responded positively to George W. Bush despite race riots that had taken place there in the previous years. Further, nearly twice as many (13 percent) of Florida's black voters chose George W. Bush in 2004, versus the 2000 election.[5] Why the change? The answer is that black church leaders in those states began to lead their flocks toward a unified Christian front. This was a risky step of faith because there was no clear guarantee that the Republican Party would address the issues that the masses of black Americans feel are important. These courageous church leaders understood the power of unity and believed that there will come a day when the entire body of Christ will move together to impact our society, both spiritually and politically. There is a growing realization among black and white Christians that the existing political structures may not accommodate such a unified effort, which has led to some talk of a third party.

A mature coalition between black and white Christians is not yet here, but new alliances are being formed, and they are absolutely necessary to change the United States. The African American church is among the most vibrant of all of the U.S.'s ethnic sectors. Let's not forget that nearly half of African American adults are born-again Christians.[6] If black voters change their minds in 2008 about their Democratic allegiances, it could rock the boat of the party. Conversely, Republicans should pay attention to black voters and the core social issues that have opened the door to this unprecedented alignment with the conservative religious political movement.

In this process we need to constantly remind ourselves that we will never succeed in uniting around political ideologies, because ideologies can never replace the unifying power of God's Word. It is the truth of God's Word that gives us the ability to be united, and therefore God's Word must be central to our efforts no matter how politically incorrect it may be. God's Word is our rallying point.

Is Integration Happening?

During the last few years there has been a movement to espouse the virtues of racial reconciliation within the church. For some this goal has become almost a Christian mantra, which they declare from the rooftops. Many pastors now will no longer speak of the white-led church versus the black-led church. Rather, they shout with religious zeal that "Jesus has only one church." They are on the right track, but with a couple of caveats. First, the "one true church" has yet to be manifest on the earth today. We are not as unified as we need to be. Thank God, however, that we are finally trying. Secondly, although this declaration can get congregational applause, the church's goal should not be racial harmony for racial harmony's sake. No—the question of the hour is, when will we work together as Bible-believing followers of Jesus Christ to improve the spiritual and moral environment of the nation? That must be our mutual goal.

Integration of churches tells only part of the story of our success. Ethnicity and race are often an integral part of a local church's assignment, and very often a church's racial mix is driven by location. Therefore, the fact that one congregation is integrated while another one is monoracial does not tell the whole story. Rather, we maintain that church services are like the huddles in football games between plays. A racially diverse huddle means nothing if we cannot run successful plays and win the game. The game the church is involved in is not a game at all; it is a battle for the heart and soul of our nation. As we—all of us—pursue social involvement and policy change, we will simultaneously solve our own internal issues of pride, division, and prejudice along with major community issues.

Make no mistake, however. We are not saying that we can ignore racism and it will go away on its own. The church must deal with racism, or God will deal with the church. Racism is a powerful stronghold that must be broken if we are to see and experience a move of God in our nation, and it must begin with each of us, as Bible-believing Christians.

Here's an uplifting story that serves as an example of how this cooperation can work. In the wake of Hurricane Katrina, there were some who claimed the government's failed response to America's worst national disaster was racially motivated. That certainly could not be said of the church. Tony was in Louisiana when both Katrina and Rita hit the Pelican State, leaving thousands of people stranded and tens of thousands displaced. Working with a network of pastors and churches that he had initiated during his time in state government, he was part of a massive church-based effort that was launched within hours of the storm.

As individuals and families escaped New Orleans in cars and buses, they sought shelter in a network of dozens of local churches in the Baton Rouge area. Tony's home church, Greenwell Springs Baptist Church, served as one of these shelters, housing dozens of evacuees for over a month. Greenwell Springs Baptist is located in a rural area outside of Baton Rouge that is predominantly white. The evacuees were black. On the Sunday night after Katrina hit, the evacuees joined the members of Greenwell Springs for the regular service. On that evening an elderly black man arrived from New Orleans, entering the service after it started. He had spent a few days stranded in New Orleans, waiting to be rescued. His wife had died during the ordeal, but he had to leave her body behind. He shared this with the pastor, Dr. Dennis Terry, during the close of that Sunday night service. Dr. Terry then shared the man's situation with the congregation, asking them to pray for him. Moments later a number of the church's deacons informally met with the pastor and volunteered to help find his wife's remains and bury her in the church's cemetery.

Also on that first Sunday, as Dr. Terry greeted the church's temporary residents with a hug, one elderly black lady told the congregation that that was the first time in her life she had been hugged by a white man. After attending a few services, a young couple from New Orleans who had been living together before the storm decided it was not right for them to go on living together without being married. Within days the membership of Greenwell Springs Baptist was witness to the first black couple to be married in the fifty-year-old church. There were other firsts, like the first black members of Greenwell Springs Baptist Church. What were the results? There were some challenges and some costs involved, but the church has experienced a powerful move of God in the months since the hurricane, with substantial growth.

This is just one example of how a church that pursues righteousness and justice according to Psalm 89:14 will automatically create an environment that reflects God's glory in practical ways. Now it's time for the church to go further and to develop a unified cultural and governmental agenda. We need a short list of policy priorities that can be considered valid by both blacks and whites.

Unfortunately, this is often where we get divided.

Policy Differences

We know that, in general terms, black Christians have prioritized social justice issues over the years, while white Christians have supported personal righteousness issues. The primary righteousness issues of our day are issues like gambling, prostitution, same-sex marriage, and abortion on demand. It is easy to say that we, the church, should universally be against these ills.

On the other hand, equally urgent social justice issues require greater personal participation and discernment to legitimately resolve. Jesus was quite clear in His declaration in Matthew 25:42–45 that His true followers will help the poor, the stranger (the foreigner or oppressed), the sick (those in need of health care), and the imprisoned. Voting for a tax increase on your neighbor to help fund government programs to help the poor across town does not fill the mandate of this scripture. Nor does the opposite of pushing for tax cuts on business for the purpose of creating more jobs. Jesus wants each of us to be hands-on in meeting the needs of others. Government should supplement the charitable work of Americans in meeting the needs of the less fortunate and those in crisis. As Christians, white and black, we need to fully embrace the simple declaration of Psalm 89:14–15 (NIV), which reads:

> Righteousness and justice are the foundation of your throne; love and faithfulness go before you. Blessed are those who have learned to acclaim you, who walk in the light of your presence, O LORD.

It's important to remember that we need both perspectives—righteousness and justice—to allow the glory of God to be seen today. Delving into social justice issues requires insight, energy, and persistence. Black and white churches can no longer be comfortable with a color-by-the-numbers approach to our culture or to policy issues. Let's take a look at the most prominent issues that divide us by race.

Affirmative Action

African Americans are often wedded to the idea that affirmative action legislation is one of the crowning achievements of the civil rights movement era. Whites, on the other hand, tend to think that America has changed so much that any kind of affirmative action is unwise and unnecessary. Before we discuss the validity of either conclusion, let's review just a few of the facts concerning the black experience in America. We will use 1978 as a benchmark because affirmative action became legally codified in the late 1970s.

The following statistics should alarm all of us:[7]

1. In 1978, a black child could expect to live fewer years than a white child. Today a black child's life expectancy is six years shorter.

2. In 1978, black family poverty was four times that of whites. Today, that rate remains unchanged.

3. In 1978, the black adult unemployment rate was twice that of whites. Today that disparity still exists. In a 2006 economy that boasted just 5 percent unemployment, black unemployment was over 10 percent.

4. In 1978, the median income of a black family was 60 percent of the median white family income. Today, the median black family income has risen to 66 percent of white income after twenty-eight years.

Analyzing these numbers, two facts stand out. First, blacks are still at a significant disadvantage in our society. Secondly, our approach to "leveling the playing field" is not working well. If black poverty is the ultimate measure of racial parity in America, history tells us that the heavy lifting was accomplished prior to affirmative action. To wit: From 1940–1947, 87 percent of black families had incomes below the poverty line. By 1960, before the legislation of that period was established, 47 percent of black families lived below the poverty line. Between 1960 and 1970, the poverty level of blacks declined to just 30 percent. Sadly, after affirmative action was formally instituted, the 1970s yielded only one more percentage point of poverty reduction among black families.[8]

Given that the data on affirmative action shows little improvement in key indicators of black success, scholars differ widely in their social prescriptions. For example, Dr. Thomas Sowell of the Hoover Institute at Stanford University has concluded that quota-based programs have not worked anywhere in the world. From India, Malaysia, Sri Lanka, Nigeria, to the United States, there has not been a true success story of poverty reduction among black families. Of course the picture in the black community is skewed because of the tremendous rise in single-parent homes during this period.[9]

On the other side of this debate, a 1995 study by Murrell and Jones posits that affirmative action has helped the income, promotion, and labor force participation rates of both women and minorities. Their research says that between 1982 and 1995, the percentage of female managers and professionals in the United States rose from 40.5 percent to 48 percent. As Edmund W. Gordon, director of the Institute for Urban and Minority Education, says, progress has been steady, but the job is not finished.[10]

Beyond the public policy of affirmative action, there are policies the church should advocate in order to change the social justice dynamic of our nation. Blacks and whites should find a point of agreement for the well-being of the nation and the advancement of the kingdom.

Let us suggest an alternative to the traditional way affirmative action is usually approached. We should target three dimensions of leveling the playing field for minorities over the next decade. These areas are: jobs, education, and business formation. We understand why many people are offended at the quota system of specifying how many blacks, Hispanics, or women should be hired in a specific job.

On the other hand, the sinful nature of man being what it is, there sometimes is reluctance on the part of majority employers and supervisors to give unproven minorities or women an opportunity to try their wings—in other words, the inability to push the right guardians of the "old boy network" to give access to people who don't look like them in many fields. The question is, *how can people get a chance to break into new fields if the gatekeepers are not motivated by fairness or the desire to impact the generations to come?*

We call upon Christian business, government, and nonprofit leaders to open their hearts and their organizational charts to train the next generation of minority and female leaders. These individuals do not want a handout, and they don't need permanent status in dead-end jobs. They need opportunities to enter a career track. Who says that this is the responsibility of Christian leadership? The Bible does. This is part of the justice agenda that the church should initiate. It is unfortunate that many conservative, evangelical Christians argue against affirmative action, yet they have never taken tangible steps to alleviate the problem. The more we as individuals do to ensure biblical fairness and equity, the less government will have to do.

On the other hand, African Americans, Hispanics, and women must teach the next generation to permanently break through the glass ceiling by exceeding the expectation of their supervisors and employers once they have been given the chance—like Hank Aaron of old, who broke all the records of his day and, because of his exemplary record, assured a place for other blacks in baseball.

As we have already alluded to, education can help minority members sidestep the land mines of prejudice that are literally strewn across the landscape of America's business world. How do we give minorities access to higher education without excluding or limiting the opportunities for whites? One answer is that outstanding colleges could set goals similar to the admission policies of great institutions like Harvard University. Harvard has sought to include ethnic groups in their classes since the mid-1800s. Their reasoning was simply that the training of their most promising pupils needed to be enhanced by personal exposure to a diverse group of fellow students. In addition, Harvard believed that part of its job was to train the leaders of the next generation.

For example, the first black to earn a doctorate at Harvard was W. E. B. DuBois. He made an amazing contribution to his community, to America, and to blacks around the world. What if Christian universities developed programs to gauge the leadership potential of Hispanics and blacks and made a commitment to train Christian leaders for these minorities in the future? This could be one of our secret weapons in America's culture wars.

Why shouldn't girls get opportunities to train in institutions like MIT? Successful models create dreams and aspirations for subsequent generations. If we want the achievement of minorities and women to rise in certain areas, we have to give them tangible measures of hope that allow them to believe that entrance into new fields is possible.

If young minorities and women see minorities and women in the generation before them only as entertainers or immoral people, we may have an even harder time winning the next generation both to Christ and to positive cultural engagement. Gangster rappers cannot be the heroes of young black children. Becoming a supermodel should not be the only goal of young girls. It's time for Christians to help create the role models for the America we envision.

What if successful Christian businessmen created a new kind of venture capital fund that focused on empowering minority people with Christian character to expand the scope and scale of their businesses while making money for the people who believed in them? During Harry's training at Harvard Business School, he found out that many businesses grow dramatically because venture capital funds identify outstanding concepts and invest in the next generation of technologies and businesses. Typically, these venture capital investors are looking for people with proven track records and a working team that they can support. The same could be true of a new breed of Christian, venture-capital people who were willing to seek two primary goals: making money and advancing the cause of Christ in the earth.

Criminal Justice System

Is Lady Justice, the symbol of America's judicial system, really blind? Ask most white Americans who have had little if any interaction with the judicial system and they would probably say that it is. Ask an African American or a member of another minority if justice is blind and the chances are the answer would be no.

In a 2004 Gallup poll, nearly two-thirds of the African Americans surveyed believe that the criminal justice system is rigged against them. Similar public opinion surveys have revealed the same distrust on behalf of minorities.[11]

Race and economic standing is clearly a defining variable that often determines the level of justice one receives in this nation. The Kobe Bryants, Michael Jacksons, and O. J. Simpsons of the world, who have the wealth to hire high-priced attorneys, do not reflect the kind of justice received by the average black man in America.

Let's review several of the facts surrounding the criminal justice system:

▸ Around 910,000 African Americans are in prison today.[12]

▸ Blacks make up 43.9 percent of the state and federal prison population, which totals 2.1 million inmates.[13]

▸ One-third of black males born in 2006 can expect to go to prison in their lifetime.[14]

▸ Only 13 percent of all monthly drug users are black, but 35 percent of arrests for drug possession, 55 percent of convictions, and 74 percent of prisoners sentenced are black.[15]

▸ These facts reveal just the tip of the iceberg. Criminals are not the only blacks who have concerns about their contact with the law. David A. Harris wrote a provocative article for the *Minnesota Law Review* titled, "Why Driving While Black Matters." His research [of data from across the country] showed that although blacks and whites violate traffic codes at similar rates, 72 percent of the people stopped and searched by the police in Harry's home state of Maryland were African American.[16]

On a national basis, one out of ten black drivers who are stopped by the police will be subjected to the ignominy of being searched or have their vehicles searched. Whites who are stopped will be searched less than four times out of a hundred.[17]

We could go on about violation of rights, excessive use of force, violent prison terms, insufficient prison aftercare, and the generational impact of prison-induced fatherlessness. It is little wonder that so many blacks are against the death penalty. After all, false imprisonment, lynching, and torture were all perpetrated on blacks in the name of "justice." Suffice it to say, there is a need for Christian-based public policy to change the way justice is both administered and perceived in our nation.

Changing racial and ethnic biases in sentencing has been a major matter of national discussion since the late 1980s. Like many areas of needed reform, we will need a new crop of godly leaders to enter this field. Our communities need thousands of Christian young people to pursue careers in the criminal justice arena as police officers, lawyers, prosecutors, and judges who will see each person as someone created in the image of God and deserving of justice, regardless of their color, their economic standing in the community or any other characteristic. These people can truly operate as "ministers" of God and restore confidence to a system of justice that was once the envy of the world.

This fairness must also be reflected in new laws.

Many whites don't realize that law and order campaigns during election seasons are often seen by blacks as racist manifestos. In the 1990s, state lawmakers took a get-tough-on-crime stance, passing "three strikes laws," which mandated the courts to give long sentences to habitual offenders, those who had committed three or more separate felony crimes.

The result has been swelling prison populations and numerous accounts of people who were unfairly sentenced to long prison terms that were not commensurate with their crimes.

Many states have recognized that unless substance abuse ends, fines and jail time are unlikely to prevent future criminal activity. As a result they have created drug courts that pursue drug treatment programs rather than prison for those offenders in the hopes of treating the source of the problem and not the symptoms. Unfortunately, funding for these alternative sentencing programs has been limited because they have the perception of being soft on crime. Policy makers should expand these types of programs by working with faith-based organizations that have successful rehabilitation programs that cost a fraction of many state-based facilities.

Additionally, our public policy should return to the biblical principle of restitution instead of incarceration for nonviolent offenders. Over 72 percent of the present incarcerated population is serving time for nonviolent offenses. The studies bear out Tony's experience from his first assignment in law enforcement as a deputy in the parish prison. Prisons are not often a place of reform; they can become high-tech training grounds for criminals.[18]

For the people who must still do time in traditional correctional facilities, specialized ministries to them are very important. During the next decade, churches must become even more hands-on in prison ministry by teaming up with organizations like Prison Fellowship, Bible Believers Fellowship, Inc., Bill Glass Ministries, and other ministries involved in the International Network of Prison Ministries. In order to facilitate effective personal ministry to inmates, one of Tony's last pieces of legislation before he left the Louisiana legislature was to pave the way for the Department of Corrections to work more closely with faith-based organizations in preparing inmates to return to the community. These types of programs, when properly staffed and managed, bring results.

In Ohio, more than 67 percent of prisoners are rearrested after their release from prison. However, for those inmates who complete a faith-based program, the likelihood of their return to incarceration was reduced by two-thirds.[19]

In addition to the approaches we have already outlined, Congress must enlarge on the good work being done through the Second Chance Act of 2004, which was sponsored by Senators Sam Brownback (R-KS) and Joseph Biden (D-DE). This legislation acknowledged that 80 percent of criminals committed their crimes while under the influence of drugs or alcohol. Therefore, personal rehabilitation treatment and specially monitored after-care programs that address drug addiction must be incorporated into our justice system. Prison aftercare programs are specifically initiated through this bill. But there needs to be more funding for this important legislation.

Poverty

We've tackled poverty in another chapter, but it's worth mentioning here that there is more to do. The middle class has quadrupled in the last fifty years, and great strides have been made in alleviating the sting of poverty among blacks. But poverty is still a major problem among blacks. In our minds, lack of home ownership is one of the most discouraging aspects of black poverty in America. Less than 50 percent of black families own their own homes, compared with more than 70 percent of whites.[20]

One solution on the horizon is presented by churches that are constructing neighborhoods adjacent to their churches with affordable housing financed by the church. Often these homes are made available to low-income single mothers who are struggling to raise their children against the backdrop of a culture that is hostile to traditional values. Not only do the houses provide a safe environment, but also the church becomes an extended family, providing the structure and support that the single moms and their children need.

In February of 2005, Harry had the privilege of being on *Focus on the Family* for the first time. It was his pleasure to present *The Black Contract With America on Moral Values*. To our great delight, he found that white evangelicals were open to embrace biblical exhortations to go after problems like prison reform and poverty. In light of this, black leaders must extend themselves to their white brothers if a morally unified church is going to rebuild the spiritual and moral walls of our nation.

The six points found in *The Black Contract With America on Moral Values* put laserlike focus upon the following areas:

1. Family reconstruction
2. Wealth creation
3. Educational reform
4. African relief
5. Prison reform
6. Health care

Harry will develop these ideas more fully in a subsequent book aimed solely at addressing the political, racial divide in America. For the purposes of this book we have made sure to widen our public policy agenda items and our strategic cultural recommendations to include things that both black and white Christians should agree upon. Therefore, we will conclude this chapter with cultural goals and strategies that can bring the church together.

Cultural Goals Concerning Racial Reconciliation

It is time to integrate our movement from top to bottom. There is a great need for faith activists to create space for blacks and women to assist in leading the movement. The most developed Christian political machinery today is led by white men. White evangelicals must invite black evangelical leaders to join in the leadership of the movement. Black leaders must bring their followers into a movement that reflects both black and white evangelicals. This will require deep relationship building and some risk taking. We have noted earlier that the early church healed the divide between Jewish believers and Hellenistic believers by making Greek deacons responsible for taking care of the support of widows. In a similar way, major black leadership needs to be raised up in key politically active ministries.

Family Research Council has just named an African American, who was the former Ohio secretary of state and candidate for governor, as a senior research fellow of their organization. This is a rare but important move that needs to be replicated in other Christian policy and advocacy groups. We can imagine a day that Tony's successor at the Family Research Council will be a black evangelical leader. Simultaneously, national Christian activist groups would do well to add black board members who are recognized as leaders in the black community. Additionally, they should look for opportunities to hire black evangelicals for key staff positions who show the potential to become movement leaders. These people should not be considered tokens but should be full partners in changing America's cultural and political infrastructure.

Black leaders, meanwhile, should begin to stand firm with their white Christian brethren even when the inevitable criticism comes from within their own ranks. Leaders like Harry, Dr. Herb Lusk of Philadelphia, and Bishop Wellington Boone have taken much heat for their stand for biblical reform of politics. Most blacks assume Harry has sold them out for money or that there is some devious agenda of personal advancement that he has developed. This is to be expected. Management theory shows that early adopters are a small percentage of any group. The black leaders who are heroically speaking out today are prophetic pioneers and early adopters. Christians of affluence should come alongside these black-led ministries and help support them as they step out in support of biblical truths in public policy that will many times put them at odds within the political structures in the black community. Black religious leaders on the Left seem to have no problem raising more than enough money to support their causes. We believe that leading media ministries also need to showcase the work of these leaders who have the capacity to create the intellectual architecture of a new moral movement in America. This means helping underwrite both ministries and biblically oriented, black lobbying and advocacy groups.

What about blacks supporting white-led ministries and political leaders? It is already happening, as blacks are some of the most supportive viewers and givers to major white-led church ministries—despite our historic differences. It must expand, however, into the area of public policy research and advocacy.

Now is the time for racial unity. To achieve this unity we must move beyond the stereotyping of the media and of Hollywood in determining how we see Christians of another race. We've allowed the worst, and arguably the smallest, representations of the races to shape how we see one another. This has kept us apart and has limited our effectiveness.

The church can change America, but we must first change the church. If Christians will take to heart the words of Paul to the Galatians and begin to see only red—the redemptive blood of Jesus Christ—our unity could very well transform our nation. We challenge you to pray for God's direction and then intentionally develop a personal relationship with a Christian of another race. As with any successful relationship there must be give-and-take. We must listen and ask the Lord for understanding and then lock arms with one another in unity if we are to successfully tackle the important moral issues of our day.

Prayer Points

▸ Give God praise for establishing the church without designation of race, gender, or class (Gal. 3:26–29). Thank Him for the freedom we have in Christ.

▸ Repent on behalf of the church for not more clearly presenting to the world a bride that includes people of all race and ethnicity. Ask forgiveness for where we have not accepted others but followed our prejudices rather than God's summons to love.

▸ Pray that the Lord awaken the conscience of the nation to conduct itself in the integrity and holiness according to 2 Corinthians 1:12.

Chapter 9

CORE VALUE #5: RELIGIOUS LIBERTIES

CROSS PURPOSES

O n a warm summer evening in June 2007, Tony made his way to the New York studio where he would appear on the *Lou Dobbs Tonight* program. Unlike on previous appearances, he was not simply going to be interviewed by Dobbs, one of CNN's most seasoned anchors. Rather, this show would host a debate between Tony and internationally known lawyer Alan Dershowitz. While Dobbs had always treated Tony with utmost respect, Tony was apprehensive because of the stature and ability of his debating opponent.

Dershowitz is widely considered to be one of America's finest legal minds. A graduate of Brooklyn College and Yale Law School, he joined the faculty of Harvard Law School at age twenty-five. (On the other hand, some would argue that anyone who would defend O. J. Simpson, Mike Tyson, and Michael Milken can't be *that* smart.) On this night the debate centered around Dershowitz's book *Blasphemy: How the Religious Right Is Hijacking the Declaration of Independence*.

Tony was placed in the position many Christians are thrust into each day, having to explain moral and biblical truths to someone who has seemingly already made up their mind not to hear them. Tony told the truth about our nation's history, combined with the truth of God's Word. The deceptively simple approach held up amazingly well in the hurly-burly of public debate.

Tony's response to Alan's book was that our Constitution offers freedom of religion—not freedom from religion. In addition, he posited that without Christianity, America would never have become the great power it is today. The bedrock value system, built on the Bible, has allowed our democracy to blossom and grow. This issue is important because an entire generation of Americans do not understand the connection of the nation's ideals to Christianity. In addition, they don't understand that our nation's tolerance of other faiths is a legacy left to us by the Founding Fathers, many of whom were men of faith.

Harry once believed that the idea that the Founding Fathers were men of faith was simply racist rhetoric and conservative propaganda. After all, he thought, how religious could slaveholders be? And what about Thomas Jefferson's alleged affair with Sally Hemings? Weren't many of our Founding Fathers cultural Christians who lived a life of double standards? In Harry's early adult world, the long, glowing statements about the faith of the Founding Fathers seemed to him an example of rewriting history. That history was far removed from the ghettos in which Harry attended school and church, and where street corner philosophers pointed out the personal failings, poor theology, and social inequities of our Founding Fathers.

But today, both of us believe that America's grassroots faith, her national attempt to honor the God of the Bible, and the values gleaned from the Scriptures have been America's biggest strength. On the other hand, we both acknowledge that America's faith has never been perfect. We envision the nation as on a journey, which at times has taken us through valleys and at other times on mountaintops. This process is similar to an individual's growth in his or her personal faith. Step by step, policy by policy, election by election, America becomes either more committed or less committed to the faith of our fathers.

There is growing evidence that the failure to engage in the shaping of public policy will ultimately limit the church's ability to openly evangelize the lost and encourage the spiritual awakening that is needed. So what is the truth about religious liberty in the nation? Is the religious Right hijacking the Constitution and therefore the nation in an attempt to establish a theocracy? Let's look into the facts about:

1. The truth about the separation of church and state
2. The effects of Christianity upon democracy
3. The current religious liberties battleground
4. What the Bible says about the freedom of religion

The Truth About the Separation of Church and State

The nation has heard too much of the Supreme Court's *misinterpretation* of what Thomas Jefferson wrote about the wall of separation between church and state. We quote: "I contemplate with sovereign reverence that act of the whole American people which declared that their legislature should 'make no law respecting an establishment of religion, or prohibiting the free exercise thereof,' thus building a wall of separation between Church & State."[1]

First, we need to know what the First Amendment actually says: "Congress shall make no law regarding the establishment of religion or the free exercise thereof." The limitation in the First Amendment is upon Congress, not the churches. To use Jefferson's metaphor, it was a wall that prevented the federal government from intruding on religion in the states or denying the people's right of free exercise of religion.

At the time the First Amendment was written and ratified, a number of the fifteen states had established state churches. The First Amendment didn't change that. The founders were concerned that the federal government would try to take over the churches and use them for its own purposes. They did not fear that Christians would influence the government. Christians *were* the government. Churches, members of the clergy, and parishioners have been, and remain, free in this country to participate in public policy debates on any subject. In fact, until the middle of the last century, it was a common practice for pastors to preach an election sermon the Sunday before an election, telling members which candidates were worthy of their support.

What liberals who misread America's original document are really saying is that the federal government should not only silence churches but also exclude their members from any influence on government. Some of these folks, like Alan Dershowitz, would essentially force Christians to choose between living out their faith in a public manner and serving in a position of governmental influence. In the name of tolerance of others, they would be intolerant to Christians. Unwittingly, many people who preach pluralism offer us a new caste system that makes Christian citizens "political untouchables." The day may soon be here, if it has not already arrived, that Christians will have to choose between being open adherents to the faith and serving in the government.

Before you reject our assertion, consider the comments of New York Senator Charles Schumer (D), who led the filibuster effort from 2003 to

2005 against former Alabama attorney general William Pryor, who had been nominated by President George W. Bush for the Eleventh Circuit Court of Appeals. Pryor, a devout Catholic, had previously stated that the Supreme Court's decision in *Roe v. Wade* was "the worst abomination in the history of constitutional law." Senator Schumer challenged Pryor's qualifications to serve on the court because of Pryor's "deeply held beliefs." It was evident that those deeply held beliefs related to his faith and his stand on the issue of abortion.

This intolerance toward religion is more advanced in Europe. Shortly after leaving office, former British Prime Minister Tony Blair made his religious convictions public. Blair acknowledged that he had intentionally kept his faith quiet for fear of being labeled a "nutter."[2]

There have been quite a few books written since the 2004 election that espouse an anti-Christian activism position here in the United States. Dershowitz's book *Blasphemy* is just one of them. He spends considerable time speaking about Thomas Jefferson. Dershowitz uses Jefferson's statements and writings on religion to "prove" the founders were not influenced by Christianity and somehow shared the same hostile view of religion that the courts and the ACLU have today: "By invoking the 'Laws of nature and of Nature's God' rather than the Judeo-Christian God, the Declaration of Independence made clear that it was not a Christian document, that it did not reflect uniquely Christian or Judeo-Christian beliefs, and that it was not a 'bridge between the Bible and the Constitution.' To the contrary, it rejected Christianity, along with other organized religions, as a basis for governance, and it built a wall—rather than a bridge—between the Bible and the Constitution."[3] This tortured version of the truth is patently skewed. The reason we can be so sure that we are right about this issue has to do with the sheer volume of writings that confirm our point of view.

For example, John Adams, the second president of the United States, was one who made clear the connection between the Christian faith and government:

> We have no government armed with power capable of contending with human passions unbridled by morality and religion. Avarice, ambition, revenge, or gallantry would break the strongest cords of our Constitution as a whale goes through a net. Our Constitution was made only for a moral and religious people. It is wholly inadequate to the government of any other.[4]

Adams actually believed that the Constitution was only viable in a religious society. It could not serve a secular government. History seems to have proven him correct as nations have copied our Constitution but not our faith, and their efforts have not succeeded. In addition, Alexis de Tocqueville, the French political scientist who traveled the young republic in the early 1830s, wrote about the connection between America's Christian faith and government:

> I do not know whether all Americans have a sincere faith in their religion—for who can search the human heart—but I am certain that they hold it to be indispensable to the maintenance of republican institutions.[5]

It is clear that Tocqueville believed that our society's foundational institutions rested on religion in America.

Francis Schaeffer, Christian theologian and founder of the L'Abri community whose ideas and writings helped spark the rise of the religious Right, has said, "The Founding Fathers of the United States (in varying degrees) understood very well the relationship between one's world view and government."[6] Why did Schaeffer make such a bold declaration? Schaeffer did what we have done—he read some of the early voices directly.

Listen to John Witherspoon, the president of Princeton, who was the only pastor to sign the Declaration of Independence. He preached a sermon on the first nationally declared Thanksgiving Day to thank God at the end of the Revolutionary War: "A republic once equally poised must either preserve its virtue or lose its liberty."[7]

He repeatedly asserted that our government rested upon the foundation of faith. Our liberty and freedom rested on the virtue established by our faith in God.

William Penn expressed a clear understanding of the bedrock foundation of democracy. He said, "If we are not governed by God, then we will be ruled by tyrants."[8] His words strike a piercing contrast: either we govern ourselves according to the truths of God or our conduct will be such that tyrannical men will lord over us.

Scores of other leaders could be quoted, but the last voice we will cite is that of Sir William Blackstone. Blackstone wrote *Commentaries on the Law of England*, which is recognized as the most important legal treatise ever written in the English language. Blackstone's work came to the colonies and became greatly influential in designing the American legal system.

Blackstone said there were only two foundations for law, that of nature and of revelation via the Holy Scripture. Every American law school graduate was required to be a master of Blackstone's book...until quite recently. It was required reading because Blackstone espoused the foundations on which our legal system is built...and the "Holy Scripture" is one of those foundations.[9]

The truth is that radical secularists are attempting to build a wall unimagined by our founders—a wall that separates people of faith from government. They project upon the founders their radical idea that the price of admission to the public square is surrendering one's deeply held religious convictions and beliefs. That is an idea that would have not only been unthinkable to the Founding Fathers, but it would have also been blasphemous.

The Effects of Christianity Upon Democracy

What was in the hearts of the founders? Were they "born again," to use a modern-day term? Does it even matter? You better believe that it matters!

Our Founding Fathers drew many philosophic tenets of government directly from the Bible. The influence of the Christian faith on what is now America has been long and profound, predating the Declaration of Independence. The Pilgrims planted what were seen as the first seeds of self-government in the Mayflower Compact, which makes clear their purpose and mission—"Advancement of the Christian Faith."[10] Freedom of religion was established to protect the free exercise of the Christian faith without the interference of an overly intrusive government. This value has given birth to a great variety of expression in the Christian community. There are many differing denominational approaches to Christianity growing side by side in the American soil. One need only look at the conflict between branches of the Islamic faith in the Middle East to see that the faith of our founders spared us from future civil war by separating the authority of the state from the practice of religion.

Some people have outrageously attempted to link Christians to radical Islamic terrorists by comparing evangelical Christian influence with images of the theocracies in the Middle East. Ironically, America's freedom has given every faith an opportunity to grow. Despite the openness of our nation, Christianity has flourished the most. We believe that this has transpired because Christianity is compatible with democracy and freedom. Radical Islam works against democracy. In addition, experts in foreign missions have repeatedly reported that Christianity has given rise to economic uplift in every nation that has adopted it. Above all, the few examples of differing faith communities living peacefully together are predominantly in Christian nations.

Several years ago, when the City University of New York did a poll of Americans' religious identification, it surveyed *more than one hundred thousand people*. This huge sample was necessary to find smaller minority religions. CUNY found that 86.3 percent of Americans identified themselves as Christians.[11] That makes America a more Christian country than Israel is Jewish or India is Hindu. Would Mr. Dershowitz and his friends really prefer to live in a country that was 86.3 percent Muslim?

Let's take a moment to talk about the freedom of religion around the world. More specifically, let's look at the Muslim faith's track record of religious tolerance. In the Islamic world there are several nations with large populations of non-Muslims who were conquered by jihad wars. Historically, Islam conquered huge territories in Africa, Asia, and Europe from A.D. 630 until 1683 or so.

Dhimmitude is a status given to non-Muslims and their formerly sovereign land. The word *dhimmitude* comes from *dhimmi*, an Arabic word meaning "protected." *Dhimmi* was the name applied by the Arab-Muslim conquerors to indigenous non-Muslim populations who surrendered by a treaty (*dhimma*). This term was coined by Bat Ye'or in 1983. This word describes the social and legal conditions under which Jews and Christians live under Islamic rule. The system differs from community to community as Sharia law is developed within that community. *Dhimmitude* is an extension of the ideology of jihad. Jihad expounds the idea of holy war to the extent that the enemies of Islam are of one body—the infidels. Jihad may be exercised through one's speech, money, or writings. As people become subject to Islamic government, *dhimmitude* is determined by the degree of their stance against Islam.

The *dhimmis*—the conquered people who remain Christian or Jewish—have a protected status under Islamic law, depending upon the way in which they were conquered. Yet they also are targets of mass discrimination. In Iran, for example, *dhimmis* may have to change the names of their children to Islamic names for them to be able to attend school. There have been attempts to silence or censor religious leadership to inhibit *dhimmis* from practicing their "protected" religion. Strict rules concerning public conduct have been imposed on *dhimmis* in certain communities.

Until the Islamic community observes the basic rights and freedoms of all people, regardless of their race, color, gender, and religion, to enjoy constitutional and legal protection, they cannot lay claim to humanitarianism. In Harry's church in Washington DC there is a Nigerian-born leader who has experienced the wrath of this kind of discrimination personally. He was raised with his family in the First Baptist Church of Kaduna, Nigeria. They lived in a majority Muslim region in which there have been frequent attacks on innocent Christians. This *dhimmi* concept is undoubtedly in the minds of the local Muslims.

In 2000, one of the associate pastors of that church was murdered by a group of angry Islamists. They abducted him from his church and demanded that he renounce his faith. When he refused, he was hacked to death with machetes and axes. Next, wooden church pews were placed upon his dismembered body and a bonfire was lit. Their final act of religious perversion was to throw his Bible on the burning funeral pyre.

The United States has historically promoted and protected religious freedom as a human right. The executive branch has been active ensuring religious minorities are protected around the globe. The efforts became more formalized when in 1993, the secretary of state initiated regular investigational reports from U.S. embassies in terms of human rights violations. The Bureau of Human Rights and Humanitarian Affairs was changed to the Bureau of Democracy, Human Rights and Labor in 1994. In 1998, the International Religious Freedom Act was passed, requiring the secretary of state to produce an annual report, titled the "International Freedom Report," in collaboration with the Ambassador at Large for International Freedom. This annual report delineated the state of religious freedom in every foreign country around the world, including citations of any violations of religious freedom as well as any improvements within those countries. In the fall of 2007 the annual report identified eight countries as Countries of Particular Concern (CPC): Burma, China, Eritrea, Iran, North Korea, Saudi Arabia, Sudan, and Uzbekistan.

We could go on about religion in the world, but it is at least safe to infer that Christianity has done no harm to this nation. Many liberals feel as though they need to throw off the restraining influence of Christianity in order to have real freedom. Both of us have experienced the ire of Americans who say to us, "We don't believe in your God." These angry citizens remind us of teenagers who can't wait to get out of their fathers' houses. They feel as though they need options, without truly knowing what those options are. They have not pressed the fast-forward button to see the results of their so-called "freedom from Christianity." Recently, many Americans were outraged by the use of the Quran to swear in U.S. Congressman Keith Ellison. Despite the outrage, it was allowed. He used Thomas Jefferson's copy of the Quran to assuage the concerns of traditionalists. This level of freedom could never exist in other nations with strong religious majorities.

As Christians, our only option is to make a commitment to the nation that we will hold true to our values and our faith. The nation needs us, even if it thinks it doesn't.

What the Bible Says About Religious Freedom

Is there a place in the Bible that gives us a road map of how to navigate our personal lives in a pluralistic society? The answer is yes, and it is found in the life of Daniel. Daniel's public service in Babylon's government was obviously blessed by God. Although he was not a traditional clergyman or religious teacher, he stood for God during a period of great religious upheaval.

The secret to Daniel's success can be used by anyone in our generation. These secrets were:

▸ Daniel held himself in covenant with God.

▸ He served his bosses well.

▸ He was a servant-leader.

▸ He influenced the policies that led to rebuilding the walls of the city of Jerusalem.

▸ In his governmental role, he made the heathen look good. He realized that regardless of the environment, he served the omniscient God and was required by conscience to do his best work.

▸ As an expression of his faith, Daniel embarked upon a lifetime of learning to master himself and faithfully serve those around him.

At the end of the day, Daniel's intimate relationship with the Lord allowed him to survive both hostile government takeovers and the transfer of power from one administration to another. Eventually, God used Daniel's position and influence to impact his nation. This story also shows us three approaches to public policy: exclusionary, accommodating, and establishing. Let's examine each one of these.

Exclusionary

Daniel's adversaries sought to discredit him and remove him from his position of coveted leadership. Unable to find fault with Daniel's professional and personal life, they decided to make a wedge issue of his religion. Not unlike the political environment today, Daniel's adversaries decided to find a way to portray him as outside the mainstream. Their desire was to exclude people of faith, like Daniel, from the political process. (See Daniel 6:4.)

Accommodation

Daniel's response is very instructive in a day when many Christians in the political process have found it better for their careers to go "undercover" in their faith. Daniel neither hid his faith nor sought to change the minds of his accusers. He continued uninhibited by the edict and maintained his daily routine of public religious display, believing that he had a right to be accommodated. It was clear that if his faith was not accommodated, he was prepared to suffer the consequences—even to the point of death. (See Daniel 6:10–11.)

Establishment

Daniel's courage to push for accommodation of his public expression of his faith brought about a third approach to public policy. Faith that unreservedly embraces the truth is transforming faith. It begins with the individual and, fully realized, has the power to transform nations. Daniel attempted to impose no religious requirement or duty upon anyone other than himself. But Daniel's testimony led the king, the highest authority in the land, to declare that Daniel's way was the best way. He established Daniel's religion as the state religion. It was not due to Daniel's political maneuvering and power moves, but because God honored his faithful service. (See Daniel 6:23–26.)

Our goal here in the United States is not establishment but accommodation. The Bible teaches that man has a free will. In other words, he can choose to run toward God or away from God. Freedom of religion is one of the "inalienable rights" mentioned in our Constitution. The concept of inalienable rights has a biblical origin. The Lord guarantees His people's dignity and their freedom to choose the course and destiny of their lives. Moses made very clear that the people had a choice, as he told them, "I have set before you life and death, blessing and cursing; therefore choose life, that both you and your descendants may live" (Deut. 30:19, NKJV). Theologians explain this inherent freedom to choose by describing man as a "free moral agent." This means he is not a robot programmed to do God's will. He can make his own decisions.

King David, whose life epitomized a checkered set of good and bad choices, acknowledged the following truths:

> If I ascend up into heaven, thou art there: if I make my bed in hell, behold, thou art there. If I take the wings of the morning, and dwell in the uttermost parts of the sea; even there shall thy hand lead me, and thy right hand shall hold me.
>
> —PSALM 139:8–10

This quotation summarizes David's experience with God. The grace and mercy of the Lord were always there for him. David accepted the negative consequences of his bad choices and the blessings of God upon his correct choices. David learned the art of repenting (or saying he was sorry) for his sinful attitudes, actions, and desires. His willingness to change course after wrong choices was crucial to David's ongoing relationship with God.

But the point of this discussion is not David's relationship with God. It is David's freedom to choose to disobey and his freedom to choose to reconnect with God. The anvil upon which the freedom of religion is hammered out is the legal system of each land. So how does the Bible direct us to reach this point of accommodation? Christianity, as most people know, has its roots in Old Testament Judaism. Among the Hebrews, both the law and the people administering it were considered sacred. Judges were God's special representatives. The law placed upon them the duty of administering justice without partiality or respect to persons (Deut. 1:17; 16:18). One of the guiding lights of each judge's responsibility was the concept that God has granted to every individual inalienable rights. One of these rights was to choose whether to serve and worship the true God or not. In addition to this freedom of choice, the Hebrew Constitution had seven additional freedoms:[12]

1. No man could be deprived of life, liberty, or property without due process of law (Num. 35:9–34).

2. No one could be convicted of a crime without two or three witnesses (Deut. 17:6; 19:2–13).

3. No one could be put to death because of the crimes of their fathers, and no one's children could receive entailed or transferred punishment (Deut. 24:16).

4. Everyone's home was inviolate (Deut. 24:10–11).

5. A freed slave who acquired his liberty through his own effort was to be protected (Deut. 23:15–16).

6. One's homestead was inalienable (Lev. 25:23–28, 34).

7. Indentured servanthood could not be made perpetual without the person's own consent (Exod. 21:2–6).

America has prospered not because it forced everyone to be a Christian; it has not, but rather America has recognized that we each have a choice. Of course, historically there has been an understanding that with choice comes both the individual and collective consequences. Today, however, the threat is not in the government forcing people to accept the Christian faith; the threat is in the government excluding people of faith from serving in government, if that faith influences their decisions. Our own liberties have come under greater threat. Instead of accommodating religion, our adversaries want to exclude it, much the way Daniel's king did before his "conversion."

Our Domestic Religious Liberties Battleground

In 2007, a major battle in the realm of freedom of speech and freedom of religion took place almost completely outside the view of most Americans. In it, Harry fought his own version of the David-and-Goliath kind of battle. The "Goliath" he faced was a major civil rights lawyer.

On Thursday, May 3, 2007, Harry entered C-SPAN's Washington DC studios to be part of a program that normally includes remarks from different points of view, call-in responses from its national audience, and commentary from its host. It was a great opportunity for him to speak to the nation concerning the encroachment that proposed a new law, H.R. 1592 "Local Law Enforcement Hate Crimes Prevention Act of 2007," represents upon our freedom of speech and freedom of religion. This law promised to grant special protected status to "sexual orientation" and "gender identity"—essentially the measure would have paved the way for the criminalizing of thoughts and religious beliefs that are contrary to politically correct ideology about homosexuals and transgender people.

Harry was opposed to this legislation for two reasons. First, as a Christian he was aware that this kind of legislation has opened the door to the arrest, fines, or incarceration of Christians in Sweden, Australia, Canada, and the United States. In fact, in Philadelphia in 2004, such an incident occurred during a protest rally at a gay convention. A seventy-five-year old grandmother of three was arrested, jailed, and charged under existing state hate crimes law for attempting to share the gospel of Jesus Christ. Ironically, no one was hurt, wounded, or even intimidated by her actions. Rather, the opposite was true. Gays can protest, intimidate, and harass anyone, anywhere, but when Christians speak up, law enforcement increasingly throws the book at them. H.R. 1592 would have emboldened this kind of muscular law enforcement against Christians.

Harry's second reason for opposing this legislation is that sexual orientation would be elevated to the same status as race or gender. Surprisingly, the African American leader he was to debate, Wade Henderson, supported elevating sexual orientation to this exalted position. He represented the Leadership Conference on Civil Rights (LCCR), founded in 1950 with over 192 national organizations. The LCCR has enjoyed the reputation of being the nation's premier civil rights coalition, coordinating the legislative campaign for every major civil rights law since 1957. Unfortunately, this powerful and formerly effective organization has been co-opted by the radical gay movement. Read this excerpt from their Web site as just one example:

> LCCR consists of more than 192 national organizations, representing persons of color, women, children, labor unions, individuals with disabilities, older Americans, major religious groups, gays and lesbians, and civil liberties and human rights groups. Its mission: to promote the enactment and enforcement of effective civil rights legislation and policy.[13]

Harry also was shocked to discover that the AARP, the American Association of University Women, and the American Federation of Teachers were organizational members of this group's board. A new generation of leaders had desecrated the memory of these groups' founders.

With all this in mind, Harry entered the C-SPAN debate with the same concern that Tony had experienced with Alan Dershowitz. For Harry, this feeling was intensified by the way Congress had fast-tracked the bill and was poised to vote on it later the same day. Further, Washington insiders predicted that the vote would go strictly along party lines. To make it worse, grassroots black ministers had not been called upon to give any input into this process until the eleventh hour. Even if Harry won the debate, the process could not be stopped. As one of Harry's friends put it, "The train has left the station." Harry dutifully followed through with the broadcast, believing that this bill could eventually be stopped by presidential veto. He realized clearly that this was the beginning of a war for America's soul that would be waged intensely for the foreseeable future.

The debate flew by. Henderson was articulate and skilled in the fine points of his argument, yet after a mile of legal rhetoric he gave no evidence that Christians would remain free from persecution. Harry left the debate more convinced than ever that the addition of gender identification and sexual preference to the list of protected groups under the new hate crimes legislation was a grave error. He was naturally skeptical of smooth-talkers who told Christians not to worry about the bill, because at the end of the day they were unwilling to change the language in the bill to truly allay our concerns. Our life experience told us that when people won't yield on such an important concern, they have a hidden agenda.

We conducted a national press conference that had been organized in a joint effort by Family Research Council and the High Impact Leadership Coalition (HILC). We wanted the nation to know that there were millions of blacks who disagreed with the "civil rights" extension of this bill. Further, white evangelicals were often dismissed out of hand as racists when they voiced their legitimate concerns about the hate crimes legislation. Thankfully, just before we arrived at the Capitol Hill location for the press conference, we got the word that President Bush was threatening to veto the bill. We could not help but think that all the prayers that had been offered had somehow stalled this masterfully organized campaign to limit our freedoms.

But in Washington, bad bills tend to die hard. Encouraged by the news of a veto, we realized we had to continue fighting the so-called hate crimes bill, and that this battle truly had to be fought by a multiracial team. Both of us began to wield whatever influence we had in the Christian community to get the word out on this problem. FRC, in conjunction with Coral Ridge Ministries, produced a forty-minute documentary that was aired several times on national television. In addition, we placed newspaper ads about the legislation in key states in which senators were on the fence about this bill.

Harry and the HILC team continued to provide a minority perspective on the religious liberties argument. Harry and Pastor Marvin Winans of Detroit, along with several other key pastors from around the country, met with Congressman John Conyers Jr. (D) of Michigan. In addition, Harry raised money to conduct a major media campaign featuring the pictures of twelve black pastors and twenty additional signatories. The full-page ad appeared in *USA Today*, *Roll Call* (a paper read by Capitol Hill staffers), and numerous local papers. The ad copy read:

> HR-1592 and S1105 "Local Law Enforcement Hate Crimes Prevention Act of 2007" promises to grant protected status to "sexual orientation" and "gender identity"—essentially mandating unequal protection under the law, which will pave the way for criminalization of thoughts and religious beliefs contrary to politically correct ideology.

We are opposed to this legislation because labeling politically incorrect views as "hate" will have a chilling effect on the free speech and religious liberty of our churches and of our members. Violent crimes should *always* be punished, no matter the victim—*but thoughts and opinions should never be.*

Laws punishing violent crime already exist in all fifty states. So, what then will define "hate"? Simply preaching biblical morality and sexual behavior, or *opposition to homosexuality*? Such laws will ultimately establish, as a matter of legal principle, that *any* opposition to homosexual or other unbiblical behavior is inherently a form of "hate," and therefore a direct threat to every American citizen's freedom of conscience. This legislation is constitutionally suspect, unnecessary, unfair, and ultimately *un-American*.

There is another story that must be told about our current state of hate crimes legislation. A student-employee of New Jersey's William Paterson

University was shocked one day to receive a university-wide e-mail from the chairperson at the Department of Women's Studies, inviting all to view a film described as a "lesbian relationship story," followed by discussion. The student e-mailed the professor only, asking that he not be copied on these types of e-mails in the future, citing that he found lesbian behavior to be a "perversion."

The professor then registered a complaint with the Office of Employment Equity and Diversity at the university. The student was accused of violating a nondiscrimination policy because the professor felt his e-mail "sounded threatening" and didn't want to feel this kind of threat at her place of employment.

The student-employee based his defense on the principle of free speech. However, New Jersey's attorney general stated that "clearly speech which violates a nondiscrimination policy is not protected." Due to the apparent violation of state discrimination and harassment regulations, a letter of reprimand was placed in the student's employment file. Thankfully, the Foundation for Individual Rights in Education was successful in removing this letter months later.*

The Legal Loopholes

There are three major problems with the kinds of "hate crimes" legislation we've been discussing, and each problem can establish precedents that will harm religious liberty for decades.

1. The definition of sexual orientation is not defined in the legislation.

If the definition is left to the courts, as is often the case, their source of definition would most likely be based on the American Psychiatric Association (APA) definition. The APA and other groups have enumerated at least twenty-five different possible sexual orientations. Our question is, who exactly is being protected in this legislation? Without attempting to be crass, this law could be applied to people involved in pedophilia, bestiality, or other particularly reprehensible behavior.

---

* These are included in a letter from Glen Lavy of the Alliance Defense Fund to Members of Congress about H.R. 1592, dated April 20, 2007.

2. This legislation introduces the phrase "bodily harm."

This means something very specific to a layperson, but it has a broader, less strictly defined meaning to the legal mind. The legal ramifications of this phrase can present a huge loophole through which speech can be included under the hate crime legislation. Consider this quote from an Alliance Defense Fund letter to Congress:

> Construing H.R. 1592 to transform any violation of a state or local "hate" crime law into an offense that can be prosecuted by the federal government would subject politically incorrect speech to federal prosecution. That is of particular concern where local officials have extreme animosity toward traditional values. For example, the San Francisco Board of Supervisors is on public record as saying that efforts to reach homosexuals with a message that change is possible is an expression of hate.[14]

If San Francisco chose to define the public expression of the belief that homosexual behavior is immoral as a chargeable "hate" crime, it would be illegal for certain organizations to advertise events there. H.R. 1592 section 4(a)(1)(C), applied to nonviolent crimes, would authorize the attorney general to prosecute Focus on the Family in federal court at the city's request if Focus on the Family advertised a "Love Won Out" event in San Francisco.[15] Given the tenor of some San Francisco City Council resolutions over the past several years, that is not an unlikely scenario.

The San Francisco Board of Supervisors passed a resolution asserting that several organizations that seek to minister to persons who engage in homosexual behavior were responsible for Matthew Shepard's death, despite the fact that evidence now overwhelmingly suggests that his death was related to his homosexual behavior and despite the fact that the organizations have never advocated violence.[16]

Of course, under current First Amendment jurisprudence, persons prosecuted for committing hate crimes because of innocuous statements or politically incorrect public statements of religious beliefs have a free-speech defense. But that does not prevent the arrest and prosecution of the persons.[17]

3. Prosecutorial zeal may create an avenue for harassment of churches.

Let's remember that just because charges are brought against an individual or church, it does not mean that the individual has committed the offense. Unfortunately, once charges or indictments have reached the newspapers, there tends to be a rush to judgment by many people in our nation. In other words, the average citizen thinks that there must be a problem if charges are made public.

Recently, Harry's church was questioned by the IRS concerning their involvement in policy advocacy because of a report given by a third party. After many hours of legal counsel and investment of management time defending themselves, the IRS closed the case without any action. Unfortunately, that has put Harry's church in a position in which it could be seen by future IRS administrations as an organization set on bending the law. The legal fees generated in this case could have bankrupted a smaller ministry. In addition, the fact that this church was harassed because of an unfounded investigation could lead other congregations in the region to avoid getting involved in any kind of public policy engagement.

Other Encroachments on Religious Freedom

By and large, evangelical Christians are not aware of how motivated the radical gay community and other anti-evangelical groups are to change biblically sound preaching into something more "politically correct." But hate crimes are certainly not the only example of recent encroachment on our religious freedoms. The following areas represent recent challenges:

The Ten Commandments

Within the last decade, we have seen the issue of whether the Ten Commandments should be displayed in a public forum rise significantly. Black Christians and liberal churchgoers have often wondered why this is important to biblically conservative Christians. Some of them question whether this is the beginning of an American Taliban. Nothing could be further from the truth.

There is a small but effective minority that desires to change America's history and to erase every symbol of genuine Christian influence in our nation. In 2003, Alabama's Chief Justice Roy Moore was suspended for failing to obey a ruling that required him to remove a Ten Commandments monument from the rotunda of the Alabama Supreme Court building. "The issue is: Can the state acknowledge God?" he said. "If this state can't acknowledge God, then other states can't....And eventually, the United States of America...will not be able to acknowledge the very source of our rights and liberties and the very source of our law.... When a court order departs from the law and tells you what you can think and who you can believe in," he said, the judge issuing that order is "telling you to violate your oath. And he can't do that. Judges simply don't have that power."[18]

In 2005, two cases came before the courts, one in Kentucky and the other in Texas, on whether it violates the U.S. Constitution to place the Ten Commandments on public property. These two cases were expected to provide clarity to the growing debate over the display of the Ten Commandments on public property, but the U.S. Supreme Court's decision tiptoed through the debate. The high Court ruled in favor of the commandments in the Texas case because of the context of the monument in question. It was less religious, more historical, and sat among other historical markers on the grounds of the state capitol in Texas. The Court ruled against the commandments in Kentucky that had been placed on the walls of two rural courthouses, saying the purpose was unconstitutional because it favored a monotheistic religion.

Most Americans have a hard time following the Court's parsing of the proper context in which the commandments can be displayed. Nearly 90 percent of evangelicals and nearly two-thirds of the entire nation do not follow the Court's segregating the past from the present as it relates to the Ten Commandments.[19] As long as moss-stained monuments are declared OK but fresh imprints of history's most important legal document are declared unconstitutional, expect the battle to continue.

The public square

Another arena of dispute within our culture is the use of religious signage or the display of religious symbols, such as the nativity scene at Christmas. This has led to a long list of cases involving displays, both public and private. For example:[20]

> ▸ *Lynch v. Donnelly* (1983): The Supreme Court ruled (5–4) that the city of Pawtucket, Rhode Island, could continue to have a nativity scene as part of its Christmas display because it represented no threat to the promotion of religion.

> ▸ *County of Allegheny v. ACLU Greater Pittsburgh Chapter* (1989): The Supreme Court ruled that a crèche display on public property was unconstitutional, yet a menorah display on another piece of the same public property was not.

▸ *Capitol Square Review Board v. Pinette* (1995): The Supreme
  Court decided that an unattended cross erected by the KKK
  on public grounds is not a violation of the separation of
  church and state because it would not give the impression
  of government endorsement.

▸ *ACLU v. Schundler* (1999): The Third Circuit Court of
  Appeals decided that a city's crèche and menorah displays
  were unconstitutional when secular symbols were not
  also exhibited, but the displays were constitutional when
  enough secular symbols were added.

These cases represent a mere handful of the many decisions made by
the courts that are inconsistent and, perhaps, even contradictory. The
Christian community needs to align itself with the Constitution and stand
together to let the courts know that they cannot amend it without the
American people standing in opposition to them through our elected
members of Congress.

Too many people have been led to believe that a decision of the Court
is the final word. That is simply not true. There are checks and balances
to the Court or the judicial branch, both the legislative and the executive
branches. Unfortunately, Congress or the legislative branch has lacked the
will to challenge the edicts of the court even though they are clearly given
that authority and responsibility in Article III of the Constitution.

Of the three branches of government, the courts were seen as the
weakest when the Constitution was created. Alexander Hamilton, one of
the Founding Fathers and one of the two authors of the Federalist Papers,
said that the judiciary would be the weakest branch because it would not
have power over either the purse or the sword.

As much as the secularists would like to have Americans believe that
the religious Right is trying to remake the nation in their image, the truth
is that Christians are simply seeking to protect their religious liberties—
religious freedoms that extend beyond their prayer closets to the nexus of
public life. For genuine Christians, it is not enough to hold their faith in
the privacy of their hearts and homes; it must guide and impact how and
what they do in all of life.

Poll after poll would confirm that the majority of Americans are OK
with the accommodationist approach of most Christians. However,
radical secularists are finding that their agenda is incompatible with

true religious liberty; therefore, they must exclude religion, primarily genuine Christianity, from the public square. So while they attempt to evoke images of the Taliban trying to establish a "theocracy" when they talk about the religious Right, this is nothing more than an attempt to distract Americans from seeing their own efforts to exclude people of faith from government.

We must resolve to defend the historical religious liberties that our nation has known. The outcome of every public policy debate rests, in large part, upon the ability of Christians to be full participants in the political and public policy process. We cannot allow Christians to be forced to check their faith at the gate of the public square.

Prayer Points

▶ Praise God for His love for the human race, that in Him only are we truly free. Thank Him for the religious liberty that we have in America. Thank Him for our unalienable rights that have been recognized by our Constitution and thus far protected by our government here in the United States.

▶ Ask for forgiveness that the church has not been as vigilant and steadfast as it should have been against the rise of secular humanism in America. Commit anew to hold the nation true to the values and faith we hold to be true, starting first in the house of God (1 Pet. 4:17).

▶ Ask that the Lord of all the earth reestablish America with the original intent of the Founding Fathers. Pray that the principles of Scripture would define the morality of our nation in every branch of government (Prov. 14:34).

Chapter 10

CORE VALUE #6: REBUILDING THE FAMILY (PART 1)

THE NEW CONFIGURATION

In January 2007, the *New York Times* carried a front-page story with the headline "51% of Women Are Now Living Without Spouse." The article proclaimed that this was a first for America. The *Times* appeared eager to announce that our nation had boldly entered a new frontier of unattached women. But a closer analysis suggests the *Times* may have been a little premature in launching the claim. The report was misleading because it did not account for women whose husbands were serving in the military and on deployment. The article also did not account for those who are married but living apart because of employment obligations. While a majority of women were living without a spouse in the household, a majority of women had a spouse.

The point of that article, and of much of the cultural chatter about marriage these days, is that marriage is an institution in decline—and that this constitutes progress. The way the numbers are spun in news segment after news segment, and article after article, it's as if there's an intentional effort to say, "If your family is falling apart, don't worry. Everybody's is. It's OK. Life may even be better without the traditional family. Go ahead and feel liberated." Even cultural conservatives find themselves riding on this bandwagon when they bemoan the sorry state of the family. They repeat the same (often misleading) statistics the secular press puts out, and this negative peer pressure causes even Christians to think that marriage really is failing and may as well be abandoned.

But while many in the media and academia are singing the same old song about the decline of the family, we see it much differently. The evidence actually suggests that amidst all the bad news, a revival of traditional marriage and family may well be in the works. It is happening mostly below the radar at the grassroots level, but in this chapter we will show you what's happening around the nation, in churches, communities, and legislatures to strengthen the family. You will see why the younger generation believes in strong families even when they act like they don't, and how legislation is tipping back toward pro-family policies for the first time in centuries.

A Season of Challenge

The state of the family is a bad news/good news situation, so let's get the obvious bad news out of the way. Little of it should surprise you. Everyone recognizes that in certain ways the institution of the family is fraying at the edges. Cultural forces are pulling at its fabric. The American family has undergone a dramatic transformation as more adults delay marriage, more divorce, more cohabitate, and fewer married couples produce children.

The concept of family has been challenged almost nonstop over the past four decades. The effects of the so-called sexual revolution are still reverberating around our culture. This "free love" movement celebrated sex and drugs and tried to redefine courtship, sex, and family life. The traditional roles of men and women were challenged both in the workplace and the home. As this redefinition was underway, the family began to go into free fall. Changing attitudes were reflected in public policy changes like the introduction of no-fault divorce in 1969, which fueled a steady rise in the divorce rate. Uncoupling sexual relations from marriage prompted an increase in out-of-wedlock births.[1] In addition, the gay lifestyle began to emerge from its "closet."

As marriages were delayed, postponed, and dissolved, children and home life began to suffer. Husbands and wives began to rethink their roles, which had a direct correlation to the roles of moms and dads. Since it is impossible to separate family life from marriage, this period was pivotal in preparing the nation to cut the anchor lines from both traditional marriage and family concepts.

Today, 45 to 50 percent of first marriages end in divorce.[2] Sixty to 67 percent of those divorced once end up getting divorced a second time.[3]

Those who try the third time have a 70 to 73 percent chance of failing.[4] Additionally, the divorce rate among Christians is running parallel to the national statistics at about 50 percent.[5] There is also a growing number of single people who will never get married at all. According to a *Washington Post* article, "Marriage Is for White People" by Joy Jones, "The marriage rate for African Americans has been dropping since the 1960s, and today, we have the lowest marriage rate of any racial group in the United States. In 2001, according to the U.S. Census, 43.3 percent of black men and 41.9 percent of black women in America had never been married, in contrast to 27.4 percent and 20.7 percent respectively for whites. African American women are the least likely in our society to marry. In the period between 1970 and 2001, the overall marriage rate in the United States declined by 17 percent; but for blacks, it fell by 34 percent. Such statistics have caused Howard University relationship therapist Audrey Chapman to point out that African Americans are the most uncoupled people in the country."[6]

Other statistics demonstrate the African American family breakdown: blacks account for over a third of all abortions in the nation, though they represent 12 percent of the population. Seven out of ten African American babies born this year will be born out of wedlock.[7] Some black women may feel that their marriage options have been limited because great numbers of formerly eligible black men are in prison, many others have contracted HIV/AIDS, and others have died prematurely due to drug use, suicide, and gang violence.

Restoring Marriage in America

But we're here to say that the church is already in the vanguard of attempting to turn things around so that marriage becomes an exalted institution once more and no longer an object of scorn in the culture. We think the cultural momentum is on our side. More people are recognizing that many of the social problems we have already discussed in this book have their ultimate origin in family dysfunction. Poverty, teen sex, out-of-wedlock pregnancies, teen drug abuse or alcoholism, juvenile delinquency, and teen suicide are all symptoms of family breakdown or trauma. Therefore, policy makers are taking a second look at traditional marriage as perhaps the single greatest issue we can solve in our nation—to help us solve many others.

So what is marriage, anyway? There's an adage that says, "If you don't know what something is intended to be used for, you are destined to abuse it!" Marriage is a sacred covenant or contract endorsed by God but simultaneously recognized by man. Marriage is a commitment made by one man and one woman to love and honor one another through the highs and lows of life. This union becomes the natural haven for raising children and developing a family.

The Bible is so clear in its support of marriage there is little need for us to go through an exhaustive definition of biblical marriage versus the types of unions allowed by law today. We will simply point out the Bible's claim, made overwhelmingly clear from Genesis through Revelation, that marriage is supposed to be between a man and a woman who love and respect one another. The scriptures say in Genesis 2:24 that a man is to leave his family and cleave to his wife. This concept is repeated in Matthew 19:5 and Mark 10:7. All the scriptures in the Bible concerning marriage presuppose heterosexual marriage.

The good news is that in the last ten years, policy changes in state legislatures across the United States reflect an increasing focus on the importance of marriage by public and government officials. As a state legislator, Tony authored the nation's first covenant marriage law in Louisiana in 1997. A covenant marriage law, which is voluntary, requires couples who chose a covenant marriage to obtain counseling prior to marriage and then puts a few obstacles in the path of divorce by requiring additional counseling and a longer cooling-off period before the court will grant a divorce. This differs from no-fault divorce, which allows one party to secure a divorce without consent from the other for no reason. Under covenant marriage, there must be grounds to terminate the marriage, and it is the aggrieved party who can initiate the divorce. The fault grounds recognized by covenant marriage are adultery, physical or sexual abuse of a spouse or child, conviction of felony, or abandonment.

At first, Tony didn't realize how significant this new policy direction was for his state or the nation. It was the first time in more than two hundred years that laws regarding divorce had become less lenient. Other states soon made efforts to do the same. More than two dozen states attempted to pass a covenant marriage law. Only two states—Arizona and Arkansas—succeeded, but the national discussion put the importance of marriage back on the table, and pro-marriage legislation remains active in many state legislatures.

Tony soon became a national advocate for covenant marriage, and he traveled to nearly two dozen states to promote covenant marriage legislation. He discovered an unexpected challenge: most civil or family law committees in legislatures are dominated by attorneys, most of whom are divorce attorneys. They want no restriction on their business! Many of these divorce attorneys blocked the advancement of covenant marriage-type legislation.

The reason that the topic of strengthening marriage remains a public policy force is because policy makers have seen the damage that divorce has done to their states. As Tony saw firsthand in Louisiana, states are running out of money to deal with problems like juvenile delinquency, welfare, incarceration, and even educational challenges. All these problems have a common denominator: breakdown of the American family. If we treat these other problems only by building prisons, hiring more teachers, creating early intervention programs, and so forth, we are treating the symptoms. But when you strengthen the family, you treat the cause. There is a clear recognition today, perhaps more than at any other time in the past several decades, that marriage and family are fundamental to the future of our society.

National Prominence

Marriage has also taken center stage in national policy. The president's Healthy Marriage Initiative explicitly seeks to undergird marriage through federal policies. It was primarily for people on welfare and in at-risk communities where government funds were used to provide marriage counseling and preparation. Some of these ideas percolated up from the states, showing what a profound effect state-level legislation can have. The federal government began working to promote marriage rather than dismantle it. Single mothers were asked who the father of their children was and if they would marry him. That question itself prompted some fathers to marry the mothers of their children, which was good for all of them. It was an almost total reversal of the Great Society approach, which provided incentives for people to leave the family structure. Now, instead of a single mother on welfare losing her housing if she married, the government removed the disincentives to keep the family together. It no longer penalizes them for doing the right thing.

The initiative gave substantial funds to nonprofits to support marriages. The Administration for Children and Families (ACF) and the Office of Family Assistance (OFA) gave millions of dollars in Healthy Marriage Demonstration grants to these organizations. These grants support innovative projects designed to strengthen existing marriages and to prepare unmarried couples for successful marriages. Public awareness and education campaigns promote the benefits and elements of healthy marriage, and teen programs explore positive relationship models and teach the core skills necessary for healthy marriage relationships.[8]

The president's efforts on behalf of family were in many ways preceded in the nonprofit realm, primarily in churches. The Catholic church has long required premarital counseling. Now there are other pro-marriage movements within evangelical churches, such as the National Association for Marriage Enhancement (NAME) founded and run by Rev. Leo Godzich out of Phoenix First Assembly of God in Arizona. These organizations hold conferences and seminars, create curricula for churches to use, and raise the level of awareness of their cause in the Christian community. They are creating subcultures of healthy marriages by giving people the tools to make themselves successful in marriage. In many churches, divorce rates have plummeted as a result of the work of these organizations.

In more and more communities, churches are also banding together to set a higher standard for marriage. Mike McManus launched something called the Community Marriage Initiative, which goes into communities, meets with pastors and even government officials, and encourages the pastors to sign a commitment not to marry a couple unless they undergo marital counseling. The result is a drastic drop in the divorce rates in these communities, some as much as 50 percent. The idea is to stop letting people "church shop" for a marriage license. The purpose of all these efforts has been to break the cycle of bad behavior by encouraging good relationship skills. Many people who get married today grew up in a culture of divorce in the 1970s and 1980s. Poor relationship skills were modeled for them. These public policies help them find different ways of solving relationship problems than calling it quits.

This is a wonderful example of churches cooperating with policy makers to set a new tone in their communities. The results are powerful. After passing the covenant marriage law in Louisiana, Tony would get wedding invitations from people who were entering into a covenant marriage. Others told him tragic stories of how they had gotten a divorce and now wished they would have waited because they feel they made a mistake and acted rashly. In some cases, couples have remarried one another.

One pastor in Louisiana taught a series on marriage leading up to a special service where people renewed their vows. One couple in the church had gotten divorced, and through this series they got back together and remarried. One of their little boys, eight or nine years old, came up to the pastor and said, "Thanks for bringing my dad home." That is the power to shape our community. It is encouraged by policy and carried out by the church. Covenant marriage laws create the discussion and set the standards. They affirm from a policy standpoint that marriage is powerful and indispensable to the health and welfare of society. Then it's up to churches and synagogues and spiritual leaders to put a renewed emphasis on marriage.

New Support for Healthy Marriages

There are other signs that the young adult generation is surprisingly supportive of marriage and family. We have noticed a trend in the past decade that has shown that the generation born and bred under no-fault divorce wants to restore family. Young people believe in loyalty, community, and putting family and friends before career. Many of them think divorce should be restricted. A lot of women are putting off their careers to raise their children, to the amazement and sometimes horror of their baby-boomer parents. It's almost as if one generation is trying to restore what the previous generation undid.

In the process of restoring family, some strange things are happening. The rate of divorce is declining, but so is the rate of marriage. On the other hand, cohabitation has skyrocketed. As disturbing as this is, we believe these are transitory statistics. Young people do not want to repeat the divorce rates and other mistakes of their parents, so they are avoiding marriage. Think of the messages young people get about marriage from most public policy, from media articles like the *Times* article referenced earlier, and from Hollywood. You rarely find a message of commitment. Is it any wonder they think marriage is antiquated? The culture has shaped their perception so much that they are groping in the darkness for the answer.

That's why we believe there has been a huge increase in cohabitation. The silver lining to these troubling statistics is that this generation is looking for a better way. They experienced the hurt and pain of broken relationships. They don't want to get a divorce—so they never get married in the first place. Often with good intentions, they decide to try out commitment while holding open the door to other possibilities if it doesn't work out. It seems like the right way out of the problem. But, of course, they are jumping out of the frying pan and into the fire, though they don't realize it.

Mike and Harriet McManus recently wrote a book on this issue titled, *Living Together: Myths, Risks and Answers*, which shows the ways in which cohabitation is disastrous and increases the likelihood that a relationship will fail.[9] There is something physical, emotional, physiological, and spiritual that happens when you become intimate with someone. And when you commit in those ways without committing to the relationship long-term, you put yourself in a state of perpetual anxiety. You worry that whoever you are with may pack up and leave. There is really nothing to keep people in the relationship other than the attraction of the moment. For a host of reasons, what you are trying to prevent (a failed relationship) becomes a monumental challenge.

The other thing cohabitating couples don't realize is that separation from a cohabitation partner can be just as damaging as divorce. When you become intimately connected with someone, it goes far beyond casual sex. It literally shapes your mind. Chemicals released during sexual intercourse, such as oxytocin and vasopressin, cause a physiological reaction that promotes bonding between the two. Studies suggest that the repeated exposure to these chemicals triggers a response that permanently alters body chemistry and behavior, making the individual more receptive toward his or her partner. Disrupting this bond creates great stress just like divorce.[10]

Additionally, research by University of Virginia psychologist Daniel Wegner on "transactive memory" suggests that when you separate, you also lose part of your external memory. According to Wegner, this is why people who go through divorce usually suffer short-term memory loss. When you've been with someone, you share responsibilities, not just household tasks but also responsibility for remembering or doing certain things. One of you may be good at remembering dates, while the other of you does the bills. When that person is suddenly gone, you lose "half your memory."[11]

Still, the younger generation is much more favorable toward committed, long-term relationships than any since the 1960s. We believe God wants to see a revival of the family and marriage in this nation because it makes people stronger, happier, more productive, and more fulfilled, and that will only benefit the entire nation. Can the church help guide this revival? Yes! Here's how.

Revival of Marriage

The ability to sustain a successful marriage is sometimes caught instead of taught, and in some ways churches have not succeeded in making marriage more attractive to many of the people they serve every week. As we make national prescriptions about improving the quality of our families, we think the church needs a renewed vision of the priority of marriage and family inside its four walls. Reversing America's family decline starts with each one of us allowing the Word of God and the power of the Holy Spirit to transform our personal lives. Just as Gideon of the Old Testament had to tear down the altars of Baal on his father's property before he could deliver the nation, we must clean house before God will move to revitalize our families nationally. Once there is a realignment of the church's core beliefs and its internal and external performance, Christians everywhere can become living billboards advertising the institution of healthy marriage. As we walk the talk, our voice will be heard and respected.

Not enough churches today put a high priority on building successful marriages. As divorce rates have grown in the church, so has the sensitivity about offending those who are divorced. If marriage and family are to rebound successfully, the church must be unafraid about promoting them. Pastors should feel empowered to preach on marriage as God designed it to be, and churches must pursue practical steps to help couples succeed in their marriages. Pastors should require premarital counseling that includes some objective evaluation tool like Prepare[12] to identify potential problem areas in a pending marriage. We understand the demands of pastoring a church today, and we are not trying to add something to the already overflowing plate of the local pastor. However, this is one area where a little investment of time, prayer, and energy today will save time, grief, and heartache tomorrow.

It's not just the pastor's responsibility. Your marriage and the marriages around you are the front line of battle for the heart and soul of our nation. Your marriage should become a top priority. Don't run from a mediocre or bad marriage. On the other hand, don't settle for a mediocre or bad marriage either. If you think you need counseling, seek help from your church or from a professional marriage counselor. If you just need a tune-up, consider going to a marriage enrichment weekend. If your church does not offer this, there are other resources like weekend conferences conducted by organizations such as Family Life Today that are enriching.

Tony often speaks of the struggles that he and his wife, Lawana, had during their first years of marriage when he was still in the U.S. Marine Corps. He jokingly says that if someone had told his wife twenty-two years ago that he would someday be a spokesman for marriage and family, she would have looked at that person like he had two heads!

Fortunately for Tony and Lawana, divorce was not prevalent in their families and not something that would have been well received. They also were a part of a church that had events designed to help couples strengthen their marriages. Because their church put a priority on successful relationships, they were encouraged to seek counseling. Tony will tell you that at the heart of their journey was a total surrendering to God. He began to see his wife as God intended him to see her, as a gift from God. Today, as a result of a little encouragement and a solid understanding of how God designed marriage to work, both Lawana and Tony testify to not just a good marriage, but a great one. Tony's personal experience was instrumental in his later policy work on covenant marriage.

There is no better preparation for our children to someday have a successful marriage than to see one modeled. It is not enough just to stay together under the same roof for your children; you need to model God's design for marriage for them. The astronomical rise in cohabitation has resulted not only because young people want to avoid the pain of divorce that they have witnessed, but also because they believe a successful marriage is beyond what their experience teaches them is possible.

Simply training our own children and grandchildren about marriage is an act of winning the war in our own families. Deciding not to get a divorce ourselves, no matter what, is an act of victory. Counseling couples in our church who are struggling in their marriage is an act of victory. Leading struggling couples to Christ and offering them personal mentorship is an act of victory. We can win the battle for marriage and family if we will begin at home.

Pro-marriage Policies

The federal government can do several important things in support of marriage. First is tax reform. In 1990 the Family Research Council championed the idea of a child tax credit. In 1997 Congress approved a $500 per child tax credit. That tax credit has now come to represent $46 billion to American families each year. In total, this has put more than $250 billion back into the hands of families. The current tax credit of $1,000 per child is set to be cut in half and then phased out for some families beginning in 2010. Congress should not only make this tax credit permanent, but they should also increase tax credits for children.

America's workforce is declining in number. By 2040 America will have only two workers paying into Social Security and the Medicare system for every retired worker drawing from the system. America's birth rate is virtually stagnant, with the average woman having 2.1 births over her lifetime. The federal government should encourage larger families with child tax credits not only for federal income taxes but also for Social Security and Medicaid. Families with children are raising not only tomorrow's taxpayers but also the workers who will fund Social Security; we should encourage large families, not discourage them with high taxes.

Michael McManus of Marriage Savers says that since 1970–1975, every state in America has allowed no-fault divorce, which allows one spouse to unilaterally end a marriage, even when no moral faults are claimed, such as adultery or abuse. Today, 80 percent of divorces are no-fault, or unilateral, divorces. Since 1970, there has been one divorce for every two marriages—42 million divorces shattering the lives of 40 million children. Therefore, there is a need to reform no-fault divorce, at least in cases involving children. Unless a major fault is proven, couples with children should not be allowed to divorce, unless both parents agree. If mutual-consent divorce were to replace no-fault divorce, experts estimate that divorce rates would fall 30 percent, saving 300,000 marriages from divorce annually.

Another way to lower divorce rates is by altering how we deal with custody issues in divorce cases. We recommend replacing sole custody with a presumption of joint custody or shared parenting in which each parent has access to the children at least one-third of the time each week. Five of the six states that created a presumption of shared parenting in the 1990s enjoyed the biggest drops in the divorce rate. This is because if a parent understands that he or she will have to interact on a regular basis with the other parent, there is less incentive to get the divorce. David Levy, president of the Children's Rights Council, and other experts estimate that if the presumption of sole custody were replaced with a presumption of shared parenting, divorce rates would fall an additional 20 percent.

These two reforms have the potential to slash divorce rates in half, saving 500,000 kids from seeing their parents divorce each year. What better strategy to support family values?[13]

The federal government has other powers it can wield over marriage as well. The federal government often encourages states to address issues that are beyond the purview of Congress by using financial incentives or disincentives. The drinking age and the speed limit are examples of state policy matters on which the Congress has repeatedly directed the activities of the states. Congress would withhold federal highway dollars if states did not raise their speed limit or lower the blood alcohol level for which a person could be charged with driving under the influence. We think the Congress should take the same approach and withhold federal monies if states alter the definition of marriage contained in the Defense of Marriage Act signed into law by President Bill Clinton in 1996.

We must educate and mobilize our own base to encourage such action. In May 2006 Harry was among a group of eighteen people who met with President Bush concerning the marriage amendment. At that juncture of history the Republican Party had thrown away the amendment in the Senate. The senators had not yet realized that backing away from moral issues would create an environment in which Republicans would be defeated the following November. Instead, they felt that they needed to be moderate and not seen as divisive. The delay coincided with the release of a book by Vice President Dick Cheney's lesbian daughter just before the marriage amendment would be voted on. Cheney's daughter and others went public with their belief that gay marriage should be reconsidered for the nation. This was a strategic political error of the highest order for the Republican Party.

In the presidential meeting Harry asked the question, "Mr. President, what can we do to help you [push the marriage amendment with the vigor that you had before the election]?" The president's answer was very simple—"Rally your people!" He was saying that there had to be a popular outcry coming from the masses to protect marriage.

We must believe 1 Timothy chapter 2, which exhorts Christians to pray for those who are in authority. Prayer gives us access to the power of

God. Prayer changes our internal attitudes, aligns us with God's scriptural agenda, and removes obstacles to His will. Prayer changes things.

And we should keep firmly in mind that state government is where most family policy is made. Values voters have often overlooked what was taking place at state capitols as we focused on Washington. For example, a recent victory came in Texas, which passed a law in its most recent legislative session giving discounts on marriage licenses to couples who undergo premarital counseling.

In Alabama a bill will probably be introduced in 2008 on the concept of shared parenting. It will also support a cooling-off period of 365 days for those seeking a divorce as opposed to the present legislated 30-day period.

Indiana is considering divorce reform and a three-part covenant marriage program that promotes premarital counseling, fault-based divorce, and pre-divorce counseling.

We must continue to watch Washington, but it is at the state level that we can advance pro-marriage, pro-family policies, as we have already seen.

Final Thoughts

A couple of years ago a story was published on Valentine's Day about Paul and Mary Onesi, a couple from Niagara Falls, New York, who were celebrating their eightieth wedding anniversary.[14] According to the couple, there were no secrets to their success. They didn't even celebrate Valentine's Day; they focused, in their words, on the sensible, not the sentimental. But the most instructive comment came from one of the couple's grandchildren in response to a question by the reporter. There had been no divorces among the couple's six children or twenty-eight grandchildren, and the reporter inquired as to why. The response from Laura Cerrillo was quite simple. "In our family, no one ever wanted to get divorced because no one wanted to tell them."

Did that little old couple from Niagara Falls really intimidate two, going on three, generations? No; it was their example of steadfastness in the face of the daily routine of marriage for over three-quarters of a century that was not only inspiring but also set a standard that others then reached for and obtained.

The Onesis may never have sat down in 1917 and planned to leave such a legacy and to impact their children and community in such a positive way, In fact, Paul Onesi thought too much attention was given to their milestone of eighty years of marriage. He felt they were doing what was expected of them.

Today it may require more than just setting out to do what is expected of us, because not much is expected and even less is required when it comes to marriage. We must determine that we will honor the covenant of marriage. Our nation is in need of covenant couples who will raise the standard for lifelong marriage again, demonstrating to hurting people in noncommittal relationships that lifelong married monogamy is the happiest, most fulfilling arrangement ever created.

It is not too late to save the family in America. Our movement simply needs to be recommitted to the biblical truth of marriage, become more organized in advancing those truths, and remain strategically focused upon creating a nation that respects marriage and the multiplied benefits it gives to our children and us.

Prayer Points

▸ Give thanks to the Lord for creating the institutions of marriage and family as vivid illustrations of His relationship with us. Praise Him for every father and mother who choose to stay married and raise their children together (1 Tim. 5:8).

▸ Ask God to forgive the church and Christians as a whole for first failing to honor the covenant of marriage and, as a result, neglecting to adequately promote and protect the institution of marriage in the public policies of our nation. Ask Him to help each one of us to defend marriage and family with both our words and actions.

▸ Ask God to press the church forward to save marriages and create community resources to help families who are struggling. Pray that He would provide mentors for spouses and parents from the churches within neighborhoods where they are needed.

Chapter 11

CORE VALUE #6: REBUILDING THE FAMILY (PART 2)

FATHERHOOD AND EDUCATION

I n elementary school, Harry had a special bond with two other boys. They did everything together—played sports, studied, and socialized. Harry was the worst athlete of the three, but he held his own with them academically. They all attended the most advanced classes that their all-black, urban school offered. Many of their classmates passed the test to enter Cincinnati's most exclusive public school, which had a college prep program.

At age twelve, Harry's life took a dramatic turn. His father took him out of the public school system. This move separated Harry from his two buddies, and they all went their separate ways. Harry Jackson Sr. sat his namesake down and explained that he would not give him an inheritance when he died. Instead, he would give him an education, which he hoped would be his son's passport to a bright future. He believed that education was America's great "class equalizer." So he enrolled Harry Jr. as one of the first black children to enter the prestigious Cincinnati Country Day School. There was no minority scholarship program. Even in 1966, this school's tuition ran several thousand dollars a year. Harry's dad began his own career working for the postal service. Despite his college degree, paid for by the GI bill, he spent years delivering and sorting mail before the days of high-speed machines. As Harry Sr. was pulling himself out of blue-collar financial limitations, he ensured that his kids would have more opportunities than he had. He footed the entire bill for his son's education from private middle school through a "Little Ivy" education at Williams College (often ranked number one in academic standing in the nation). Harry was an all-city wrestling champion in high school, a "Small College All-American" football player in college, and signed a pro football contract his senior year in college with the New England Patriots. After his father's death, Harry pursued an MBA at Harvard Business School largely because his dad had always dreamed of Harry attending Harvard University.

The Jackson family's decision to invest in education changed Harry's destiny and the course of his life. He was exposed to things he would not have ever experienced otherwise. But Harry's two buddies were not as fortunate. Neither of them succeeded in high school sports. One of them wound up in prison at age eighteen for killing a man in a fight. The other, who had been the fastest sprinter in their school, had to get a job while he was in high school. This kept him from playing sports. He eventually became a bus driver for the city of Cincinnati.

A world-class education was Harry's ticket out of the financial limitations of the ghetto and was a formal invitation into America's middle class. Harry's story illustrates two important components in economic uplift and family development. First, the leadership of fathers is essential in charting a child's life course. Second, securing a strong educational foundation is essential for preparing children for success. These two areas can be strengthened by public policy so that fathers and the educational system come alongside American families to undergird the training children receive.

Fathers: A Healing Factor

Most everybody, liberal or conservative, can agree, or at least should agree, that as the father goes, so goes the family, and as families go, so goes the nation. Therefore, if fathers are strengthened, the family and country are strengthened. In June 2000, former Vice President Al Gore said, "Don't ever doubt the impact that fathers have on children. Children with strongly committed fathers learn about trust early on. They learn about trust with their hearts. They learn they are wanted, that they have value, and that they can afford to be secure and confident and set their sights high."[1]

An article written in the *Journal of Men's Studies* in 2002 showed nine important dimensions of a father's involvement.[2] These nine dimensions are imperative to a child's healthy development, and when they are encouraged, men and their families will blossom. They are:

1. Providing
2. Supporting the mother
3. Disciplining and teaching responsibility
4. Encouraging success in school
5. Giving praise and affection
6. Spending time together and talking
7. Being attentive to the child's needs
8. Reading to their children
9. Encouraging children to develop their talents

Each of these activities is more difficult, even impossible, when the birth father is not living with the child's mother in the same household. David Blackenhorn, author of *Fatherless America*, said, "Fatherlessness is the most harmful demographic trend of this generation."[3] Rightly, most Americans view the increased number of single-parent households as a major problem. A 1999 poll discovered that 64 percent of Americans are concerned about this.[4] A separate *New York Times* poll performed one month later showed that 77 percent of Americans believe that increased divorce and single parenting have weakened family ties.[5] Over half of Americans studied in a survey in 2001 by Harvard University's Kennedy School of Government believe that the high number of single-parent families is a major cause of poverty.[6] Studies also reveal that most Americans believe that welfare programs encourage single-parent families and teenage pregnancy.[7]

These opinions have been validated repeatedly by social scientists. Sharon E. Lock and Murray L. Vincent completed a survey of 564 adolescent young women in rural South Carolina that showed something we have known for years. That "being from a two-parent family increased the likelihood of not engaging in premarital sexual intercourse."[8]

Malcolm D. Williams made an amazing discovery in 1997 using a sample of 1,610 ten- to thirteen-year-olds. He found that children who learn to share significant ideas with their fathers had fewer behavior problems than their peers. In addition, these children developed stronger cognitive abilities.[9]

Similar results were found by researchers who studied African American boys. In a 1995 study of 254 black adolescents living with both of their biological parents, 96 percent of these boys said their fathers were their role models. No doubt these dads had been available to talk to, to encourage, and to impart values. In this study, only 44 percent of black adolescents who were not living with their fathers said their fathers were their role models.[10]

The *Journal of Family Psychology* in 2000 wrote up the findings of a study of 116 African American students ages ten to thirteen. The boys with married parents were found to have much higher levels of self-esteem and a better sense of personal power and self-control compared to single-mother homes. Of special interest to us was the fact that even when parental education levels and income were the same, intact families produced more secure young people.[11]

The final piece of social research we will quote was especially shocking. Over and over again, scholarly studies focused on adolescence show that early onset of puberty in girls is a major problem. It is associated with psychological, social, and health problems. Things like depression, alcohol consumption, and higher teenage pregnancy rates are some of the results. An eight-year study of 173 girls and their families showed that a father's presence in the home, with appropriate involvement in his children's lives, contributed to later pubertal timing of the daughters in the seventh grade.[12]

These studies suggest what most Americans have always known: children, both boys and girls, are deeply affected in both biological and psychological ways by the presence of their fathers.

The Father Wound

But the problem of fatherlessness in America has become greater. According to the U.S. Department of Health and Human Services, over the last four decades there has been a dramatic increase in the number of children growing up in homes without fathers. In 1960, fewer than 10 million children did not live with their fathers. Today, the number is nearly 25 million. More than one-third of these children will not see their fathers at all during the course of a year. Studies show that children who grow up without responsible fathers are significantly more likely to experience poverty, perform poorly in school, engage in criminal activity, and abuse drugs and alcohol.[13]

Over the years, the Family Research Council (FRC) has done a great deal of research on current trends in the family, including research on father absence. FRC has discovered that:

1. Children from single-parent homes are likely to suffer economic poverty.

2. Children from single-parent homes are more likely to develop emotional problems.

3. Children from single-parent homes are more likely to experience abuse.

4. Single mothers are more likely to live in poverty than married mothers.[14]

These are not the only penalties associated with the absence of fathers. According to a 2003 study, divorce in the United States eats up $33.3 billion per year. This number includes costs to federal and state government for child support enforcement, Medicaid, Temporary Assistance to Needy Families (TANF), food stamps, and public housing. There are a host of additional costs rolled into this number, like expenses related to drug use, delinquency, the maintenance of correctional facilities, and social problems related to divorce.[15] The average divorce costs state and federal governments $30,000 in direct and indirect costs, according to the same study.

Plan of Action to Restore Fathers

Polls suggest that Americans are willing and eager to invest time and even tax dollars to create policies that will encourage fathers to settle down and help to raise their own children. We plainly need to pursue these major goals for fatherhood:

▸ Increase the number of crisis pregnancy centers in black communities

▸ Lower black and Hispanic prison recidivism so that fathers may create stability in their families

▸ Lower the number of out-of-wedlock births

Churches must also get involved and:

▸ Develop mentoring programs for young fathers

▸ Develop programs that celebrate fatherhood at other times during the year than Father's Day

▶ Encourage the development of local church prison reentry programs in conjunction with Prison Fellowship

Our public policy strategies should be to encourage state correction agencies to partner with faith-based organizations to help ex-convicts successfully transition back into society. We should seek increased funding for the Second Chance Act, which helps prisoners reenter society. We should increase tax benefits for married couples at or near the poverty level and not penalize single mothers who marry their baby's father by immediately cutting off benefits. We should also develop first home ownership programs for couples at the poverty level who have children.

Local churches should also develop adoption ministries as recommended by Dennis Rainey's Family Life Today and modeled by churches like Antioch Bible Fellowship, pastored by Dr. Ken Hutchinson. If Christians use these vehicles to redeem the lives of discarded domestic children, this could make a major impact on generational cycles of racism and poverty.

Educational Reform

Education is the other pillar of family success. Parents have been charged by God with the responsibility of training their children. For this reason, Christians made up a large portion of parents who began homeschooling their kids in large numbers about twenty years ago. Christian cultural leaders like Dr. James Dobson helped the average family evaluate their ability to teach their kids at home. Once considered highly experimental, homeschooling has stood the test of time. The National Home Education Research Institute says "there were an estimated 1.9 to 2.4 million children (in grades K to 12) home educated during 2005–2006 in the United States," and the number is growing.[16]

Many bright, stay-at-home mothers have made their young prepubescent children true disciples of Christ through godly curricula and parental involvement in their children's lives. Three-fourths of homeschooled children are white, 9 percent are black, and 5 percent are Hispanic, according to 2003 statistics. Eighty-five percent of homeschooling parents say their concern about school environment is their reason for undertaking such a demanding endeavor. And the results they put up year after year are phenomenal. On average, homeschoolers scored an average of 1.7 points higher on the ACTs (36 is the maximum score) than non-homeschoolers. On the SAT, out of 1600 points, homeschooled students scored an average of 1083, 67 points more than the national average.[17] Additionally, some U.S. military academies are actively recruiting homeschool students, not only for their academic achievements but also for their strong discipline and moral conduct.[18]

Tony and his wife, Lawana, homeschool their children. Tony first became aware of homeschooling while he was a television reporter and was assigned to do a story on the socialization of homeschooled children, an issue that is used as an objection to homeschooling. At the time, Tony and Lawana did not have school-age children, and he actually had a biased view against homeschooling because of the portrayal of homeschooling by the media.

What Tony discovered, not only anecdotally but also from the research of others, was eye-opening. Research by Larry Edward Shyers at the University of Florida not only disproved the claims of homeschool detractors, but also it actually revealed that homeschooled children are better socialized than their peers.[19]

Lawana was reluctant to homeschool at first. Beyond the way homeschool families have been stereotyped as throwbacks and oddballs, there was real concern over the mechanics of homeschooling and replicating the high-quality educational experience she and Tony had received in public schools. But when it came time for their daughter to enroll in kindergarten, Lawana decided to try homeschooling for the first year. Nine years later she is homeschooling all of their school-age children and would not consider any other options. Once she was able to break free of the public education system's rigid, one-size-fits-all model, educating their children became easier to conceive and carry out successfully. Today there are vast amounts of resources available to homeschool parents. More and more parents of all races are taking back the role of educator.

As a fitting coda to Tony's experience, one of the homeschool students from the family that Tony interviewed back in 1993 for his news story is now the chief of staff of Louisiana Governor Bobby Jindal.

That said, 90 percent of America's students still attend public schools. Therefore, the main cultural battleground in education is the public school system. Many Christians now encourage their brightest and best children, who are spiritually mature and well grounded, to go confidently into public schools. Students supported by alert parents and vigilant local churches can make a major difference in every corner of the nation. With strong Christian students in public schools, we can begin looking for revival and a major cultural change within student bodies. Being "good" and studious can once again become cool if the right students take leadership among their peers.

Other important changes, however, cannot be made by students. We need to send an army of adult educational missionaries into the school systems. The nation needs an inside force of professional educators and elected school board members who will advocate for moral and academic change. In order to reinvigorate education in America, we must recognize that the power of the public school system is vested in three different locations—local schools, leading universities, and the U.S. Department of Education. Four very different types of educational missionaries are needed: classroom teachers, school administrators, university professors, and educational policy makers. Let's look at each more closely.

Classroom teachers

A new breed of classroom teachers is needed to permeate every sector of American public schools. The new breed is especially needed in lower-income, urban environments. These proven teachers with excellent classroom skills will take on the task of challenging, correcting, and encouraging marginal and unmotivated students. We realize that we cannot re-create fictional characters from movies like *To Sir With Love* and *Freedom Writers* in which Sidney Poitier or Hilary Swank appear on the scene and suddenly cure all the ills of the school. On the other hand, we are aware that teachers with proven track records and years of exceptional service can do wonders if they are compensated well and given the tools they need to do their jobs. Local churches need to help recruit these kinds of teachers to work in the schools in their communities. The teachers may have to temporarily receive lower salaries or work in tougher conditions than they might working in some private schools. But the nontangible rewards for such labor will be immeasurable.

School administrators

School administration has become a complex, even daunting field. Many of Harry's uncles and family friends have joyfully taken on the task of putting their mark on a high school or elementary school by becoming principals and committing to living and working in the local community in a way that produces generations of solid, productive citizens in marginal or troubled neighborhoods. The need for great administrators is not simply in the ghetto. That need is also felt widely in both suburban and private school systems. Supply and demand being what it is, however, the most gifted leaders often wind up in the environments that need them the least. In the 1970s, there was a term that described how upwardly mobile, white citizens left neighborhoods that began to erode economically. It was called "white flight." In education, it seems to us there is sometimes a leadership parallel that occurs in troubled school districts. We call it "leadership flight." Churches and Christian service organizations can help to turn these things around. We need a Christian version of "Teach America." This kind of program can be led by some of our larger denominations or developed by private foundations with a commitment to both teach and administrate with excellence.

University professors

For far too long, Americans have decried the fact that institutions of higher education have become intellectually corrupt and undisciplined in their training. Jim Nelson Black explores this problem in depth in his book *Freefall of the American University,* in which he describes what happens to our brightest young minds as they become "intellectually scarred, morally neutered, socially and intellectually programmed." Black goes on to say, "Universities are responsible for the collapse of educational standards and a debasement of morality that is unprecedented in American history."[20] We believe that Dr. Black is correct in his assessment and that it will take more than simply creating Christian universities to turn this trend around. We must send seasoned Christian apologists—those who argue in defense of the Christian faith—into the most influential academic environments, such as Harvard, Yale, and the best of our universities. To accomplish this, parents and policy makers who pay the bills must insure the voices of the professors are afforded the same rights and privileges as those on the Left.

Educational policy makers

Abraham Lincoln was credited with saying, "The philosophy of the classroom in one generation will be the philosophy of the government in the next." America's schools today will probably determine what America will look like tomorrow. There is a growing movement in America that recites the mantra, "Whoever controls the schools rules the world." In fact, this is the title of a book written by Gary DeMar. "Over time, most Christians adopted the false premise that facts are neutral. It didn't matter who taught math, science or history, because facts are facts. The humanists took advantage of this type of thinking by gradually shaping and controlling education in terms of materialist assumptions. . . . Our world view opponents understand that education is where the war of ideas is fought."[21] In their book *Children at Risk*, James Dobson and Gary Bauer state, "A great civil war of values rages today . . . two sides with vastly differing and incompatible worldviews are locked in a bitter conflict that permeates every level of society. . . . A struggle now is for the hearts and minds . . . the war is not fought with bombs and bullets, but with ideas."[22] Most people do not realize that educational policy makers are the architects of how our educational house will be built for generations to come. An army of Bible-believing PhDs needs to invade the educational field and work hard to rise to high levels of leadership so they can pave the way for Christian ideologies to have free course. Some are doing this, but many more must join them.

In addition to missionaries, we believe that there must be a savvy use of the following elements to improve our educational system:

1. Productive public schools
2. Competitive charter schools
3. Parental choice in education decision
4. World-class private education
5. Teacher accountability

Race and Education

We cannot neglect the racial aspect of education's problems as well. The National Center for Education statistics tell us that the majority of white kids go to mostly white schools, and large numbers of black kids go to predominantly black schools. Today racial separation in various neighborhoods is not by government fiat or prejudice—it is by choice.

Unfortunately, racial separation often coincides with stark differences in rates of success. Prince George's County, Maryland, where Harry pastors, is said to be America's wealthiest predominantly black county. Unfortunately, the school system is one of the worst in the Washington DC region. In a community in which million-dollar homes and Mercedes Benz automobiles are commonplace, quality educational programs in the schools are rare. The poor performance of students cannot be blamed on poverty or segregation alone.

The No Child Left Behind (NCLB) Act of 2001 helped close the nation's racial divide in its first six years of existence. The achievement gap between black and white children closed at the elementary school level and is at the lowest level that it has been in thirty years. Yet there remains a huge problem at the high school level.

During the days of the *Brown v. Board of Education* decision, only 24 percent of blacks under the age of thirty had finished high school. Today that number has grown significantly—86.3 percent of black adults aged twenty-five to twenty-nine have graduated from high school. Unfortunately this lags behind the 93.4 percent graduation rates of whites.[23] Why are these numbers important? Educational standards have gradually been watered down over the years. Blacks and Hispanics who do not substantively progress beyond high school will never achieve economic equality with whites.

In 2007 the Supreme Court ruled that voluntary plans to create racial balance in schools should stop. They voted that forced racial integration mandated by *Brown v. Board of Education* was not truly serving the current needs of the average child. The Supreme Court decision was an indictment of the current educational system. What is needed today is not a Supreme Court ruling but a positive plan to change the structure of education. Kids of all races are in academic danger. Black and Hispanic children are especially vulnerable.

Overall Education Goals

During his experience as an elected official, Tony discovered that educational policy is usually focused on the educational system and not the children. Public education has seen tremendous growth in public funding. Between 1960 and 1995, per pupil spending rose 212 percent, yet increasingly we are seeing less return on each dollar invested in public education.[24] The unions and educational hierarchy are focused on preserving a system and stifling any educational competition that could be beneficial to students. Our goal should be to produce well-educated children who have the academic essentials and work ethic to make them globally competitive. We must move beyond seeing public schools as the only means of education. Our state and federal policy should acknowledge that parents are in the best position to determine what educational approaches would afford their children the best opportunity for success.

America's educational policy should:

1. Empower parents
2. Equip children with the tools to succeed
3. Ensure taxpayers the best return for every educational tax dollar

As we have already stated, Christians can play a big role in education. Churches should develop special support groups and prayer ministries similar to Moms in Touch that support the successful education of children. Churches should also develop private and charter schools with public money in neighborhoods in crisis. Christian schools should develop scholarship programs for outstanding minority and disadvantaged students. And once again we emphasize the fact that churches should encourage high school and college students to answer the call of God to educational "ministry."

An easy way to remember the strategic actions we recommend for education is by using the acrostic TIP:

1. TOUCH the lives of as many children as possible by raising up independent Christian schools, starting charter schools with predominantly Christian boards, or becoming part of existing schools and taking leadership.

2. INFLUENCE the public school system. This can be done by running for school boards, critiquing and evaluating curriculum, and leading PTA and other school-related associations.

3. PROMOTE effective godly programs. Get positive feedback concerning things that work. All too often Christians are only heard complaining about what is wrong with the system. It's time to become a positive force.

Public Policy Goals

In the arena of public policy, believers should support a revised version of the No Child Left Behind (NCLB) Act, the A-Plus Act, which gives states more control over education and allows them to end inefficient and effective one-size-fits-all federal programs. The goals of NCLB of accountability for public schools are laudable and much needed; however, the result has been the accountability of educational outputs rather than educational outcomes. The best accountability for public education is first the parents of the students, secondly the local community, followed by the local school board, and then the state.

Despite the fact the NCLB Act only represented 8.5 percent of the total funding for public education, some constituencies were accused of reaching for the dollars—while compromising effective educational processes. Some states lowered standards, others changed how tests were evaluated, and many regions attempted to keep parents from understanding what their children were actually learning. Some groups have dubbed these changes as a "race towards the bottom."[25]

Early on, states responded to the pressure of NCLB testing by lowering state standards. Testing targets were altered in many schools, which allowed for children with test performances lower than grade level to receive social promotions. Parents, citizens, and policymakers were denied basic information about student performance in our schools. On a micro level, the loss of academic transparency in some jurisdictions hindered parents from knowing whether or not their children were learning. On a macro level, the lack of academic transparency prevented policy makers from judging how well some of their schools were performing.

Overall, though, we believe that NCLB started with a pure and noble vision. This vision, unfortunately, has often been obscured because of territorial infighting and poor implementation. The accountability that NCLB is striving for is crucial to our improving education in America. After all, if you don't know where you are or where you're going, it's impossible to map out a strategic plan. Just as importantly, when the plan is set, we must know how we are doing in student learning, teacher instruction, and school administration. It seems to us that the process of removing students from ineffective schools and improving public schools has not been fully developed. We need to let the worst schools die and give support to the schools that are striving for excellence.

In addition to these macro issues, we must also support development of teacher incentive programs that deploy skilled teachers to the neediest arenas. In recent years school districts all over the country have gotten into the habit of rewarding the best teachers with easy teaching environments instead of bonuses and incentives to take on the most challenging students and the most challenging educational environments.[26]

Finally, states should advance policies that put educational decisions back into the hands of parents. Empowering parents to decide where and how their children will be educated could revolutionize education in America. States should establish refundable education tax credits or educational vouchers that give parents true choice in how their children are educated. These tax credits should be applicable to the costs of public, private, and homeschool education, letting parents decide where their children and their tax dollars will go.

Personal Goals

Although many in our increasingly secular society, including Christians, fail to recognize this truth, the Bible's instructions for the family work. Children are a gift from God to parents, not burdens placed upon the state. Our children are our future, and they are truly the way in which we leave a lasting impact upon the world (Ps. 127:3–5). Fathers are not extra accessories in this process, as some feminists would suggest. Fathers are absolutely critical for the spiritual, emotional, and physical well-being of both boys and girls.

There is only one specific instruction given in the New Testament to fathers in terms of their relationship to their children. Twice, fathers are instructed not to provoke their children to anger or to exasperate them (Eph. 6:4; Col. 3:21). Rather, fathers are to nurture their children and advise them in the ways of God. This is an important instruction to fathers because unresolved anger can lead to bitterness, antisocial behavior, and unrealized potential. This anger in children is not necessarily created by an overt act of being too stern or exerting arbitrary authority over a child; in more cases than not, today it is created by fathers neglecting their children or walking out of their lives. Increasingly, the greatest need that children have today is a father who is actively involved in their lives.

This in no way diminishes the nurturing role that mothers play. God created children to be raised by moms and dads. To moms and dads, God gave the instruction to train up their children in the ways of life, teaching them the truths that would make them successful.

Teaching goes beyond reading, writing, and arithmetic. It is the instruction in how to live in a way that honors God. It is instilling character and the ability to see beyond oneself. It is raising children who become responsible, respectful, and resourceful citizens. These are key aspects of our children's education that schoolteachers, public or private, cannot and should not be expected to provide. Parents must assume the God-assigned responsibility to raise their children.

This begins with fathers. Fathers must provide the example of servant leadership to their children and their wives. Even if fathers are not married to the mother of their children, a nonideal situation, they must remain involved in the lives of their children.

The church, the community, the courts, and Congress should make strengthening marriage, family, and fatherhood a top priority. As Christians we should seriously heed the warning given by God's "messenger" in the last verse in the Old Testament: "And he [God] shall turn the heart of the *fathers* to the children, and the heart of the children to their *fathers*, lest I come and smite the earth with a curse" (Mal. 4:6, emphasis added).

Prayer Points

▸ Thank God for being our perfect heavenly Father and loving us as His children. Thank Him for establishing faithful and loving fathers all across the land who will encourage, nurture, and develop the next generation. Pray that more men would join the ranks of these faithful fathers.

▸ Ask forgiveness for the way the church has allowed humanism to permeate the school systems in America (2 Chron. 7:13-15). Repent for any way you may have missed opportunities to be a voice to the schools in your area through voting, publicly promoting truth, or writing local school administrators.

▸ Ask the Lord to build godly men in this country who will love their wives and their children.

▸ Pray that parents would once again assume their role as the educators and trainers of their children (1 Cor. 4:15).

Chapter 12

CORE VALUE #7: THE ENVIRONMENT AND GLOBAL WARMING

CAN WE BEAT THE HEAT?

I n recent years we found ourselves confronted by an increasingly alarming approach to the issue of environmental stewardship from some within the leadership ranks of our movement. In response, we helped draft a private letter addressed to the chairman of the board of the National Association of Evangelicals (NAE), Dr. L. Roy Taylor, asking that the NAE confer with other Christian groups regarding its increasingly dissonant stance on the issue of global warming. Very unfortunately, this letter was leaked to the press, by whom we do not know, and its contents appeared on the front page of the *Wall Street Journal*. Our attempt to bring unity to evangelicals on the issue of environmental stewardship had inadvertently created more division. The media, ever willing to herald the crack-up of our movement, pounced on the letter and attempted to drum up as much division as it could within our ranks.

Because Harry was a part of this attempt to bring unity to the conservative Christian movement, he was asked to discuss global warming on CNN's *Anderson Cooper 360°*. Another evangelical minister, Rev. Jim Ball, president and CEO of the Evangelical Environmental Network, presented the case of evangelicals who believe that global warming and the environment are among the most important issues of our day. Harry winced when he originally received the invitation because he knew the host or the producers likely wanted to see a brawl between Christian brothers on the issue of global warming. After talking about the interview with Tony and several other evangelical leaders, Harry decided that he would not let the session dissolve into a name-calling contest. He would not be baited into attacking one of his fellow evangelicals. Rather, he would approach the opportunity seeking to bring peace and unity when possible. But he was all too aware that the reporters could cast him as a Neanderthal or, worse, a mean-spirited, religious zealot.

As a nonscientist, Harry also wanted to avoid trying to sort through the research or declaring that he had some kind of epiphany or divine revelation concerning global warming. Few of the people debating global warming are scientists, and that most definitely includes us. But all too often Christians and opponents of the radical environmentalist agenda are made to look like we are antiscience. Nothing could be further from the truth, as we shall see.

Thankfully, the Anderson Cooper interview came off without any bitter fighting or name-calling between Harry and the other guests, though the debate was informative and even sharp at times. Since that time, we have been considering how the evangelical movement can retain its unity in its approach to this issue. We have also become more aware and more concerned about the underlying philosophy of the radical environmental agenda and how it may actually lead people away from God and into humanism. We approach this topic now with a strong desire to set the stage for our movement's success on this issue in the years to come. The environment does not need to be a wedge issue that our opponents use to drive us apart. Rather, we can stand together on common ground, taking a principled and balanced approach to the stewardship of our planet and environment, while avoiding the at times egregious policies and philosophies put forth by green evangelists, for whom the environment has almost become a secular religion.

Polls tell us that the environment is at the bottom of most evangelicals' concerns. This doesn't mean evangelicals don't care about proper stewardship of the planet, just that they don't see it as the most pressing issue facing our nation. If you are like us, with so many contradicting voices on this topic, you've probably been scratching your head wondering who to believe. Or maybe you've just decided to ignore the issue. As we begin this chapter, we want to make clear that we do not hold ourselves out to be scientific experts on the topics of pollution, the environment, and global warming. But we have both made it a point to study the issue of global warming because of its growing importance in public policy discussions. In this chapter we want to look at the claims being made about global warming and report our take on the solutions that are being trumpeted around the world. We will follow our analysis by a look at what the Bible has to say about our environmental responsibilities and specifically the issue of global warming.

Let us state our positions right up front. We are for good steward-ship of this planet God has given to us to inhabit. We are for good science that can help us measure our stewardship efforts. We are for good policies. We are for clean forests and unpolluted lakes, air, and oceans. We believe there is little true division within the religious Right, or in the population at large, over what kind of environment we want to live in. What causes the division is some people's rush to bad conclusions, bad science, bad policy, and bad results.

How Warm Is It Really?

One morning in the fall of 2005 as Tony was headed to a breakfast meeting with then U.S. Senator Rick Santorum, he was glancing through the *New York Times* on the way to the Capitol. A full-page ad by Allstate Insurance caught his eye. Large dominos were lined up and trailing out of the picture. Each domino bore a year, beginning with 2006. A man was peering out from behind the domino marked 2006, and the domino was beginning to tilt backward toward the 2007 domino, which upon falling would cause a chain reaction. The ad read, "Eight Out of the 10 Largest U.S. Catastrophes Have Happened in the Last Four Years. Are We Ready To Deal With The Next Four?" It then went on to address proposed legislation.

That ad, and the fear it seemed to promote, reflected the current debate over the environment. Fear seems to have trumped reason. Quick, drastic solutions seem to draw favor while measured, studied approaches are tossed out because of the so-called urgency of the situation. When even a major insurance company is caught up in what amounts to scare tactics, you know that fear is gripping an entire society.

But the science about global warming is a tangled mess. Some people, including well-respected scientists, are convinced that the data point to human-caused warming. Other people, including well-respected scientists, say nothing is happening to the climate that doesn't normally happen in the earth's fluctuating temperature cycle. There are zealots on both sides who won't listen to anyone who opposes them, and there are also reasonable people on both sides. Unfortunately, many of the reasonable voices seem drowned out, not by melting glaciers, but by fear, panic, even hatred. Muddled reporting on the issue makes it even worse.

The planet's average global temperature is increasing one degree Fahrenheit every thirty years. On average in the past, the temperature has risen by about one degree Fahrenheit per century. Over the past fifty years the increase has been twice this rate. There is a widely accepted consensus that the earth is in fact warming. It is the cause of the warming that is in question. Many scientists believe human activity, such as the burning of fossil fuels, contributes to the warming. Others say these temperature cycles are related to internal dynamics of ice accumulation and loss. In addition, changes in the tilt of the earth's axis of rotation and the elliptical, rather than circular, path of the earth's orbit may also contribute to these changes.

Global warming alarmists claim that it will cause a host of planetary disasters. We are told, for example, that sea levels will rise because of melting ice caps and glaciers, causing catastrophic flooding. Al Gore's documentary film, *An Inconvenient Truth*, shows a large part of New York City underwater as a result of sea levels rising twenty feet. But Jim McCarthy, the head of the American Academy for the Advancement of Science (AAAS) and a Harvard University professor, questions Gore's claims: "There is no reasonable climate scenario whereby this is likely to happen in the next century or two," he told us. "However, three feet of sea level rise, which is not at all out of the question for this century, would be devastating for many regions—especially with amplified storminess." It's also worth noting that it is not easy to project the exact impact of climate change upon the sea levels. For example, the UN's climate panel has downgraded their predicted sea rise between now and the year 2100 from nearly three feet to seventeen inches. That didn't get much attention, and certainly there were no sighs of relief from the alarmists. They seem too taken with their ideas to notice. We are not attempting to minimize the potential impact of a rise in sea level. We simply are concerned about the wide numeric discrepancy.

In fairness to Dr. McCarthy, he generally supports Gore's view of the environmental issues of the day. In fact, McCarthy and the thousands of scientists he represents at the AAAS believe that global warming, left unchecked, will be a major problem in the future. They declare that the overwhelming majority of scientists line up on their side. As far as global warming as a whole is concerned, the issue we have focused upon is what we can do to prevent a loss of human life and unsure, realistic, measurable results. In other words, if we spend $10 billion, what will we get?

What about the dramatic changes we are seeing in the weather? Some scientists claim that global warming will cause an increase in extreme weather events like Hurricanes Katrina, Rita, Dean, and Felix. While there is consensus that there has been an increase in tropical storm activity in the North Atlantic over the last thirty years, there has not been a corresponding increase in tropical storm activity in other regions of the world that would challenge the claim that these storms are the result of human-induced global warming.[1] A study by the National Oceanic and Atmospheric Administration (NOAA) found that linking global warming and hurricane intensity was premature.[2]

Other environmental activists warn that there will be an increase in diseases because of increased temperatures and weather-induced migrations. According to a report commissioned by the Center for Naval Analyses, "human-driven warming of the climate" will result in an increase in civil unrest globally and as a result poses risks to the security of the United States.[3] It is interesting to note that the idea of weather-induced migration is being included in the military curriculum taught at West Point.

But this present global warming scare was not the first climate panic. In the spring of 1975, *Newsweek* published an article on climate change that read, "There are ominous signs that the earth's weather patterns have begun to change dramatically and that these changes may portend a drastic decline in food production—with serious political implications for just about every nation on earth. The drop in food output could begin quite soon, perhaps only 10 years from now."[4] The article cited as evidence of radical climate change an experience that both of us can remember living through as young men. On April 4, 1974, the United States experienced the worst outbreak of tornados in U.S. history; 148 twisters touched down in 13 states. Before it was over, 330 people were dead and 5,484 were injured in a damage path covering more than 2,500 miles, evidence (at least to *Newsweek*) that radical climate change was taking place. However, the fear wasn't of global warming but of global cooling. According to many news reports, the earth was moving into another ice age. Just thirty years later, not only did the ice age not appear, but now we are told the world is on the verge of unprecedented global warming.

Back in the 1970s a pattern was taking place that is similar to the pattern of today. Scientific journals of the day were saying there would likely be warming because of greenhouse effects, sooner than the return of an ice age. But these predictions did not make headlines. Rather, people were fixated on global cooling. Similarly, all scientists nowadays don't agree on how to handle global warming. No wonder it has been difficult to create clear-cut plans of action that synchronize local, regional, and international environment agendas. In the present, as in the past, we often get a blend of media hype and personal prejudice. Unfortunately for the nation, the media seem to have a script already written, which may or may not be completely accurate.

Take, for example, the story of John Coleman, long-time meteorologist and founder of the Weather Channel. According to Coleman, the science that supports arguments favoring global warming "has been manipulated" and much of the data has been "manufactured," resulting in what he calls "bad science" that, unfortunately, passed peer review.[5] He states that natural cycles in weather are more responsible for any climate change, and that over the next two decades there is an equal chance for a cooling trend as there is for a warming trend. He also believes that once the dire predictions of some of our environmental scientists fail to occur, people will realize they have been "duped."

Other experts remain unconvinced of any major human culpability in the global warming phenomenon at all. Such a contrarian view of global warming is offered by Dennis T. Avery, an environmental economist, and S. Fred Singer, a physicist and professor from the University of Virginia. In their book *Unstoppable Global Warming—Every 1,500 Years*, they point out that the earth moves in 1,500-year cycles of significant warming and cooling. The earth warms, and then it cools, it warms again, and then it cools again. Could it be that that is the way that God designed the earth?

In a study of the media's coverage of "climate change," R. Warren Anderson and Dan Gainor examined how major media outlets covered the issue of climate change over the last one-hundred-plus years.[6] What they discovered was that there have been four climate change scares; a concern over global cooling beginning in 1895, followed by fears of global warming in 1929, only to be replaced by alarm over global cooling; now we are back to global warming. With each succeeding crisis, the call for a government solution has grown louder and louder.

Why the flip-flop in the media and among alarmists? We are not sure, except that once a sensational story runs its course, they need another.

Despite their best efforts, the global warming alarmists have yet to convince most Americans that we are facing a crisis. A *crisis* is defined as an unstable condition requiring an abrupt or decisive decision or change. It essentially moves the matter to the top of the list of public concerns, diverting limited resources away from other issues such as health care, national defense, protection against terrorism, and education. However, they do have their "solutions" waiting in the wings, and these solutions mostly involve more and greater government intervention. But with global warming, the solution is bigger than even the federal government; the solution must be global. Alarmists propose grand, sweeping, global policies that ask nations to surrender their national sovereignty. Environment zealots, like political ideologues, rarely come up with good solutions. In our opinion, and the opinion of the American public, environmental alarmists have failed to present a clear case concerning how much money must be spent to "fix" the problem.

In global warming, some people have found their life cause; unfortunately, it may lead to spiritual imbalance and even deception.

Jesus and Global Warming

The Bible gives two clear points of reference for an environmental theology. The first discourse about creation comes from Genesis, while the second can be inferred from the teaching of Christ. In the beginning, Adam was given stewardship over both the Garden of Eden, in particular, and Earth, in general. He was called to take oversight or dominion over Earth. The word *dominion (radh)* in the Hebrew means to tread down, that is, to subjugate. In the King James Version, it especially means to prevail against, reign, or rule over.[7] As we discuss the global environmental issues of our day, there is a great need for the church to take an active stewardship role. We must exercise dominion and lead the way in the caring for the earth. We cannot simply repeat the new mantra, "I do not believe in global warming," even if we don't. We have a responsibility to encourage our political leaders and scientists to give real options for bettering our stewardship of this planet God has given to us to tend and rule over.

The second Hebrew word used by the Lord to describe man's interaction with the earth is the word *subdue*. The Hebrew word here is *kabash*.[8]

It means to conquer or subjugate by force. In the King James Version of the Bible, it carries a meaning of keeping something under, subduing, or bringing into subjection. We must never forget that as the planet changes and goes through various cycles, our call to subdue the earth never changes. As a practical matter, this would mean that we should treat the matter of working with nature and the earth as someone would approach breaking a horse or taming a wild animal. Wisdom, strength, focus, and even force may be necessary to exert our will over the planet. Scientists are in the position to tell us what should be done. Theologians, however, are in the best position to tell us what should be done morally. Politicians are in the best position to determine what should be done practically. However, everyone on the planet, as well as the animals and plants, will benefit from the right things being done.

In the New Testament, Jesus Himself actually has something to say about the changes in the weather and our environment. Although He does not mention global warming directly, He does help us perhaps understand the role disruptions in our weather patterns may play in the days leading up to His return. In the twenty-first chapter of the Gospel of Luke, Jesus discusses with His disciples what is going to happen in the future—the destruction of Jerusalem, which occurs in A.D. 70, and His second coming to the earth. Jesus makes clear to them that they need to be able to discern the times by looking at the signs so they will not be deceived by what others are saying and they will not be surprised.

> And they asked him, saying, Master, but when shall these things be? and what sign will there be when these things shall come to pass? And he said, Take heed that ye be not deceived: for many shall come in my name, saying, I am Christ; and the time draweth near: go ye not therefore after them. But when ye shall hear of wars and commotions, be not terrified: for these things must first come to pass; but the end is not by and by. Then said he unto them, Nation shall rise against nation, and kingdom against kingdom: And great earthquakes shall be in divers places, and famines, and pestilences; and fearful sights and great signs shall there be from heaven. But before all these, they shall lay their hands on you, and persecute you, delivering you up to the synagogues, and into prisons, being brought before kings and rulers for my name's sake.
>
> —LUKE 21:7-12

We believe it is possible that Jesus is referring to dramatic, national weather changes in this passage. These could be related to the famines and pestilence He says will come. While we cannot state scientifically that there is a direct correlation between pestilence and famine and global warming, it is not unreasonable to see them as linked. The word *pestilence* (Greek *loimos*[9]) is a plague—literally a disease or figuratively a pest. During a recent trip to Alaska, Harry observed a major natural change in which beetles ate up miles of forest as the old natural order in that area was altered due to climate changes.

Notice that Jesus warns us that there will be "fearful sights" in the earth and "great signs" in the heavens. Amazingly, the Greek word for fear (*phobetron*) comes from a root word from which terror and terrorism come. Jesus was literally telling His disciples over two thousand years ago that there will be acts of terror preceding His second coming. In addition, according to Jesus, there will also be great signs from heaven or astrological occurrences, eclipses, falling stars, and comets.

It's possible that the End-Time signs that Jesus referred to were part of God's warning the world of His imminent return. This declaration is not meant to be fatalistic; it is meant to alert us to the fact that we are entering into "crunch time" or the last phase of the game. Professional football teams often practice something called the two-minute drill. This drill includes the plays that are reserved for the critical last two minutes of the game. When the two-minute signal is given, the best teams know what to do. From the above passage of scripture, many believers conclude that the following things should be signs of the second coming of Christ:

▸ Increased civil disturbances (v. 9)
▸ Increase in war (v. 10)
▸ Extreme weather events (v. 11)
▸ Famines (v. 11)
▸ Pestilence (v. 11)
▸ Acts of terror (v. 11)
▸ Unusual astronomical events (v. 11)

Did you notice that what Jesus warned would occur in the last days are almost identical to what some global warming theorists are saying is going to happen?

God's Warning vs. Global Warming	
Increase in civil disturbances[10]	Increase in civil disturbances and security threats[11]
Increase in war[12]	Nuclear war[13]
Extreme weather events[14]	Extreme weather events[15]
Famines[16]	Famines[17]
Pestilence[18]	Pestilence/disease[19]
Acts of terror[20]	Increase in terrorism[21]

Jesus also said there will be an increase in spiritual deception that is intended to get Christians off our game and render us ineffective when we should be running our two-minute drill. Deceived people are, by definition, not in tune with the priorities of Christ's kingdom. They put their faith in something other than God. And this is exactly what environmental alarmists ask us to do. The language they use and the policies they promote are humanistic. How many times have you heard them appeal to others to "help save the planet"? The whole premise of the statement presupposes that mankind is ultimately in charge of the fate of our planet. It springs from the same idea that we can save ourselves and that we don't need the atoning work of Christ on the cross. If the problems of pollution, the environment, and global warming are man-made, their logic goes, then the solution can be man-made too. We don't need God. If undue focus on the environment is indeed a type of spiritual deception, then its proponents are conditioning people to look to government and to the powers of man—not God—to save them.

It is disheartening to see some Christians unwittingly embrace the environmentalist agenda without looking seriously at its philosophical underpinnings. As believers in Jesus Christ we should not be fearful. Knowing that there will be efforts to deceive the church and Christians in the last days, true believers should be careful to whom they listen. John 10:27 reads, "My sheep hear my voice and I know them, and they follow me." John states in 1 John 4:18 "There is no fear in love, but perfect love casteth out fear: because fear hath torment. He that feareth is not perfect in love." David reflects on this truth in Psalm 46 when he says, "God is our refuge and strength, a very present help in trouble. Therefore we will not fear, even though the earth be removed, and though the mountains be carried into the midst of the sea; though its waters roar and be troubled, though the mountains shake with its swelling" (vv. 1–3, NKJV). No matter what happens, even if the mountains are thrown into the seas, God is our refuge and our strength, a very present help in a time of trouble. Therefore, He will not be gripped by fear. Likewise we should not be gripped by fear, nor should we act rashly because of fear.

Population Control?

Just as alarming to us as the potential subjugation of our nation's economy to a global body, and the potential spiritual deception we have just discussed, are the adjacent calls for population control as part of the global warming solution. We are concerned that human life will be devalued in order to "protect the ecosystem." As believers, we must make sure that population control is not chosen as a way of balancing out the CO_2 equation.

Population control is a loaded term that includes not only abortion, contraception, and sterilization, but also infanticide and promotion of same-sex relations. Women from China have testified before the U.S. Congress of forced abortions, as late as nine months into the pregnancy, as well as forced sterilizations because of China's population control measures.

It is hard to imagine that there are evangelical leaders who are calling for population control in response to the global warming crisis. In a speech delivered to the World Bank in May of 2006, the vice president of the National Association of Evangelicals, Rich Cizik, said, "I'd like to take on the population issue, but in my community global warming is the third rail issue. I've touched the third rail...but still have a job. And I'll still have a job after my talk here today. But population [control] is a much more dangerous issue to touch.... We need to confront population control and we can—we're not Roman Catholics, after all—but it's too hot to handle now."[22]

Before including Rev. Cizik's comments here, we verified with him that the comments were true. He responded by saying the comments were a part of a question-and-answer period and do not reflect his record in support of life. We therefore believe his comments were well intended. But that does not allay our concern that these kinds of comments could lead other evangelicals into the deception of the radical environmental movement. Some may even go as far as to fail to function as watchmen who are to protect the human life. Our concern is more than just a matter of semantics. There is nothing in Scripture to suggest that God's instruction to man to be fruitful and multiply had an expiration date that has passed. At the heart of the push for population control is an unbiblical view of children and of life. David makes clear that children are the "heritage of the LORD: and the fruit of the womb is his reward. As arrows are in the hand of a mighty man; so are children of thy youth" (Ps. 127:3–4). Rather than being a drain on our limited resources, children represent the potential of the future. While we applaud Richard Cizik's zeal and commitment to trumpet his message to the nations, we think that each believer must be concerned about his focus and priorities. We, the evangelical community, have needed Richard Cizik's input to wake us up. But now we need to continue to engage Cizik and other Christian environmentalists in a closed-door discussion about the practical next steps that this message should take.

The present call for population control by secular environmental activists is not unlike the warnings sounded by Thomas Malthus in 1798, who said the world's growing population was growing exponentially while the earth's food supply could at best be increased only arithmetically. According to Malthus, the population would soon overtax the planet's ability to sustain the human race. He argued for policies that would result in a decreased population among the poor classes. He warned that if both private and public policies to limit population were not enacted and wars did not decrease the population, disease and famine would. He obviously underestimated the power of "witty inventions" (Prov. 8:12) that fueled the Industrial Revolution and increased the average yield per acre.

Beyond the devaluing of children, population control says we have all we are ever going to have, and we know all we are ever going to know, so we must therefore allocate what we do have so we don't run out. There is nothing in history that suggests that to be true of the world God created for us.

A similar warning was sounded in 1968. Stanford University professor Paul R. Ehrlich, in his book *The Population Bomb*, predicted millions of people would die of starvation in the 1970s and 1980s without population control.[23] The hysteria created by Ehrlich paved the way for the United Nation's Population Fund, which was established in 1969. Ehrlich believed that those nations who refused to institute his population controls were willing to let citizens of those nations starve to death. He also believed that Indian men who had more than three children should be sterilized by force.[24] Fortunately for us, Ehrlich was not a prophet. Virtually nothing he wrote came to pass.

Global population control became a major focus of the United Nations as they projected the planet to be overrun with 11.5 billion people. The UN now admits that the human race that now stands at 6.6 billion people will fall far short of their projections and peak at 8.5 billion. Demographers say that once the population peaks, it will start a long-term decline because of falling birth rates.

Even though the fertility rate is declining across the board in Western nations, it is the most Christian nations that have the highest birth rates. Ireland has the highest fertility rate among the European Union countries with a rate of 1.86 births per average woman. The United States stands out among the industrialized nations with a fertility rate of 2.1 children per female, a rate that is declining but is still higher than most. The U.S. rate is higher in part because of religious conservatives who have a higher-than-average fertility rate.[25]

Christian conservatives, however, are not keeping pace with Muslims, who have the highest fertility rates. For instance, Muslims in Europe have a fertility rate that is three times higher than non-Muslims, leading some like Islam scholar Bernard Lewis to predict Europe will have Muslim majorities by the end of the twenty-first century at the latest.

We are beginning to see the long-term consequences on the horizon for seeing children as the consumers of limited resources rather than a reward and heritage from Lord.

The Bible and the Environment

Unfortunately, a number of religious leaders have joined the alarmist crusade and are attempting to make the environment the most important issue in the church. In some ways they are correct in pushing for the church to get involved. In other ways, many of them are like the young prophet who ran to King David before he heard the message. (See 2 Samuel 18:22–28.) They have zeal and a desire to change things, but they do not have the message that the church needs at this time. There has to be a clear, proven approach to protecting the environment and forestalling the damages of global warming.

We must be positive and deliberate in our stewardship of this planet, not just to fulfill God's mandate to us, but so we can maintain the moral high ground in our society. While environmental issues remain a low priority for most evangelicals, it is an issue of increasing interest among young people, evangelicals included. Young people see stewardship of the environment as a basic responsibility of our civic leaders. If we are reactionary or disdainful toward those on the other side of us on this issue, we risk alienating the next generation. It is time for the church to add their voice to the discussion of environmental issues without adopting the at times godless tactics, agenda, and philosophy of the more extreme alarmists. In shaping our future environmental agenda, we will need to hear from Richard Cizik, Jim Ball, Carl Betsner, and a host of other committed Christians. We believe we can have a strong, balanced, reasonable agenda that will gain far more support from Americans than the alarm-based agenda now being offered.

The Bible says, "The heavens declare the glory of God" (Ps. 19:1). In other words, nature and science belong to God. They reveal His glory. They are an extension of Him. They do not compete with His current work in the earth. Rather, science completes the revelation of God—it does not compete. In fact, some of the most devout Christians we have ever met have been born-again scientists. We want to make it perfectly clear that we are proscience. Scientists are not the enemy of the conservative community on the issue of the environment.

Our biggest challenge is to set forth clear steps of action that are in the best interests of our nation and the world. We would both describe ourselves as conservationists, and here we believe there is much common ground for Christians and all Americans to stand on even if we disagree on other aspects of the debate. While we've made great progress in the last twenty-five years of cleaning up our air and water, everyone can agree that we can still do more. Every day people such as asthma sufferers can attest to the fact that automobile emissions, industrial waste, and factory fumes impact people's health. The same goes for polluted water sources.

There are other policies we can promote as well. We have all heard the exhortations from civic leaders to use energy more efficiently by running the air conditioning less, keeping our water heaters at lower temperatures, planting trees to give cooling shade, and buying cars that get good gas mileage. As mundane as this sounds, these things do make a difference. It is interesting to note that because of the state's standards program on conservation and energy reduction, California's per capita electricity consumption has not increased since 1978. The rest of the country has increased 50 percent on average.[26] This has not diminished the standard of living for Californians, but it has helped the environment.

Here are some other basics. Don't litter. It sounds simplistic, but litter remains a serious problem. Roadside litter alone costs an estimated $115 million a year to remove. We can all conserve electricity by turning off lights when they are not in use. Reduce the number of miles you drive by better planning of your commute and/or errands. Consider carpooling or taking public transportation if it is available. In Washington DC you can *slug*. Slugging is a unique form of commuting. If you don't have a car or someone to carpool with, you simply stand in a designated area and a total stranger in need of another person or two to qualify for the high-occupancy lane (HOV) will pick you up. Slugging can certainly make for some interesting rides!

We also believe the church can and should provide leadership on this issue because it affects national security. The war in Iraq and our challenge with global terrorism make America more vulnerable because of our dependence upon foreign oil. This must be overcome. We have been "tithing to terror," as one scientist put it, by allowing nearly 60 percent of our oil to come from foreign sources. Reducing consumption and diversifying sources will simultaneously increase national security and help appease the cry of environmentalists. Expanded nuclear power and more efficient use of the present facilities should be part of this comprehensive energy strategy. For instance, we can increase the effectiveness of the output of our existing nuclear power plants by using heated water that comes from these reactors, just as European nations do, rather than discharging it. This would reduce our use of less efficient fossil fuels.

We should also remind people that until we get a clearer, measurable game plan for reducing global warming, we should avoid spending huge amounts of money on unproven solutions. Those dollars could go toward other global problems for which we have more immediate answers, such as sickness and poverty. Every dollar we spend on a perhaps chimerical crusade to decrease global temperature is a dollar we can't spend helping the poor or curing disease. Also, as the scientific research gets better, it may lead us to a two-prong solution that will eliminate some CO_2 emissions while reducing the impact of an ever-warming globe.

Dr. Calvin Beisner, in *A Call to Truth, Prudence and Protection of the Poor: An Evangelical Response to Global Warming*, points out that it would be more cost effective to mitigate the projected effects of global warming on the poor than to spend trillions to reduce carbon emissions.[27] For instance, investing additional dollars to assist developing countries in solving agricultural problems in projected drought areas could have a much greater impact upon hunger than a slight reduction in CO_2 emissions. Coastal areas vulnerable to flooding, if sea levels rise, could be protected by sea walls or levees at a fraction of the costs of compliance with the Kyoto Protocol. The Kyoto Protocol is a part of a United Nations treaty addressing climate change that was crafted in 1997 in Kyoto, Japan. The industrialized nations that are party to the Kyoto Protocol are required to reduce carbon dioxide emissions and five other greenhouse gases by varying degrees before the year 2012. As of today, over 172 countries have ratified this protocol.

Shortly after taking office, President George W. Bush said the United States would not participate in the treaty, and he refused to send it to the U.S. Senate for ratification. President Bush cited the negative economic impact that U.S. compliance with the international treaty would have on the country. If the United States were to ratify the protocol, in order to achieve the mandates under this UN treaty, some have estimated that the United States would have to reduce its present energy use by as much as one-third. Such a reduction in energy use would result in an estimated decline in the Gross Nation Product (GNP) of 1 to 4 percent. For example, Harry visited the Alaskan village of Shishmaref, located on Sarichef Island in the Chukchi Sea just north of the Bering Strait, that will be destroyed within the next decade due to rising temperatures, reduction in sea ice, and thawing of permafrost along the coast. This problem is coming on too quickly for current CO_2 emissions plans to work. Alaskan officials will have to decide how to relocate the natives of this Eskimo settlement who have been there for four thousand years.

As Bible-believing Christians, we should not be gripped or motivated by fear of what the future may hold. We should view the future with optimism, not pessimism. That does not mean that we deny reality; rather, we see these great challenges of our day as an opportunity for God to unlock yet further secrets of His magnificent creation. We should see the challenges of stewardship of this planet as opportunities for other witty inventions that will allow us to pollute less, use less energy, and keep our environment cleaner and healthier.

As Christians we have the opportunity to be a voice of calm in the midst of crisis, whether real or perceived. With the Bible as our guide, we can provide the balanced solution that the world needs on global warming and other environmental ills. The Bible calls us to be good stewards of what

God has given us to inhabit, not to worship the creation but to use our ingenuity to manage it in a way that honor's God's original intentions.

Prayer Points

▸ Thank God for the blessing of the beautiful earth where we live. Praise Him for His creative genius to order the seasons and the times of man. Give thanks for the bounty we have in America because of His faithfulness and goodness (Job 5:10).

▸ Ask forgiveness that the church has not consistently been a faithful steward in caring for God's creation. Pray that the church would have a proper balance between honoring the Creator and caring for His creation (Job 35:11).

▸ Pray that scientists and the church would grow a strong bond to speak to the nation with intelligence and wisdom in terms of our environment. Ask that the Lord would open the ears of leaders in our government to promote public policy that will benefit human life, the family, our economy, and the environment simultaneously.

Conclusion

TAKING THE LAND

History fails to record a single precedent in which nations subject to moral decay have not passed into political and economic decline.

There has been either a spiritual awakening to overcome the moral lapse, or a progressive deterioration leading to ultimate national disaster.

—GENERAL DOUGLAS MACARTHUR
SUPREME COMMANDER OF THE ALLIED FORCES IN THE PACIFIC

On a warm autumn day in the fall of 1999 on the campus of St. John's College, the nation's third-oldest college, a four-hundred-year-old tulip poplar tree was cut down. The tree, which had succumbed to years of disease and decay, was dealt a final blow by the winds of Hurricane Floyd. Experts had examined the old tree and declared it was in danger of collapsing. Because it posed a safety hazard, it had to be cut down.

But this was not just any old tree; it was the last of the Liberty Trees, the trees that served as meeting places for the local chapters of the Sons of Liberty throughout the thirteen original colonies. It was under trees like this one in Boston that Samuel Adams, the "father of the revolution," the "last of the great Puritans," and eventual governor of Massachusetts, planned events like the Boston Tea Party that led to the War of Independence. A bell was tolled thirteen times as this tree, a significant historical reminder of how our nation was founded, became a forgotten object of the past.

Like the fate of that old tree, it is not only possible but also likely that the Christian values upon which our country was founded and that led to its prosperity will be laid to rest by this generation. Yet many Christians wonder why they should be involved in the defining public policy debates of our day, debates that include the value of life and the fundamental definitions of marriage and family. Lately there has been a move among some well-meaning Christians and their leaders to abandon the public arena altogether. They say that the church has been corrupted by a desire for power and has been used by those who see the faithful as a stepping-stone to higher office. This may be true to a certain degree, but is it a good reason to head for the exit doors?

Let us answer that question with another question: What kind of government do you want? Do you want honest, efficient government under which there is security for private property, life, and personal freedom? Our nation's first president, George Washington, in his farewell address to the nation in 1796 said such government cannot be maintained without morality and religion, what he called the "great pillars of human happiness." Was he speaking of a state-sponsored church? Certainly not. Such an arrangement, where the church is under the influence of the government, is bad for both bodies. It corrupts the church's calling as a moral check and balance on the direction of that government. This concern for church independence gave rise to the First Amendment to the Constitution, which says, "Congress shall make no law respecting an establishment of religion, or prohibiting the free exercise thereof; or abridging the freedom of speech, or of the press; or the right of the people peaceably to assemble, and to petition the Government for a redress of grievances."

If there is no state church or Office of Public Morality within government, how then do we preserve these "great pillars of human happiness" that George Washington spoke of? It is through the character, influence, and actions of those who serve in government. Proverbs 29:2 says, "When the righteous are in authority, the people rejoice; but when the wicked beareth rule, the people mourn." The founder of Pennsylvania, William Penn, described it this way: "Governments, like clocks, go from the motion men give them: and as governments are made and moved by men, so by them they are ruined too. Wherefore governments rather depend upon men than men upon governments. Let men be good, and the government cannot be bad; if it be ill, they will cure it. But, if men be bad, let the government be never so good, they will endeavor to warp and spoil it to their turn."[1]

Very simply, our government reflects the people who serve in it. Transformed people are the only people who can transform nations. If you want to change the character of government, you must change the characters in it!

This means that we must work hard at getting Christians and others who share our values and worldview elected to office regardless of party affiliation. Our founders did not envision a day when non-Christians would lead our land. Fortunately, the entire New Testament was written during a period in which Christians were a minority faith. Many researchers have lamented about the "post-Christian" style that America exhibits today. Yet, the Scriptures give us clear guidelines on how to operate in this kind of environment.

Government Is of God

Christians must realize that God has ordained and sanctioned civil government. It is part of His plan. He specifically ordained four institutions of authority for this earth. The first and most basic is self-government (Gen. 2:16–17; 4:7; 1 Pet. 1:15–16). Unless individuals govern their own conduct, there is little hope for civil order. For most of our nation's history, basic standards of conduct came from the Bible.

The second institution is the family (Gen. 1:26–28; 2:24; 3:16; Eph. 6:1–4). The third is civil government (Gen. 9:5–6), and the fourth is the church (Acts 2). Think of it like a structure with self-government as the foundation, and the family, the church, and civil government as the three supporting pillars that uphold a civil society. For society to be properly balanced, all three must bear their proper load.

Our point is that God has said government is necessary and we are to be subject to it (Rom. 13:1). Government is God's idea. But if we want a government that honors God and protects our freedoms, then we have to have a government that is made up of people who honor God and value freedom. It's that simple.

There Is Right and Wrong

The most frequent objection we hear from opponents of Christianity who fear the presence of believers in government is, "What right do you have to impose your morals on us?" Tony likes to tell them, "The same right you have to impose your lack of morals on us." Someone's values will always be reflected in public policy. Almost every government policy decision is a value judgment. In this postmodern world, where moral relativism is the philosophy of choice, these value judgments are often based on the conditions of the moment rather than objective, transcendent, biblical truth. This is where the two sides diverge. As Bible-believing Christians we believe there is absolute truth, a view, incidentally, that was held by all Christians and many Americans until the turn of the twentieth century. This view, as we discussed earlier, holds that the Bible is the inspired and infallible Word of God even when it speaks to the topics of history or the cosmos. A Christian worldview says that there is a personal God who is directly involved in the activities of man and who authoritatively communicates to man through His Word and the Holy Spirit.

Shortly after the Civil War, the Protestant church began to divide over this belief in a literal interpretation of Scripture. Liberals began to move away from Scripture as the sole authority in order to accommodate "rational truth," which they saw as incompatible with the Bible.[2] These liberals embraced the "essence of Christianity" rather than the inerrancy of Scripture so they could synthesize their Christian thought with so-called scientific findings of the day, most notably Darwinism and social Darwinism. Incidentally, the same is true today for those who are embracing the latest scientific findings on issues like global warming and are now clamoring for drastic government actions to solve the "crisis."

One of the preeminent voices to emerge in defense of absolute truth shortly after the turn of the century was a Princeton Theological Seminary professor and Presbyterian minister, J. Grescham Machen. Machen, who would later lead a split within the Presbyterian church over the rejection of biblical orthodoxy, wrote in 1923 what became the definitive work for Bible-believing Christians in their battle with liberalism. It was titled *Christianity and Liberalism*. Machen said that liberalism was not only theologically wrong but was not connected at all to true Christianity. "What the liberal theologian has retained after abandoning to the enemy one Christian doctrine after another is not Christianity at all, but a religion which is so entirely different from Christianity as to belong in a different category."[3] In Machen's description the argument was no longer between two views of evangelicalism, conservative and liberal, but rather a conflict between two religions. Liberalism is "a type of faith and practice that is anti-Christian to the core," Machen wrote.[4]

What has transpired in the mainline Methodist, Presbyterian, and Episcopalian denominations over the last one hundred years gives us clear evidence of the results of this abandonment of absolute truth. These mainline denominations have shrunk in size and are no longer debating the inerrancy of Scripture but issues such as the ordination of homosexuals. As we look at their decline, we can only wonder what will be next for a church or a society that has rejected absolute truth.

Drifting From Orthodoxy

In spite of this stark example of what happens to churches and movements that untether themselves from absolute truth, there is a similar division occurring within evangelical ranks today. Some believers and their churches are drifting from Scripture to the call of the cultural sirens. The present divide among evangelicals that the media frequently point to as "evidence" of the declining influence of the conservative Christian movement is not new. Christian theologian Francis Schaeffer in his last work before his death in 1984, *The Great Evangelical Disaster*, spoke to the cause of this divide, and it was the same as it is today—a rejection of absolute truth. Schaeffer chastised those who had compromised their view of Scripture and had accommodated the culture in the name of "love."

Unfortunately, a growing number of Christians are being influenced more by the popular culture than Scripture in terms of their worldview. Even younger evangelicals, who tend to track conservatively on most core social issues, do not consistently view the world from a biblical perspective. In late 2003, Christian sociologist and pollster George Barna conducted a fairly extensive poll on the prevalence of a "biblical or Christian worldview" in the United States. He defined biblical worldview as being based upon a foundation of eight beliefs:

1. Absolute moral truths exist.
2. The Bible defines these absolute moral truths.
3. Jesus Christ lived a sinless life during His ministry on the earth.
4. God created the universe and continues to rule it today. He is omnipotent and omniscient.
5. Salvation is a gift from God. It cannot be earned through good works or behavior.

6. Satan is a real living entity.
7. Christians have an obligation to share the gospel with the unsaved.
8. The Bible is accurate in all of its teachings.

What did he find?

▸ Only 4 percent of the total population of American adults has a biblical worldview.
▸ Nine percent of born-again Christians have a biblical worldview.
▸ Seven percent of Protestants, including those attending conservative, mainline, and liberal churches, have a biblical worldview.
▸ Two percent of adults who attend mainline churches have a biblical worldview.
▸ Fewer than 0.5 percent of persons who attend Roman Catholic churches have a biblical worldview.

The churches that are most effective in teaching a biblical worldview to their membership are:

▸ Nondenominational churches, mostly fundamentalist congregations; 13 percent of their membership holds a biblical worldview.
▸ Pentecostal churches: 10 percent of the membership.
▸ Baptist churches: 8 percent of the membership.[5]

Loving Confrontation

In light of these dispiriting statistics, we must get back to emphasizing God's truth and God's love. Schaeffer pointed out that absolute truth requires confrontation. One cannot simultaneously accommodate the culture and stand for truth. But he also challenged those who defend truth to simultaneously display God's love. If there is only one concept that you grasp in this entire book, we hope it is this: We must defend truth, but we must defend it in love. As Bible-believing Christians, we are instructed to speak the truth but to speak it in love (Eph. 4:15).

An Old Testament example of this confrontation is found in Numbers 25 where Phinehas, the grandson of Aaron, confronted a man of Israel who was flaunting his sin before the people. This confrontation took place before a backdrop of some twenty-four thousand people who died from a plague that had broken out as a result of their spiritual and sexual sin. Phinehas, a priest, could have easily justified looking the other way, thinking that someone else would confront the problem. In the meantime the plague threatened to take more lives. Phinehas chose to act with the "zeal" of the Lord. This means he acted out of regard for God's holiness and love. Had he not acted, God's truth would have continued to be mocked and the people would have continued to die. It is interesting that Phinehas's reward for this act of confrontation was a "covenant of peace." This shows us a truth that is uncomfortable for some: confrontation, not conflict resolution, is the surest path that leads to peace and unity.

Some people will no doubt read this section in an attempt to exploit something that we say or level a charge of "hate speech" against us, so let us acknowledge again that the Old Testament is a shadow of the New Testament. Where the Old Testament speaks to the physical, the New Testament speaks to the spiritual. A parallel to Phinehas today would be a pastor who not only preaches the truth as it pertains to the issues of our day—like abortion, embryonic stem cell research, sexual immorality, or state-sponsored gambling that preys upon the poor—but also confronts the public policies that promote behavior that is individually and corporately destructive.

Phinehas's actions show us the two essential, inseparable characteristics of God: His holiness and His love. It is His holiness that points us to His love (Rom. 7:7). The challenge for us as Christians is to simultaneously display truth and love as God does. If we veer toward the truth and leave love behind, we become judgmental and hinder the redemptive work of God's love. Likewise, if we head toward love, avoiding truth, we will cause people to miss the depth and reality of God's eternal love. It may seem easier to embrace one or the other—truth or love—as a guidepost, but then we will not reflect the true nature of God to the world. The challenge for us is to hold to His truth and His love simultaneously, confronting that which is wrong, but confronting it in a redemptive way.

God's purpose and therefore our purpose is not to catch people doing wrong, but to defend the truth, allowing it to reveal what is wrong so that we all are drawn to the forgiveness that is found in God's love. The confrontation that truth requires is not pleasant, nor does it make you popular. You will be accused of being judgmental, but defending absolute truth is not judging; it is holding up a standard by which people must judge themselves or ultimately be judged by God.

But be warned: if you actually enjoy the confrontation that comes from defending the truth, then you may have lost your balance and strayed from God's love into unholy judgmentalism. The opposite is true as well. If nothing in society today stirs you to confrontation because you are concerned it might offend someone, you may have lost your grip on the truth.

Strength in Unity

The key to the religious Right's success has been its unity, based in the understanding that absolute truth exists and that we can know it through both God's general and specific revelations. Because conservative Christians acknowledge the Bible as the divinely inspired and infallible Word of God, they remain unified not only on the basic tenets of the Christian faith but also on most of today's public policy issues. That's not to say there are no disagreements or disputes over priorities and methods, but generally speaking, the authority of the Bible keeps us in a place of unity, or at least civility, on most issues.

Consider the opposite scenario. The World Council of Churches, which claims to represent some 550 million Christians in over 100 countries, is not a force in the shaping of public policy, though its size and budget dictate that it should be. Their problem is simple: they lack unity. They are able to coalesce only around ill-defined yet noble issues such as stopping violence, ending poverty, and addressing the AIDS epidemic in Africa. But when it comes to agreeing on specifics, they fragment. It's a perfect picture of how moral relativism leads to disunity.

Bible-believing Christians, on the other hand, are able to find and remain on common ground because they believe in right and wrong, and they view God's Word as the final authority. They stand unified on such issues as the sanctity of life, the preservation of marriage, the importance of the traditional family, and a personal and corporate responsibility to help those in need and be hands-on in alleviating suffering. More than any other factor or characteristic, the issue of absolute truth provides the dividing line on today's religious and political landscape.

Stop, Look, and Listen

When Tony was about seven years old, he attended a bicycle and pedestrian safety course during the summer. The course covered the traffic laws and safety rules using songs and cute phrases. One of the phrases he learned, and which many of us remember to this day, was "Stop, Look, and Listen." This is what you are supposed to do before crossing a railroad track.

This simple slogan is also helpful for Christians as we seek to make godly decisions. Too often we rush into making decisions or value judgments without pausing to consider what is right. We should stop and pray and ask for guidance on every personal or policy decision we make, realizing that no issue we face is beyond the wisdom or direction of God. We should look to see what the Bible has to say about the matter that is before us. If there are no direct statements, we should look for general principles that may apply. If there is no clear answer still, we must listen to what the Holy Spirit may say through an overlooked scripture or through godly counsel.

You may look around and think, "There are not very many of us. How can we make a difference?" Here's how:

The Three Ps

Pray

As we have worked together over the last few years in defense of biblical marriage and to protect the rights of pastors to preach the whole Word of God, the challenges facing this country have never been clearer. While these matters have manifested themselves in the public policy arena, at their core they are spiritual problems. Almost every issue we are dealing with today is either the product or the symptom of a spiritual ill. First and foremost we need to pray for a revival in the church and an awakening that would turn this nation around. We cannot approach public policy, or any other challenge in life, the same way the world does. Paul said in 2 Corinthians 10:3 that "though we walk in the flesh, we do not war according to the flesh: (For the weapons of our warfare are not carnal, but mighty through God for the pulling down of strong holds;)." Therefore we must use our spiritual weapons and pray.

Nehemiah is a great Old Testament example of someone who worked for public policy change. When Nehemiah of the Old Testament was confronted with the dire situation his countrymen faced in Jerusalem, his first reaction (after grief) was to pray. Do you pray? Do you really pray? Are you emotionally gripped by what you see happening in the world around you? Are you driven to your knees in prayer before the almighty God? We have to go beyond checklist prayers. It's time to make heartfelt, passionate prayer a priority every day. Men must also begin to pray. We are grateful for the prayer warriors, many of them women, who have sustained the church through the generations, but the challenges of today require the rest of us, and men in particular, to get serious about prayer.

We challenge you to make prayer a priority in your life. Begin to not only pray for your family, but also begin to intercede for your local church and especially your pastor. Begin to pray for your community. If it is experiencing a problem with rampant drug activity or other types of criminal activity, make it a matter of prayer. Maybe there is a visible problem with homelessness in your town—begin to pray about it. It could be something in your local school or some other need. Be sensitive to the needs of your community and begin to pray. Pray also for our nation and the mounting issues we face as a country. If you need prayer resources, the organization that Tony heads, the Family Research Council, has a prayer team that provides a weekly prayer guide, which can be found at http://www.frc.org. In addition, Harry's organization, the High Impact Leadership Coalition, will also provide you with frequent email alerts which can be found at http://thetruthinblackandwhite.org. Prayer is the essential first step, but it is just the first step toward changing your world.

Prepare

Nehemiah prayed when he was confronted with the ongoing devastation of Jerusalem, but he did not stop with prayer. As he prayed for many days, no doubt God began to speak to him and give him a plan. Four months passed between when he received the discouraging news from Jerusalem and the opportunity to speak to King Artaxerxes was given. When the opportunity came, he was ready with a plan.

As we pray we need to listen to the Holy Spirit and prepare as we are directed. We hope this doesn't scare you, and it shouldn't, but when you begin to pray about a situation in your community or your city, the answer or the solution you receive to your prayers may involve you. Nehemiah probably was not looking for something else to do, but as he prayed, it became clear that he was to do more than just pray. He was to prepare for the opportunity to participate in the solution to the problem.

Participate

Like us, Christians have heard many times the words "I'll pray for you!" Those are often comforting words, but when you are trying to enlist the support and assistance of other Christians in the effort to impact your community, those can be discouraging words. Why? Because some people believe all we need to do is pray. James made clear that such faith is dead; it must be accompanied by action (James 2:20).

Nehemiah prayed; then he prepared and participated in solving the problem. Don't just curse the darkness—turn on the light! This is where the instructions given by James gain traction. If we are going to change the world, it is going to require our hands-on involvement. This could be as simple as writing a letter to your senator or making a phone call to your congressman. It could be spearheading a community impact team in your church so that the people in your church are kept informed of what is happening locally and nationally on the key issues of the day. Once again, FRC is a great resource in this area and has guidance available at www.frc.org.

It even could be that your path takes a similar course to Tony's, when he was praying for his home state of Louisiana and about the increased influence of decriminalized gambling in the mid-1990s and he was stirred to run for public office. We must be willing to take this third critical step of participation; if not, our prayers and even our preparation will leave us short of changing anything.

Pick up the newspaper or turn on the television on any given day, and the headlines will show the signs of moral and social decay. We are at the fork in the historical road of nations that General MacArthur described in the opening quote of this conclusion. We can either take the path toward a spiritual awakening that will not only touch our churches but also reform our nation's policies, or we will veer left and take the path littered with once great nations.

It's ours to decide.

Notes

Introduction—Is the Religious Right Really Dead?

1. J. D. Hunter, *Evangelicalism: The Coming Generation* (Chicago: The University of Chicago, 1987).

2. UPI, "Views of the Religious Right Are Assailed by Carter," *New York Times*, June 1, 1981, http://query.nytimes.com/gst/fullpage.html?res=980CE7D61538F932A35755C0A 967948260 (accessed November 13, 2007).

3. Jimmy Carter, *Our Endangered Values: America's Moral Crisis* (New York: Simon and Schuster, 2006).

4. E. J. Dionne Jr., "The Bloom Is Off the Religious Right," *Washington Post*, November 30, 1990, http://www.highbeam.com/doc/1P2-1161336.html (accessed November 13, 2007).

5. Michael Weisskopf, "Energized by Pulpit or Passion, the Public Is Calling," *Washington Post*, February 1, 1993, http://pqasb.pqarchiver.com/washingtonpost/access/72107934 .html?dids=72107934:72107934&FMT=ABS&FMTS=ABS:FT&date=Feb+1%2C+1993 &author=MichaelWeisskopf&pub=The+Washington+Post+(pre-1997+Fulltext)&edition =&startpage=A.01&desc=Energized+by+Pulpit+or+Passion%2C+the+Public+Is+Calling (accessed November 13, 2007).

6. Gustav Niebuhr, "G.O.P. Candidates Divide Religious Right," *New York Times*, January 19, 1996, http://query.nytimes.com/gst/fullpage.html?res=9907EFDE1E39F93AA25752C0 A960958260 (accessed November 27, 2007).

7. Alexandra Alter, "Religious Right at Political Crossroads," *Miami Herald*, May 8, 2007, viewed at http://pewforum.org/news/display.php?NewsID=13422 (accessed November 13, 2007).

8. David D. Kirkpatrick, "Evangelical Crackup," *New York Times Magazine*, October 28, 2007, http://www.nytimes.com/2007/10/28/magazine/28Evangelicals-t.html (accessed November 27, 2007).

9. Ann Coulter, *Godless: The Church of Liberalism* (New York: Three Rivers Press, 2007).

Chapter 1—Who Is the Religious Right Anyway?

1. The Barna Research Group, "Catholic Vote May Tip the Scales for Bush," http://www .barna.org/FlexPage.aspx?Page=BarnaUpdate&BarnaUpdateID=171 (accessed November 13, 2007).

2. Frances Fitzgerald, "The Evangelical Surprise," *The New York Review of Books*, vol. 54, no. 7, April 26, 2007, http://www.nybooks.com/articles/20131 (accessed November 13, 2007).

3. The Pew Research Center, "The Voters Liked Campaign 2004, but Too Much 'Mud-Slinging,'" November 11, 2004, http://people-press.org/reports/display.php3?ReportID =233 (accessed November 13, 2007).

4. Ibid.

5. Noah Feldman, *Divided by God* (New York: Farrar, Straus and Giroux, 2005).

6. Samuel P. Huntington, *Who Are We?* (New York: Simon and Schuster, 2005).

7. Frank Newport, "One-Third of Americans Believe the Bible Is Literally True," Gallup News Service, May 25, 2007, http://www.gallup.com/poll/27682/OneThird-Americans-Believe-Bible-Literally-True.aspx (accessed November 13, 2007).

8. Huntington, *Who Are We?*

9. Martin Tolchin, "Amendment Drive on School Prayer Loses Senate Vote," *New York Times*, March 21, 1984, http://select.nytimes.com/gst/abstract.html?res=F40816F63B5D0 C728EDDAA0894DC484D81&n=Top/Reference/Times%20Topics/People/W/Weicker,%20 Lowell%20P.%20Jr. (accessed November 13, 2007).

10. Bryan Ott, "School Prayer: Teen Support Hinges on Type," Gallup.com, July 26, 2005, http://www.galluppoll.com/content/?ci=17494 (accessed November 13, 2007).

11. Alan Sears and Craig Osten, *The ACLU vs. America: Exposing the Agenda to Redefine Moral Values* (Nashville, TN: B&H Publishing Group, 2005).

12. YouthWorkers.net, "United in Prayer," October 5, 2007, http://www.youthworkers .net/PDF/syatp2007_2.pdf (accessed November 13, 2007).

13. SYATP.com, "See You at the Pole History," http://www.syatp.com/info/history/index .html (accessed November 13, 2007).

14. Ibid.

15. SYATP.com, "See You at the Pole is September 26, 2007," Press Release, http://www .syatp.com/media/journalists/pressrel/index.html (accessed November 13, 2007).

16. Scott S. Greenberger, "Gay-Marriage Ruling Pushed Voters, Mobilized Bush, Left Kerry Wary," *Boston Globe*, November 7, 2004, B1, http://www.boston.com/news/specials/ gay_marriage/articles/2004/11/07/gay_marriage_ruling_pushed_voters/ (accessed November 13, 2007).

17. Gregg Sangillo, "GOP and Blacks: An Inch at a Time," *National Journal*, January 1, 2005, as quoted in Robert P. Jones, PhD, and Dan Cox, "African Americans and the Progressive Movement: A Background Report for Strategic Communications," Center for American Values in Public Life, April 2006, http://media.pfaw.org/pdf/cav/aareport.pdf (accessed November 13, 2007).

18. Martin C. Evans, "Gay Marriage Gained Bush Black Votes," NewsDay.com, November 14, 2004, http://www.edisonresearch.com/home/archives/Newsday11-14-2004.pdf (accessed November 13, 2007).

19. Harry Jackson, "Black Power: the New Conservative Stronghold—Part 2," Townhall.com, November 27, 2006, http://www.townhall.com/Columnists/ HarryRJacksonJr/2006/11/27/black_power_the_new_conservative_stronghold_--_part_ 2# (accessed November 13, 2007).

20. Tony Harris, "The Soul Factory," CNN.com, October 22, 2006, http://www.cnn .com/video/#/video/us/2006/10/22/harris.soul.factory.cnn?iref=videosearch (accessed November 13, 2007).

21. Juan Williams, *Enough* (New York: Three Rivers Press, 2007).

22. Max Blumenthal, "Justice Sunday Preachers," *The Nation*, April 26, 2005, http:// www.thenation.com/doc/20050509/Blumenthal (accessed November 13, 2007).

23. Kevin Phillips, *American Theocracy* (New York: Penguin, 2007).

24. Alan Brinkley, "Clear and Present Dangers," *New York Times*, March 19, 2006, http://www.nytimes.com/2006/03/19/books/review/19brink.html?pagewanted=all (accessed November 13, 2007).

25. *The View*, September 12, 2006.

26. David Kuo, *Tempting Faith* (Washington DC: Free Press, 2006).

27. Luis Lugo and Scott Keeter, "Election 2004: Religion and Politics," August 25, 2004, http://www.washingtonpost.com/wp-dyn/articles/A29588-2004Aug24.html (accessed

December 28, 2007).

28. Scott Sonner, "Dean Urges Dems to Court Evangelical Christians," Associated Press, June 11, 2007, http://www.sfgate.com/cgi-bin/article.cgi?f=/n/a/2007/06/11/politics/p211100D09.DTL&type=politics (accessed November 13, 2007).

29. Associated Press, "Religion and Politics Go Hand-in-Hand in 2008 US Presidential Campaign," WorldWide Religious News, June 1, 2007, http://wwrn.org/article.php?idd=25247 (accessed November 13, 2007).

30. Audrey Barrick, "How Does the Faith of Republicans, Democrats Measure Up?" ChristianPost.com, March 6, 2007, http://www.christianpost.com/article/20070306/26175_How_does_the_faith_of_Republicans_Democrats_measure_up%3F.htm (accessed January 16, 2008).

31. Dan Cox, "Young White Evangelicals: Less Republican, Still Conservative," Pew Research Center, September 28, 2007, http://pewresearch.org/pubs/605/young-white-evangelicalsless-republican-still-conservative (accessed November 13, 2007).

32. Ibid.

33. Ibid.

Chapter 4—Core Value #1: The Value of Life (Part 2)

1. Shana Schutte, "Focus Celebrates Option Ultrasound Success," Heartlink, http://www.heartlink.org/OUP/A000000422.cfm (accessed November 14, 2007).

2. AbortionBreastCancer.com, "Medical Groups Recognizing Link," http://www.abortionbreastcancer.com/medicalgroups/index.htm (accessed November 28, 2007).

3. Dr. Jamie Love, "The Cloning of Dolly," November 27, 1997, http://www.synapses.co.uk/science/clone.html (accessed November 28, 2007).

4. Associated Press, "Embryo Rescued After Hurricane Katrina Born," FOXNews.com, January 16, 2007, http://www.foxnews.com/story/0,2933,243885,00.html (accessed November 14, 2007).

5. Rick Weiss, "400,000 Human Embryos Frozen in U.S.," Washington Post, May 8, 2003, http://www.washingtonpost.com/ac2/wp-dyn/A27495-2003May7? (accessed November 14, 2007).

6. National Institute of Health, "The Human Embryonic Stem Cell and the Human Embryonic Germ Cell," Stem Cell Information, http://stemcells.nih.gov/info/scireport/chapter3.asp (accessed November 14, 2007).

7. Stem Cell Research Enhancement Act, Susan B. Anthony List, http://www.sba-list.org/legislation.aspx?page=2leg (accessed November 14, 2007).

8. Cord Blood Registry, "Diseases Treated With Stem Cells," Cord Blood Registry, http://www.cordblood.com/cord_blood_banking_with_cbr/banking/diseases_treated.asp (accessed November 14, 2007).

9. Fred08.com, Statement by Fred Thompson on Adult Cell Research Breakthrough, November 20, 2007, http://www.fred08.com/NewsRoom/PressRelease.aspx?ID=f186d721-31ee-4462-9cc7-e81ebdbb740c (accessed November 27, 2007).

10. Mother Teresa's Letter to the US Supreme Court on Roe v. Wade, http://www-swiss.ai.mit.edu/~rauch/nvp/roe/mothertheresa_roe.html (accessed November 14, 2007).

11. Vincent Iannelli, MD, "Child Abuse Statistics," About.com, July 15, 2007, http://pediatrics.about.com/od/childabuse/a/05_abuse_stats.htm (accessed November 14, 2007).

12. Ibid.

13. National Right to Life Committee, "Number of Abortion by Year," National Right to Life News, March 2007, http://www.christianliferesources.com/?/library/view

.php&articleid=1042 (accessed November 28, 2007).

14. Maria Sophia Aguirre, PhD, "Family, Economics, and the Information Society: How Are They Affecting Each Other?" The World Congress of Families II 1999, November 1999, http://www.worldcongress.org/wcf2_spkrs/wcf2_aguirre.htm (accessed November 14, 2007).

15. Human Rights Education Associates, "The Rights of the Aged," http://www.hrea .org/learn/guides/aged.html (accessed November 15, 2007).

16. Butler County Department of Job and Family Services, "Elderly Protection," FAQs, http://www.butlercountyohio.org/workplace/faq.html (accessed November 28, 2007).

17. Ibid.

18. PlannedParenthood.org, "About Us: 1914–1979," http://www.plannedparenthood .org/about-us/who-we-are/1914-1929-9923.htm (accessed November 15, 2007).

19. Randy Hall, "Planned Parenthood Reports Record Abortions, High Profits," CNSNews.com, June 15, 2007, http://www.cnsnews.com/ViewCulture.asp?Page=/ Culture/archive/200706/CUL20070615a.html (accessed November 15, 2007).

20. PlannedParenthood.org, Planned Parenthood Federation of American, Inc., Annual Report 2005–2006, page 16, http://www.plannedparenthood.org/files/PPFA/Annual_ report.pdf (accessed November 15, 2007).

21. Euthanasia ProCon.org, "State Laws on Assisted Suicide," http://www .euthanasiaprocon.org/statelaws.htm (accessed November 15, 2007).

22. Euthanasia.com, "Arguments Against Euthanasia," http://www.euthanasia .com/argumentsagainsteuthanasia.html (accessed November 15, 2007).

23. ABCNews.com, "Teen Girls' Stories of Sex Trafficking in U.S.," *Primetime*, February 9, 2006, http://abcnews.go.com/Primetime/story?id=1596778 (accessed November 14, 2007).

24. Richard J. Estes and Neil Alan Weiner, "The Commercial Sexual Exploitation of Children in the U. S., Canada and Mexico," University of Pennsylvania, April 2002, http:// www.sp2.upenn.edu/~restes/CSEC_Files/Abstract_010918.pdf (accessed November 14, 2007).

25. Melissa Farley, PhD, and Howard Barkan, DrPH, "Prostitution, Violence Against Women, and Posttraumatic Stress Disorder," *Women & Health* 27 (3): 37–49, http://www .prostitutionresearch.com/ProsViolPosttrauStress.html (accessed November 14, 2007).

26. Joseph Mettimano, "Examining U.S. Efforts to Combat Human Trafficking and Slavery," World Vision Congressional Statements, July 7, 2004, http://www.worldvision .org/worldvision/wvususfo.nsf/stable/globalissues_criticalissues_trafficking (accessed November 15, 2007).

27. Julian Sher and Benedict Carey, "Debate on Child Pornography's Link to Molesting," *New York Times*, July 19, 2007, www.nytimes.com/2007/07/19/us/19sex .html?ex=1342497600& (accessed November 15, 2007).

28. CNN Law Center, "Supreme Court Strikes Down Ban on 'Virtual Child Porn,'" CNN .com, April 18, 2002, http://archives.cnn.com/2002/LAW/04/16/scotus.virtual.child.porn (accessed November 28, 2007).

29. D. W. Hamilton, "The Different Shades of Death," *European Weekly*, http://www .europeanweekly.org/pages/features/fea_editorial18.htm (accessed November 15, 2007).

Chapter 5—Core Value #2: Immigration

1. U.S. Department of State, "Chinese Immigration and the Chinese Exclusion Acts," http://www.state.gov/r/pa/ho/time/gp/82014.htm (accessed January 18, 2008).

2. University of Houston, "Landmarks in Immigration History," http://www
.digitalhistory.uh.edu/historyonline/immigration_chron.cfm (accessed January 18, 2008).

3. Ibid.

4. Documents of American History II, "1940s: Displaced Persons Act of 1948," http://
tucnak.fsv.cuni.cz/~calda/Documents/1940s/Displaced%20Persons%20Act%20of%201948
.html (accessed January 18, 2008).

5. U.S. Citizenship and Immigration Services, "Immigration and Nationality Act,"
http://www.uscis.gov/portal/site/uscis/menuitem.eb1d4c2a3e5b9ac89243c6a7543f6d1a/
?vgnextoid=f3829c7755cb9010VgnVCM10000045f3d6a1RCRD&vgnextchannel=f3829c
7755cb9010VgnVCM10000045f3d6a1RCRD (accessed January 18, 2008).

6. Jana Evans Braziel, "History of Migration and Immigration Laws in the United
States," Spring 2000, http://www.umass.edu/complit/aclanet/USMigrat.html (accessed
January 18, 2008).

7. U.S. Citizenship and Immigration Services, "Immigration Reform and Control Act of
1986," http://www.uscis.gov/portal/site/uscis/menuitem.5af9bb95919f35
e66f614176543f6d1a/?vgnextoid=04a295c4f635f010VgnVCM1000000ecd190
aRCRD&vgnextchannel=b328194d3e88d010VgnVCM10000048f3d6a1RCRD (accessed
January 18, 2008).

8. Encarta.com, "Immigration," http://encarta.msn.com/encyclopedia_761566973_4/
Immigration.html (accessed January 18, 2008).

9. Joseph A. Whitt Jr., "The Mexican Peso Crisis," http://www.frbatlanta.org/
filelegacydocs/J_whi811.pdf (accessed January 18, 2008).

10. Citizen.org, "The Ten-Year Track Record of the North American Free Trade
Agreement: The Mexican Economy, Agriculture and Environment," http://www.citizen
.org/documents/NAFTA_10_mexico.pdf (accessed January 18, 2008).

11. National Immigration Forum, "Chronology: Changes in Immigration and
Naturalization Law," http://www.itvs.org/outreach/workers/workers-Chronology.pdf
(accessed January 18, 2008).

12. Administration for Children and Families, "The Personal Responsibility and Work
Opportunity Reconciliation Act of 1996," fact sheet, http://www.acf.dhhs.gov/programs/
ofa/prwora96.htm (accessed January 18, 2008).

13. U.S. Department of Homeland Security Press Office, "Border Reorganization Fact
Sheet," January 30, 2003, http://www.dhs.gov/xnews/releases/press_release_0073.shtm
(accessed January 18, 2008).

14. Manual Miranda, "Immigration Policy Reform Proposal: Good Steward, Good
Neighbor," policy paper prepared for Family Research Council, December 2006.

15. Letter from Theodore Roosevelt to Richard Hurd, January 3, 1919, available from
the Library of Congress Manuscript Division, http://www.snopes.com/politics/quotes/
troosevelt.asp (accessed January 20, 2008).

16. Federation for American Immigration Reform (FAIR), "Chain Migration," http://
www.fairus.org/site/PageServer?pagename=iic_immigrationissuecenters3e2a (accessed
November 29, 2007).

17. Ibid.

Chapter 6—Core Value #3: Poverty and Justice (Part 1)

1. Arthur C. Brooks, *Who Really Cares: America's Charity Divide* (New York: Basic Books,
2006).

2. Ibid.

3. James M. Henslin, *Sociology* (Boston: Pearson and AB, 2007), 278.

4. Robert E. Rector and Kirk A. Johnson, "Understanding Poverty in America," January 5, 2004, http://www.heritage.org/Research/Welfare/bg1713.cfm (accessed November 15, 2007).

5. Ibid.

6. Merrill Frederick Unger, *The New Unger's Bible Dictionary* (Chicago, IL: Moody Press, 1988).

7. Greg Bensinger, "Taxi Medallions Fetch a Record $600,000 Each," *New York Sun*, May 30, 2007, http://www.nysun.com/article/55479 (accessed November 29, 2007).

8. Quickest-Cash-Advance.com, Frequently Asked Questions, http://www.quickest-cash-advance.com/faqs.asp (accessed November 15, 2007).

9. U.S. Census Bureau, "Historical Poverty Tables," http://www.census.gov/hhes/www/poverty/histpov/hstpov3.html (accessed December 28, 2007).

10. Mike Stobbe, "37 Percent of U.S. Births Out of Wedlock," Nov. 21, 2006, CBS News, http://www.cbsnews.com/stories/2006/11/21/ap/national/mainD8LHNMSG0.shtml (accessed November 15, 2007).

11. David J. Eggebeen and Daniel T. Lichter, "Race, Family Structure, and Changing Poverty Among American Children," *American Sociological Review* 56 (December 1991): 807.

12. Paul R. Amato and Bruce Keith, "Parental Divorce and the Well-being of Children: A Meta-Analysis, *Psychological Bulletin* 110 (1991).

13. Elaine Kamarck and William A. Galston, "Putting Children First: A Progressive Family Policy for the 1990s," whitepaper from the Progressive Policy Institute (September 27, 1990).

14. Wikipedia.org, "Gullah," http://en.wikipedia.org/wiki/Gullah (accessed November 29, 2007).

15. "Higher Education Is the Major Force in Closing the Black-White Income Gap," *Journal of Blacks in Higher Education*, http://www.jbhe.com/news_views/55_closing_the_income_gap.html (accessed November 15, 2007).

16. Scott Dyer, "Panel Hears Conflicting Views on La. Gambling," *The Advocate*, September 12, 1998, 12A.

17. John M. Barron, Michael E. Staten, and Stephanie M. Wilshusen, "The Impact of Casino Gambling on Personal Bankruptcy Filing Rates," August 18, 2000, http://www.ncalg.org/Library/Studies%20and%20White%20Papers/Bankruptcy/Gambling%20Impact%20on%20Personal%20Filings.pdf (accessed December 31, 2007).

18. "The Personal Bankruptcy Crisis, 1997: Demographics, Causes, Implications & Solutions," SMR Research Corporation, 1997, p. 117.

19. Muhammad Yunus, *Banker to the Poor* (New York: Public Affairs, 2003), 57–58.

Chapter 7—Core Value #3: Poverty and Justice (Part 2)

1. Michael Jacobsen, *The Word on Health* (Chicago, IL: Moody Publishers, 2000), 11.

2. Ibid.

3. Encyclopedia Britannica Online, "Constantine I," http://www.britannica.com/eb/topic?idxStructId=133873&typeId=13 (accessed November 15, 2007).

4. Encyclopedia Britannica Online, "Danubian Principalities (Historical Area, Europe)," http://www.britannica.com/eb/topic?idxStructId=151307&typeId=13Danube.

5. National Coalition on Health Care, "Health Insurance Cost," http://www.nchc.org/facts/cost.shtml (accessed December 27, 2007).

6. John Donnelly, "47 Million Americans Are Uninsured," Boston.com, http://www

.boston.com/news/nation/washington/articles/2007/08/29/47_million_americans_are_ uninsured/ (accessed November 29, 2007).

7. Steve Sternberg, "18,000 Deaths Blamed on Lack of Insurance," USAToday.com, May 22, 2002, http://www.usatoday.com/news/health/healthcare/2002-05-22-insurance-deaths.htm (accessed November 29, 2007).

8. FamiliesUSA.org, "The Health Care Crisis in America," http://www.familiesusa.org/assets/pdfs/Health-Care-Crisis-in-America.pdf (accessed November 29, 2007).

9. "DNC Winter Meeting—Remarks as Prepared for Delivery," February 2, 2007, http://johnedwards.com/news/speeches/dnc-winter-meeting/ (accessed November 16, 2007).

10. "Universal Health Care Through Shared Responsibility," http://johnedwards.com/issues/health-care/health-care-fact-sheet/ (accessed November 16, 2007).

11. Thomas Sowell, "No 'Health Care' in America?" *Capitalism Magazine*, September 9, 2007, http://www.capmag.com/article.asp?ID=5015 (accessed November 16, 2007).

12. Brownback President 2008, "Issues," http://www.brownback.com/s/Issues/tabid/60/Default.aspx (accessed November 16, 2007).

13. "Empower Patients and Families, Not the Government," press release, July 30, 2007, http://www.joinrudy2008.com/commitment.php?num=7 (accessed November 16, 2007).

14. Oz Garcia and Sharyn Colberg, *Look and Feel Fabulous Forever* (New York: HarperCollins, 2003).

15. Jordan Rubin, *The Great Physician's Rx for Health and Wellness: Seven Keys to Unlock Your Health Potential* (Nashville, TN: Nelson, 2005).

16. Don Colbert, MD, *The Seven Pillars of Health: The Natural Way to Better Health for Life* (Lake Mary, FL: Siloam, 2007).

Chapter 8—Core Value #4: Racial Reconciliation

1. *The Biblical Illustrator*, copyright © 2002, 2003, 2006 Ages Software, Inc. and Biblesoft, Inc.

2. George Barna and Harry R. Jackson Jr., *High Impact African-American Churches* (Ventura, CA: Regal Books, 2004), 106–107.

3. Martin Luther King Jr., "Letter From Birmingham Jail," http://thekingcenter.org/prog/non/Letter.pdf (accessed November 16, 2007).

4. The Oyez Project, *Bob Jones University v. United States,* 461 U.S. 574 (1983), http://www.oyez.org/cases/1980-1989/1982/1982_81_3/ (accessed November 16, 2007).

5. USAToday.com, "Campaign 2004, USA Today/CNN/Gallup Polls," May 20, 2005, http://www.usatoday.com/news/politicselections/pollsindex.htm (accessed November 16, 2007).

6. Barna.org, "Americans Have Commitment Issues, New Survey Shows," April 18, 2006, http://www.barna.org/FlexPage.aspx?Page=BarnaUpdate&BarnaUpdateID=235 (accessed November 16, 2007).

7. Warren Richey, "Affirmative Action's Evolution: How the Debate Has Changed Since 1970s," *Christian Science Monitor*, March 28, 2003, http://www.csmonitor.com/2003/0328/p01s01-usju.html (accessed November 16, 2007).

8. Ibid.

9. Thomas Sowell, "'Affirmative Action' Quotas on Trial," *Capitalism Magazine*, January 8, 2003, http://www.capmag.com/article.asp?ID=2340 (accessed November 30, 2007).

10. A. J. Murrell and R. Jones, "The Paradox of Affirmative Action: Examining Its Impact and Future for Women and Minorities in Employment," manuscript submitted for publication. Reported in Faye Crosby et al., "Affirmative Action: Who Benefits?" a briefing

paper of the American Psychological Association, Society for the Psychological Study of Social Issues, Society for the Psychological Study of Ethnic Minority Issues.

11. Gallup.com, "Race Relations," http://www.gallup.com/poll/1687/Race-Relations .aspx#3 (accessed January 20, 2008).

12. Human Rights Watch, "Incarcerated America," Figure 1, April 2003, http://www.hrw .org/backgrounder/usa/incarceration/us042903.pdf (accessed January 17, 2008).

13. Ibid.

14. Marc Maurer and Ryan Scott King, "Schools and Prisons: Fifty Years After *Brown v. Board of Education*," The Sentencing Project, http://www.sentencingproject.org/Admin/ Documents/publications/rd_brownvboard.pdf (accessed January 17, 2008).

15. The Sentencing Project, "Young Black Americans and the Criminal Justice System: Five Years Later" April 2001 Report Summary, http://www.sentencingproject.org/Admin/ Documents/publications/rd_smy_youngblack5yrslater.pdf (accessed January 17, 2008).

16. David A. Harris, "The Stories, the Statistics, and the Law: Why 'Driving While Black' Matters," *Minnesota Law Review* 84 (1999): 265.

17. U.S. Department of Justice, "Contacts Between Police and the Public: Findings From the 2002 National Survey," Bureau of Justice Statistics, Washington DC, April 2005, 10.

18. The Sentencing Project, "The Federal Prison Population: A Statistical Analysis," http:// www.sentencingproject.org/Admin/Documents/publications/inc_federalprisonpop.pdf (accessed January 17, 2008).

19. U.S. Department of Justice, "Prisoner Reentry and Community Policing: Strategies for Enhancing Public Safety," http://www.urban.org/uploadedpdf/411061_COPS_reentry _monograph.pdf (accessed January 17, 2008).

20. National Urban League, "National Urban League's The State of Black America 2005," April 6, 2005, http://www.nul.org/publications/SOBA/2005SOBAEXCSUMMARY.pdf (accessed November 30, 2007).

Chapter 9—Core Value #5: Religious Liberties

1. Thomas Jefferson, "Jefferson's Letter to the Danbury Baptists," January 1, 1802, http://www.loc.gov/loc/lcib/9806/danpre.html (accessed November 27, 2007).

2. *The Guardian*, "Blair Kept Quiet About His Faith for Fear of 'Nutter' Jibes," November 26, 2007, http://politics.guardian.co.uk/tonyblair/story/0,,2217072,00.html#article _continue (accessed December 3, 2007).

3. Alan Dershowitz, *Blasphemy* (Hoboken, NJ: Wiley, 2007), 53.

4. John Adams, *The Works of John Adams, Second President of the United States*, Charles Francess Adams, editor (Boston; Little Brown and Company, 1854), Vol.IX, p.229, to the officers of the First Brigade of the Third Division of the Militia of Massachusetts on October 11, 1798, as quoted in AmericanDestiny.com, "Historical Quotes: John Adams," http://www.americandestiny.com/john_adams.htm (accessed November 30, 2007).

5. Alexis de Tocqueville, "Principal Causes Which Tend to Maintain the Democratic Republic in the United States," *Democracy in America*, http://xroads.virginia.edu/~HYPER/ DETOC/1_ch17.htm (accessed November 27, 2007).

6. Francis A. Schaeffer, *A Christian Manifesto* (Wheaton, IL: Crossway Books, 1981), 31.

7. Ibid., 33.

8. Ibid., 34.

9. Ibid., 38.

10. HistoryPlace.com, "The Mayflower Compact," http://www.historyplace.com/ unitedstates/revolution/mayflower.htm (accessed November 30, 2007).

11. Footnote TV, "Issues: Religion," http://www.newsaic.com/mwreligion.html (accessed November 27, 2007).

12. International Standard Bible Encyclopaedia, s.v. "Courts, Judicial," Electronic Database copyright © 1996, 2003 by Biblesoft, Inc. All rights reserved.

13. CivilRights.org, "About LCCR," http://www.civilrights.org/about/lccr/ (accessed November 27, 2007).

14. *American Family Association, Inc. v. City and County of San Francisco*, 277 F.3d 1114, 1119 (9th Cir. 2002).

15. Love Won Out is a ministry by Focus on the Family that "exhorts and equips the church to respond in a Christlike way to the issue of homosexuality" (http://www .lovewonout.com).

16. *American Family Association, Inc. v. City and County of San Francisco*, 277 F.3d 1114, 1119–1120 (9th Cir. 2002); ABC News, "New Details Emerge in Matthew Shepard Murder," November 26, 2004, http://abcnews.go.com/2020/story?id=277685 (accessed November 27, 2007).

17. Foundation for Individual Rights in Education, "William Paterson University Tramples Student Constitutional Rights," FIRE press release, July 20, 2005, http:// thefire.org/index.php/article/6119.html (accessed November 30, 2007).

18. CNN.com, "Judge Suspended Over Ten Commandments," August 23, 2003, http:// www.cnn.com/2003/LAW/08/22/ten.commandments/index.html (accessed November 27, 2007).

19. PewForum.org, "Survey Shows Broad Support for Ten Commandments Displays," The Pew Forum on Religion & Public Life, http://pewforum.org/publications/surveys/ten -commandments.pdf (accessed January 16, 2008).

20. Austin Cline, "Constitutionality of Religious Displays on Public Ground," About.com, atheism.about.com/od/religioussymbolsholidays/a/nativitydisplay_4.htm (accessed November 27, 2007).

Chapter 10—Core Value #6: Rebuilding the Family (Part 1)

1. Department of Health and Human Services, "Report to Congress on Out-of-Wedlock Childbearing," September 1995, http://www.cdc.gov/nchs/data/misc/wedlock.pdf, pages 3–4 (accessed January 16, 2008).

2. DivorceStatistics.org, "Divorce Statistics," http://www.divorcestatistics.org/ (accessed January 16, 2008).

3. Ibid.

4. Ibid.

5. ReligiousIntolerance.org, "U.S. Divorce Rates for Various Faith Groups, Age Groups, and Geographic Areas," http://www.religioustolerance.org/chr_dira.htm (accessed January 16, 2008).

6. Joy Jones, "Marriage Is for White People," March 25, 2006, http://www .washingtonpost.com/wp-dyn/content/article/2006/03/25/AR2006032500029.html (accessed December 3, 2007).

7. Maryann Reid, "First Comes Baby, Then Comes Marriage?" *Christian Science Monitor* online, http://www.csmonitor.com/2006/0424/p09s02-coop.html (accessed December 27, 2007).

8. Administration of Children and Families, The Healthy Marriage Initiative, "Funding Opportunities," http://www.acf.hhs.gov/healthymarriage/funding/index.html (accessed December 3, 2007).

9. Mike and Harriet McManus, *Living Together: Myths, Risks and Answers* (West Monroe, LA: Howard Books, 2008).

10. PhysiciansForLife.org, "The Two Become One: The Role of Oxytocin and Vasopression," http://www.physiciansforlife.org/content/view/1492/36/ (accessed December 3, 2007).

11. Daniel Wegner, "Transactive Memory in Close Relationships," *Journal of Personality and Social Psychology* 61, no. 6 (1991).

12. Life Innovations, Inc., Prepare: Build a Stronger Marriage by Developing a Closer Relationship With Your Partner, http://www.prepare-enrich.com/couples.cfm?id=32 (accessed December 3, 2007).

13. Michael J. McManus, "Ethics and Religion," http://www.marriagesavers.org (accessed January 16, 2008).

14. Carolyn Thompson, "Nation's Longest-Married Couple Never Celebrated Valentine's Day," Associated Press, February 14, 1998.

Chapter 11—Core Value #6: Rebuilding the Family (Part 2)

1. Al Gore Jr., "Remarks as Delivered by Vice President Al Gore Jr.: Service of Celebration and Thanksgiving for the Life of Senator Albert Gore Sr." Tuesday, December 8, 1998, http://clinton3.nara.gov/WH/EOP/OVP/speeches/ags.html (accessed December 3, 2007).

2. Kay P. Bradford et al., "The Inventory of Father Involvement: A Pilot Study of a New Measure of Father Involvement," *Journal of Men's Studies* (2002): 183–196.

3. David Blackenhorn, *Fatherless America: Confronting Our Most Urgent Social Problem* (New York: Harper, 1996).

4. Hart and Teeter research companies performed this poll for NBC News and the *Wall Street Journal*, June 16–19, 1999.

5. *New York Times* poll conducted July 17–19, 1999.

6. NPR.org, "Poverty in America," http://www.npr.org/programs/specials/poll/poverty/ (accessed December 3, 2007).

7. Isabel V. Sawhill, "Teen Pregnancy Prevention: Welfare Reform's Missing Component," November 1998, http://www.brookings.edu/papers/1998/11metropolitanpolicy_sawhill .aspx (accessed December 3, 2007).

8. Sharon E. Lock and Murray L. Vincent, "Sexual Decision Making Among Rural Adolescent Females," *Health Values* 19, no. 1 (1995): 47–58.

9. Malcolm D. Williams, "Reconceptualizing Father Involvement," Master's Thesis, Georgetown University, 1997.

10. Mark Zimmerman, Deborah Seiler, and Kenneth Maton, "Family Structure and Psychological Correlates Among Urban African American Adolescent Males," *Child Development* 66 (1995): 1598–1613.

11. Jelani Mandara and Carolyn B. Murray, "Effects of Parental Marital Status, Income, and Family Functioning on African American Adolescent Self-esteem," *Journal of Family Psychology* 14 (2000): 475–549.

12. National Fatherhood Initiative, "Father Facts," http://www.fatherhood.org/ fatherfacts (accessed January 16, 2008).

13 National Child Care Information Center, "Promoting Responsible Fatherhood Through Child Care," http://www.nccic.org/pubs/resp-fatherhood.html (accessed December 3, 2007).

14. FRC, *The Family Portrait—a Compilation of Data and Public Opinion on the Family*, 127–134.

15. David G. Schramm, "What Could Divorce Be Costing Your State? A Costly Consequence of Divorce in Utah: The Impact on Couples, Communities, and Government, a Preliminary Report," June 25, 2003, publication in process, Department of Family, Consumer and Human Development, Utah State University.

16. Brian D. Ray, PhD, "Research Facts on Homeschooling: General Facts and Trends," July 10, 2006, http://www.nheri.org/content/view/199/ (accessed December 3, 2007).

17. National Center for Education Statistics, "Homeschooling in the United States: 2003," February 2006, http://nces.ed.gov/pubs2006/homeschool/ (accessed August 8, 2007).

18. Home School Legal Defense Association, "Military Recruitment of Homeschoolers," March 2006, http://www.hslda.org/docs/nche/000010/200506150.asp (accessed January 16, 2008).

19. Karl M. Bunday, "Socialization: A Great Reason Not to Go to School," http://www.learninfreedom.org/socialization.html (accessed December 3, 2007).

20. Jim Nelson Black, *Freefall of the American University* (New York: WND Books, 2004), back cover.

21. Gary DeMar, *Whoever Controls the Schools Rules the World* (Powder Springs, GA: American Vision, 2007), back cover.

22. James Dobson and Gary Bauer, *Children at Risk* (Nashville, TN: Thomas Nelson, Inc., 1994).

23. U.S. Census Bureau, "Educational Attainment in the United States: 2006," http://www.census.gov/population/www/socdemo/education/cps2006.html (accessed December 3, 2007).

24. William J. Bennett in *School Reform News*, October 1, 1999, published by the Heartland Institute.

25. Eugene Hickok and Matthew Ladner, PhD, "Reauthorization of No Child Left Behind: Federal Management of Citizen Ownership of K-12 Education," June 27, 2007, http://www.heritage.org/research/education/bg2047.cfm (accessed January 16, 2008).

26. National Center for Education Statistics, "Monitoring School Quality: An Indicators Report," December 2000, http://nces.ed.gov/pubs2001/2001030.pdf (accessed January 16, 2008).

Chapter 12—Core Value #7: The Environment and Global Warming

1. World Climate Report, "Global Hurricane Intensity Not Increasing," February 27, 2007, http://www.worldclimatereport.com/index.php/2007/02/27/global-hurricane-intensity-not-increasing/ (accessed November 20, 2007).

2. *NOAA Magazine* Online, "NOAA Attributes Recent Increase in Hurricane Activity to Naturally Occurring Multi-Decadal Climate Variability," November 29, 2005, www.magazine.noaa.gov/stories/mag184.htm (accessed November 20, 2007).

3. Andrew C. Revkin and Timothy Williams, "Global Warming Called Security Threat," *New York Times*, April 15, 2007, http://www.nytimes.com/2007/04/15/us/15warm.html (accessed November 20, 2007).

4. Peter Gwynne, "The Cooling World," *Newsweek*, April 28, 1975, http://www.denisdutton.com/cooling_world.htm (accessed November 20, 2007).

5. Pete Chagnon, "Founder of Weather Channel Disses 'Global Warming,'" OneNewsNow.com, November 14, 2007, http://www.onenewsnow.com/2007/11/founder_of_weather_channel_dis.php (accessed November 20, 2007).

6. R. Warren Anderson and Dan Gainor, Fire and Ice, May 17, 2006, Business and Media Institute.

7. James Strong, *Strong's Exhaustive Concordance of the Bible* (updated) (N.p.: Riverside World, 1996), s.v. *radh*, OT:7287, "dominion."

8. Ibid., s.v. *kabash*, OT:3533, "subdue."

9. Ibid., s.v. *loimos*, NT:3061, "pestilence."

10. Luke 21:9.

11. Revkin and Williams, "Global Warming Called Security Threat."

12. Luke 21:10.

13. Mark Townsend and Paul Harris, "Now the Pentagon Tells Bush: Climate Change Will Destroy Us," *The Observer*, February 22, 2004, http://observer.guardian.co.uk/international/story/0,6903,1153513,00.html (accessed January 17, 2008).

14. Luke 21:11.

15. CNN.com, "Extreme Weather on the Rise," July 3, 2003, http://www.cnn.com/2003/WEATHER/07/03/wmo.extremes/.

16. Luke 21:11.

17. ABC News Online, "Climate Change Likely to Increase Famine: FAO," http://www.abc.net.au/news/newsitems/200505/s1378213.htm (accessed December 3, 2007).

18. Luke 21:11.

19. Associated Press, "Global Warming Causes Disease to Rise," MSNBC.com, http://www.msnbc.msn.com/id/15717706 (accessed December 27, 2007).

20. Luke 21:11.

21. Tom Regan, "Global Warming: A Threat to World Security?" *Christian Science Monitor* Online, http://www.csmonitor.com/2005/0208/dailyUpdate.html (accessed December 27, 2007).

22. ChristianNewsWire.com, "Evangelical Leaders Exploited by Global Warming—Population Control Lobby," news release, September 29, http://www.christiannewswire.com/news/429601108.html (accessed December 3, 2007).

23. Overpopulation.com, "Paul Ehrlich, http://www.overpopulation.com/faq/people/paul-ehrlich/ (accessed December 3, 2007).

24. Paul Ehrlich, *The Population Bomb* (New York: Valentine Books, 1968), 146–148, 151.

25. Lisa Jordan, "Religion and Fertility in the United States: A Geographical Analysis," http://paa2006.princeton.edu/download.aspx?submissionId=60812 (accessed January 16, 2008).

26. Energy Design Resources, "e-News," issue 44, December 2004, http://www.energydesignresources.com/resource/191/ (accessed January 16, 2008).

27. Calvin Beisner et al., *A Call to Truth, Prudence and Protection of the Poor* (no publishing information available).

Conclusion—Taking the Land

1. Constitution.org, Excerpts from William Penn, "Frame of Government of Pennsylvania," 1682, http://www.constitution.org/bcp/frampenn.htm (accessed December 3, 2007).

2. Thomas A. Askew and Richard V. Pierard, *The American Church Experience: A Concise History* (Grand Rapids, MI: Baker Academic, 2004).

3. J. Grescham Machen, *Christianity and Liberalism* (New York: William B. Eerdmans, 1923).

4. Ibid.

5. The Barna Group, "A Biblical Worldview Has a Radical Effect on a Person's Life," *Barna Update*, December 1, 2003, http://www.barna.org/FlexPage.aspx?Page=BarnaUpdate&BarnaUpdateID=154 (accessed December 3, 2007).

Index